My Days in Court

> "In so far as the examinations are conducted according to the university rules and regulations and duly approved and ratified by the university senate, the court has no jurisdiction in the matter. A court of law which dabbles or flirts into the arena of university examinations, a most important and sensitive aspect of university function should remind itself that it has encroached into the bowels of university authority. Such a court should congratulate itself of being party to the destruction of the university and that will be bad not only for the university but also for the entire nation."

That's the Supreme Court of Nigeria saying its hands were tied even against the weight of the evidence, by declining jurisdiction in a matter bordering on the very process the court intended to preserve. Here the court is not saying that the student did not deserve his hard earned certificate, since the due process of postgraduate examination was satisfactorily followed, rather that the process followed at University of Agriculture Makurdi for student Magit, though manifestly flawed *ipso facto*, simply did not matter. This implies that the court was not favourably disposed to overrule the university on matters of postgraduate examination, even if it was clear that the student had been victimised on malicious grounds, as is obvious in the case of Magit. Therefore the collateral damage is done forever, given the role of supreme court as the final arbiter humanly available – collateral because, in fairness to the trio of Umeh, Njike and Gyang, I as the student's supervisor was the primary target intended to be nailed down by them, not student Magit.

Nonetheless, the verdict of Supreme Court in this case is worrisome regarding the plight of the Magits of this world facing oppression in malicious circumstances and at the hand of university authorities. Here I rest my case, as the farthest limit of a supervisor's ability to defend his innocent student has now been reached. The journey was truly tortuous, and also strenuous, from the High Court to the Appeal Court and finally to Supreme Court of the land. So at this stage, I am but only spirit-bound, to turn over the rest of the matter to the Supreme Being, Almighty God for Him to judge between the righteous and the wicked, in the matter of fundamental human rights enforcement at the instance of the victim, student Magit on the one hand and the villain, lecturer Umeh and his associates on the other hand.

My Days in Court

Travails and Hullabaloos in a University

Gbolagade Ayoola

Copyright © 2018 by Gbolagade Ayoola.

Library of Congress Control Number:	2018913616
ISBN: Hardcover	978-1-5434-9015-2
Softcover	978-1-5434-9016-9
eBook	978-1-5434-9017-6

All rights reserved. No part of this book may be reproduced or transmitted in any form or by any means, electronic or mechanical, including photocopying, recording, or by any information storage and retrieval system, without permission in writing from the copyright owner.

Any people depicted in stock imagery provided by Getty Images are models, and such images are being used for illustrative purposes only.
Certain stock imagery © Getty Images.

Print information available on the last page.

Rev. date: 02/20/2019

To order additional copies of this book, contact:
Xlibris
800-056-3182
www.Xlibrispublishing.co.uk
Orders@Xlibrispublishing.co.uk
776348

CONTENTS

Dedication ix
Prologue xi

Part One: Backstory

How the Hostility Brewed Against me 26
And the Bubble Finally Burst at Abuja 30
My Three Stalkers...40

Part Two: Onslaughts

Sporadic Offensives...71
Strange Illness..96
How Umeh Lost the Deanship Election to My Ghost 123
The Coming of Seven Gunmen...129
In the Aftermath 157

Part Three: Legal Tussle

Case 1: Direct Criminal Prosecution of Professor M. C. Njike for Forgery in the Matter of My Postgraduate Student Patrick Magit 186

Case 2: Libel Suit against Professor M. C. Njike, Mr I. U. Odoemenem and Dr J. C. Umeh................................196

Case 3: Fundamental Human Rights Enforcement in the Matter of Centre for Food and Agricultural Strategy (CEFAS) 211

Case 4: Direct Criminal Prosecution of Dr J. C. Umeh for Mischief and Related Offences in the Matter of My Wrongful Suspension 221
Case 5: Fair Hearing in the Matter of Student Rampage 232
Case 6: Fair Hearing in the Matter of My Postgraduate student Mr Patrick D. Magit 238
Case 7: Fundamental Human Rights Enforcement in the Matter of another Postgraduate Student Victor Ehigiator 246
Case 8: Fundamental Human Rights Enforcement in the Matter of My Wrongful Suspension 257
Case 9: Direct Criminal Prosecution of Professor M. C. Njike for Defamation in the Matter of My Student Victor Ehigiator 280
Case 10: Originating Summons in the Matter of General Maladministration of the Federal University under Professor E. O. Gyang 293

Part Four: Afterword

Lessons Abound 316

Annexe

Notarization 321
Appreciation 323

Notarised by J. S. Okutepa SAN

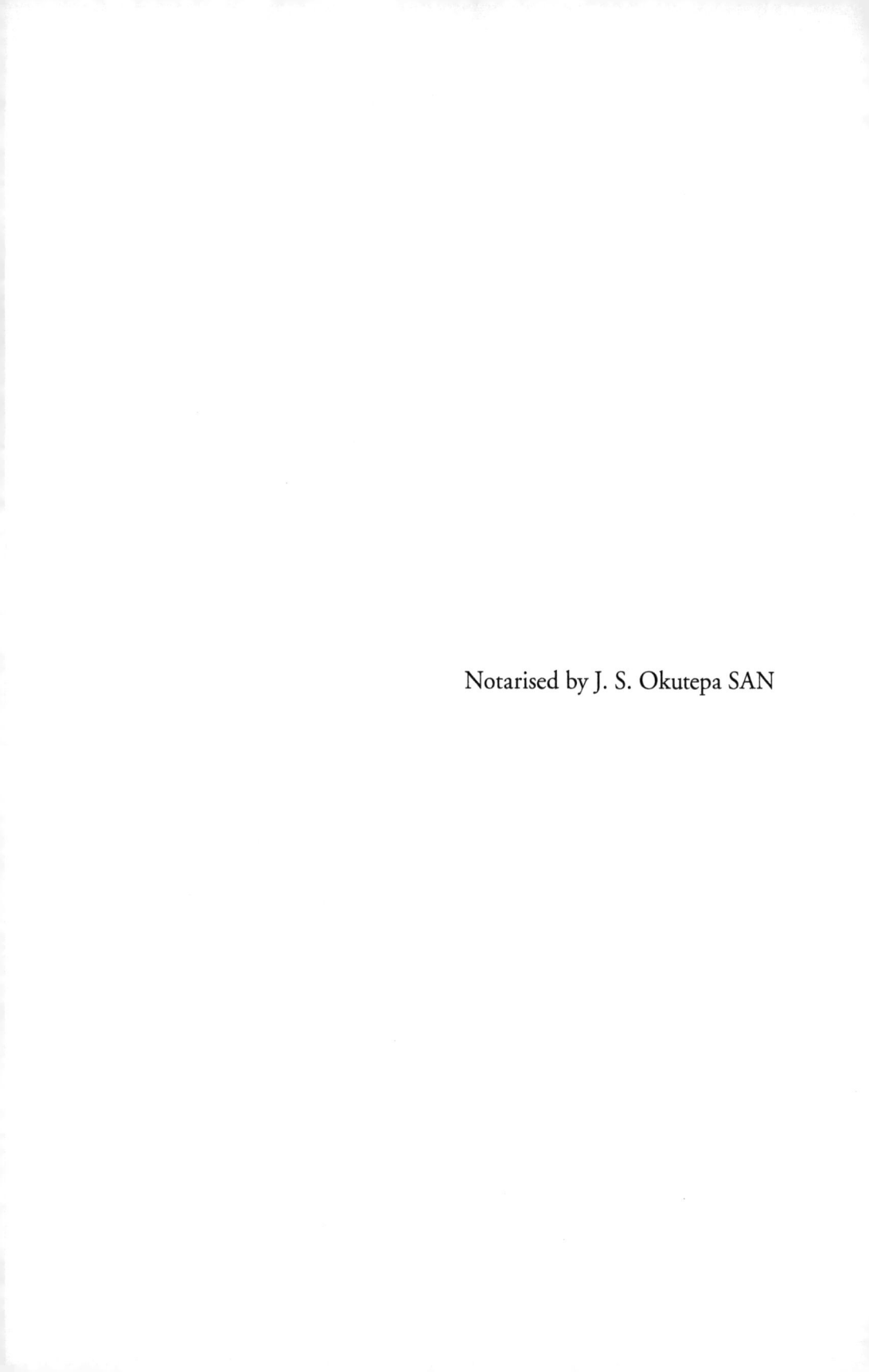

Dedication

To the cherished memory of my teacher and mentor, the late Professor Francis Sulemanu Idachaba (1943–2014), a stickler for merit and excellence in academia and public service; as well to my two postgraduate students – Patrick Magit and Victor Ehigiator, who for no fault of their own they fell victim of the consequential travails, thereby dying my own death at UNIAGRIC Makurdi; and also to the good nature of Bose, my soulmate who gave the utmost support required when things turned bad, and who demonstrated extreme resilience while the trouble lasted for me and the family at Makurdi.

Prologue

I met Professor F. S. Idachaba for the first time during my postgraduate training at the Department of Agricultural Economics, University of Ibadan (1982–1988), during which he was my teacher in econometrics, planning, and project analysis. He was highly impressed by my excellent performances in these courses, and so he invited me to join his team as a research associate on the Rural Infrastructure Survey (RIS) project; he had secured a line item vote for its implementation on the annual budget of the federal government. That relationship was sustained throughout the period of my postgraduate training and beyond, to earn me his admiration as, in his own words, a "most faithful disciple" of his.

In the year of my doctoral graduation, 1988, I headed for Makurdi and joined the new University of Agriculture as a lecturer in agricultural economics at the instance of Idachaba, who was appointed by the federal government of Nigeria as the pioneer vice chancellor of the institution. However, during his two-term tenure of eight years, Idachaba faced protracted hostility from the native Tiv elites, who expressed preference for a "son of the soil" as chief executive of the university. Nonetheless, he triumphed to put the university on the global intellectual map as a world-class institution before he left the position in December 1995. My own undoing was the naive decision I took to stay back at UNIAGRIC Makurdi. I faced a horrendous transfer of aggression from Idachaba's adversaries and an extremely horrific persecution by his successor, Professor Erastus Gyang, a Tiv man from Ahmadu Bello University, Zaria.

From the outset, apart from my classroom performance, I was quite conscious of the most important aspects of my conduct that glued me to Idachaba so tightly: disciplined hard work and impeccable moral behaviour. At Ibadan and later at Makurdi, Idachaba and I had no time for frivolities. Over the time I also imbibed from him a spirit of zero tolerance for fraud or corruption in both private and public life, or shades of corrupt practices of any conceivable kind. His penchant for merit and excellence knew no bounds, and he never found me wanting in any of these areas. At Makurdi when he was busied by administrative workload, he almost totally relinquished all his research projects to me as manager of the desk and field works involved, as well as the financials. He would assign me to represent him professionally anywhere and everywhere, so much so that I became very visible on and off campus.

Even though Idachaba groomed me to full professional maturity, he would not pamper me even a foot, and indeed in many instances he would consider me last for a special advantage at his disposal or willfully deny me such advantage altogether. In particular, even in his exalted position as VC, while incentivizing other staff to build a critical mass of staff for the university's takeoff, my boss would insist I pass through the mill, such as my normal movements through the ranks, from Lecturer II to Lecturer I and to senior lecturer positions at the mandatory minimum intervals of three years in each case.

Meanwhile, with the prompting of his kitchen cabinet, Gyang had quickly identified me as the foremost Idachaba boy along with other endangered staff that he met on ground. We were surreptitiously earmarked to be crushed at all costs and sacked from the university. As I put up resistance by running incessantly to courts, a hullabaloo engulfed the institution, during which Gyang became so embattled, embittered, and battered that he could not organise the convocation for any set of graduating students as statutorily required of him. Gyang failed woefully in office for not having his signature appended on their certificates during his tenure of five years as VC of UNIAGRIC. In the aftermath, I triumphed as a plaintiff in ten criminal and civil proceedings that I filed in various courts against Gyang and his hatchet men. Sadly, aside from the psychological stress caused me during the period and the professional setback I suffered when my promotion to the rank of professor was delayed for seven years after the due date, the ensuing crisis also led to a rapid decay of the university, which soon diminished its image so badly and almost wiped it out entirely from institutional memory.

My Days in Court is a documentary of my travails and the consequential hullabaloos at the University of Agriculture Makurdi. It's somewhat a separate chapter from but critically linked to my yet to be written *Makurdi Files* in a section of my forthcoming autobiography. As a memoir of generational value at this stage, it is purposed to not only expose the evildoing in Nigeria's higher educational system but also illuminate the inner mechanisms of the academic system wherefrom important lessons abound for all and sundry to be learnt—students, lecturers, administrators, legal practitioners, and even filmmakers in search of fascinating scenes of uncommon types. Herein, my experiential story demonstrates the fact that contrary to popular expectation or belief, the typical Nigerian university, or possibly universities in other parts of the world, is not immune to criminality, corruption, and application of non-merit criteria, amongst other societal ills commonly observed in government ministries, departments, and agencies in public service. Given its rich factual and empirical contents, *My Days in Court* is my own stylized antidote to falsehood or future misrepresentations of the facts by tattlers about what happened to me at Makurdi at the hands of Gyang, a deep-pocketed bully and, borrowing the word of the High Court judge in one of my cases, a quintessential "despot" dressed in academic robes.

Gbolagade Ayoola

Part One
Backstory

♪
*O Lord my God, When I in awesome wonder,
Consider all the worlds Thy Hands have made;
I see the stars, I hear the rolling thunder,
Thy power throughout the universe displayed.*

In September 1996, when Erastus Gyang, a professor of veterinary medicine, assumed duty as vice chancellor of the University of Agriculture, Makurdi (UNIAGRIC Makurdi), there was no governing council in place for the federal institution of higher learning. The term of the last council had expired at the same time that Idachaba had successfully completed his two terms of eight years as the pioneer vice chancellor in December 1995. The federal government had not appointed another council yet. The implication of that situation was that the new VC was more or less sole administrator and at liberty to lord himself over the university system without the usual checks and balances from higher authorities. It was under these circumstances that Gyang came with the mindset of a despot of sort and launched an authoritarian regime at UNIAGRIC. This development is much contrary to the democratic tenets of academia worldwide and is in obvious contrast to the cherished principles of Idachaba's administration which we were all used to.

At that moment, I was in the United States as a joint visiting scholar to the Economics Department and the Centre for Agricultural and Rural Development (CARD) at Iowa State University, Ames, for three months (since mid-1996). It was most gratifying for me that during the visit, I propounded the "deathly embrace" theory of the dual economy structure (agriculture and industry), which was so well received by the faculty of agricultural economics that Professor Stanley Johnson, then director of CARD and provost for extension at ISU, moved quickly to approve the seminar paper on the topic for special publication in a monograph of the centre.

It was towards the end of my stay at ISU that I learnt that a new VC had been appointed for UNIAGRIC different from Professor Ikenna Onyido, contrary to popular expectation. I had never met Gyang, who as I later understood was a professor of veterinary medicine from Ahmadu Bello University, Zaria. The story was told how the members of Mzough U'Tiv (a sociocultural and political association of Tiv-speaking people on campus) rolled out drums to welcome Gyang to Makurdi from Zaria, singing and dancing in a motorcade. The celebration was because a "son of the soil" had taken over the university from the *ukes* (Tiv word for strangers). The term is commonly used for people dwelling in Benue State who belonged to other states of the federation. And as to be established shortly in this introductory overtures and subsequent chapters of this memoir, the ethnic bigotry marked the beginning of a new era for the institution—an era of retrogression and eventual institutional decay. The ardent pursuit of merit and excellence in the university that had characterized Idachaba's era was deeply eroded, ushering another era ruled by inordinate ambition, frivolity, and incompetence of people in authority at the institution.

Since I'd come to Makurdi in 1988, it had largely been the viewpoint of the native Tiv community that UNIAGRIC, a federal institution, was their own share of the national cake. Although they could grudgingly share the staffing and students population with other tribes in the state, the position of the chief executive was not negotiable as their birthright (or at least so they thought). This mindset explains why Idachaba, though initially an indigene of Benue State at that time, was an Igala man by tribe and therefore was not welcomed as the pioneer VC. He faced the wrath of the native Tiv elites from the word go, and hostilities came in quick succession: the revolt of students within a couple of months of his assumption of office; the fire disaster in the university bursary before the institution could settle down; the avalanche of petitions to federal government that a Tiv man or woman, not an Igala man, was preferred as head of the institution; the heightened altercations between Idachaba and Farther Adasu, then state governor, even on the pages of newspapers; the refusal of indigenes to vacate the land procured by the federal government for the development of the permanent site of the institution; the devastating student rampage that threatened the life of Idachaba, when he was nearly captured inside the temporary lodge; and the torching of two or three buildings occupied by some staff loyal to Idachaba.

To many people, including myself, Gyang was an interloper whose appointment was manifestly crooked, to say the least. Indeed, it was an ill-considered appeasement of the Tiv people from the onset, who had promised fire and brimstone if a "son of the soil", was not appointed as VC of UNIAGRIC at the end of Idachaba's tenure. The right person to be appointed was Professor Onyido, who had come tops amongst contestants to the position before the expiration of Idachaba's tenure. The governing council had advertised the post during the last six months, and we learnt that twenty-two were shortlisted based on a long list of applicants from UNIAGRIC and other Nigerian universities, which included Gyang and Onyido; it also included Professor M. C. Njike. At the end of the succession race, the choice of the council was Onyido; we were told Gyang had finished sixth and Njike had finished twenty-second. Accordingly, the governing council recommended Onyido for the appointment by the federal government.

However, in the face of intense Tiv pressure, the federal government dilly-dallied until the tenure of Idachaba expired in December 1995, and even until I left for the United States in July 1996. Instead of ratifying the decision of the university council for the substantive appointment of Onyido, who was Idachaba's deputy for the entire period, the federal government appointed him as the acting VC only—a position in which he was kept for close to a year before the announcement of Gyang. No sane person would have thought that merit could so easily give way to mediocrity in a university setting, but it indeed happened at UNIAGRIC with the wrongful appointment of Gyang as VC. Nothing infuriated me more in that appointment than the injustice demonstrated and the bottomless pit that our educational system had reached by that singular action. The culture of excellence and merit that Idachaba had instituted in the university, and which had sprouted and blossomed during his tenure, had totally gone.

In the case of Gyang, as the story had it, in order to pull the federal officials to their side, the Tiv elite had traded their block vote for the military head of state at the time, General Sanni Abacha, in his bid to transform himself into a civilian president. One of the aberrant political parties created to achieve this for Abacha had Mr Gemade, a Tiv man, as its chairman. He was said to have delivered the message of the Tiv elites to the government, which led to the unfair substitution of Onyido's name for Gyang's, with the instrumentality of Gambo Jimeta, a former police chief and the then agriculture minister, thereby thwarting the recommendation of the governing council.

For that to be done, it took the mindlessness of the then Abacha's agriculture minister to superintend over this corrupt act. Later, we heard the story of how the minister had directed the officers of the federal agriculture ministry to rewrite the council's report on the succession exercise in order to change the recommendation on the choice of VC from Onyido to Gyang, which eventually led to the announcement of the warped appointment. The fraud manifested in the open when it was later rumoured that Gyang became VC of the university merely by radio announcement organised by some rent-seeking officials in the presidency, and that he was not issued any official letter by Sani Abacha to that effect.

In fairness, playing the devil's advocate, and at the risk of rationalising an absolutely corrupt act, the warped appointment of Gyang also reflected the sustained pressure of the Tiv elite on government. They were hell-bent on having a son of the soil as the VC, and they promised bloodshed on campus if there was failure. It was an agitation that had succeeded to put the appointment on hold for about one year already.

Nonetheless, I quickly got my act together and, realising my current position as the director of the university's Centre for Food and Agricultural Strategy (CEFAS), I wrote a letter of congratulation from my base in the United States to Gyang and sent it to Nigeria by courier. I also sent a letter of encouragement to Professor Onyido, as the victim of a policy failure on the part of government to uphold merit as a desirable trait of the institution. Before then, I had sent an e-mail to inform Idachaba about this development at his base in The Hague, the Netherlands. At the time, he was a senior research fellow and deputy director-general of the International Service for National Agricultural Research (ISNAR), a job he took upon leaving the University of Ibadan, soon after his exit from UNIAGRIC. He simply admonished me to put the matter behind me and focus on my job of reforming CEFAS, which he knew I had commenced before my departure to the United States—or in case my circumstances changed when I returned, as a single-minded lecturer in the university.

* * *

Gyang received my letter probably within two weeks of his assumption of duty, which I addressed to him through the registrar of the university, Mr Lawrence Tsumbu, and in which I misspelt his name as Gang, the way it sounded on telephone when the news came. It was Dr Sule Ochai, my colleague in the department and also on leave in the United States at the time, who called me by phone to break the news to me. I wrote a letter of solidarity to Professor Onyido, who was the acting VC at that time. That made three letters in a row.

IOWA STATE UNIVERSITY
OF SCIENC.E AND TECHNOLOGY

Department of Economics
Heady Hill
Ames, Iowa 50011-1070
515 294-6740
FAX 515 294-0221

6 September 1996

The Registrar,
Mr Lawrence Tsumbu
University of Agriculture, Makurdi,
P. B. B. 2373, Benue State
NIGERIA

Dear Mr Tsumbu,
I am writing to congratulate you and the university community on the appointment of a new Vice Chancellor for UNIAGRIC. I am not sure if I got the name correct but I have written a letter of official congratulation to him which is being passed through you (attached).

If the new Vice Chancellor has not assumed office yet I request you to kindly assist to forward it to him at ABU in good time.

Let me thank you for the opportunity to visit the United States at this time on the intellectual mission. It has been a wonderful experience for me and beneficial venture for CEFAS and UNIAGRIC as my report will show on arrival in early October.

How is Dorcas at Gboko, madam and all? I miss everybody here.
God Bless.

Sincerely,

Signed

Dr G. B. Ayoola
Visiting Scholar

IOWA STATE UNIVERSITY
OF SCIENC.E AND TECHNOLOGY

Department of Economics
Heady Hill
Ames, Iowa 50011-1070
515 294-6740
FAX 515 294-0221

6 September 1996

The New Vice-Chancellor
Professor E. O. Gang
University of Agriculture, Makurdi,
P. M. B. 2373, Benue State,
NIGERIA
Through: The Registrar
Mr Lawrence Tsumbu

Dear Professor Gyang,

I have received the news of your appointment as the new Vice-Chancellor of the University of Agriculture, Makurdi (UNIAGRIC) minutes after the announcement through the internet (E-mail) communication directed to me from Texas A&M, some 1500 miles away from my present location at Ames, Iowa State.

I must congratulate you on this important assignment and the confidence of the federal government of Nigeria therein.

I am a foundation member of the academic staff of the university and the Acting Director of the Centre for Food and Agricultural Strategy (CEFAS). I am presently visiting the United States of America under the World Bank (staff development) project. My academic programme entails active interaction with the faculty in the Economics Department and the university at large on intellectual grounds and explore opportunities for institutional collaboration with CEFAS specifically and the UNIAGRIC generally.

I am convinced, given my original involvement right from the conception stage (pre-1988) through the drawing board or design stage (1988/89) to the implementation stage (1989 till date), beyond any shadow of doubt that the University of Agriculture concept holds the key to the scientific transformation of the Nigerian agricultural landscape. And the concept, as pursued in the mission and mandate of UNIAGRIC, is crystal clear: A strong background of academic colleges for active teaching and research enterprise, coupled with sharp arrow heads in terms of outreach programmes, i.e., CEC for agricultural extension and CEFAS for agricultural policy analysis; I should be able to brief you fully about the activities and status of CEFAS upon my return to the country at the end of this month and resumption of work at Makurdi early October.

I have chosen to visit the Iowa State University for what it is in relation to UNIAGRIC; it is one of the oldest agricultural universities in the United States established in 1858. The United States itself is the most fertile environment for understudying the workings of an agricultural university both in concept and in practice. Since passing the erstwhile Morill act by Congress in 1862 to establish the "Land-Grant" colleges known as agricultural universities, these institutions have grown in great numbers and in qualitative development. I should also be able to brief you fully about my most eventful stay here interacting with key functionaries of the advanced system for realising the goals of an agricultural university.

I fervently desire that our own UNIAGRIC maintains the clear lead to Nigeria's agricultural greatness through the systematic and relentless pursuit of excellence and disciplined hard work among us the staff. Sir, if there is something you are inheriting at Makurdi, it includes a strong and committed core of academic and professional staff who had burnt the candle in both ends to put the system in place for productive work. In my own little way I hope to continue in the direction of raising the limelight status of CEFAS and the university for their successful launching on to the world intellectual map. The contributions of other staff—academic and nonacademic alike—are also significant in this respect.

Let me wish you a very productive leadership at UNIAGRIC. You are welcome in God's name.

My love to your family as a whole.

While pledging my unalloyed loyalty during your tenure of office as Vice Chancellor of a pioneer agricultural university in Nigeria, I request that you please accept my congratulations together with the felicitations from Bose, my wife, and children, all in Makurdi.

Utmost personal regards.

Sincerely,

Dr G. B. Ayoola.
Visiting Scholar

IOWA STATE UNIVERSITY
OF SCIENC.E AND TECHNOLOGY

Department of Economics
Heady Hill
Ames, Iowa 50011-1070
515 294-6740
FAX 515 294-0221

6 September 1996

The Acting Vice-Chancellor,
Professor Ikenna Onyido,
University of Agriculture, Makurdi,
P,M,B. 2373, Benue State,
NIGERIA

Dear Professor Onyido,

I have received the news of the appointment of a new Vice Chancellor for UNIAGRIC which is contrary to our expectations. This is to sympathize with you on this turn of events as another one in the series of the lessons of life in our thankless struggle to impact on the system. I am sure that the little you have been able to do for the system and more forthcoming for you to do in the micro or macro sense of the system will surely go down in your history as a dedicated professional we have had and worked with.

Anyway, our own hope as Christians is, according to Paul's second letter to Corinth, not focused on the seen but the unseen. Therefore, I urge you to remain firm in your close relation with the Lord. My estimation is to the effect that you have fought a good fight after all.

I remain with you at this time, proud as ever before, of the basic elements upon which you contested and excelled in the process, based just on the merit criteria set. I am sure God will replenish you many fold for the huge investment in terms of the psychological, emotional and time commitments; in particular I pray for the fullest restoration of your physical health as well.

Give my love to Madam and children.

God Bless.

Sincerely,

Gbolagade Ayoola
Visiting Scholar

But soon after dispatching the letters by courier, word came from Makurdi advising me to stay in the United States and seek another job with my hosts. I understood that I had been labeled the "most faithful Idachaba boy" and that my name came on top of the hit list of the new VC, amongst those earmarked for him to crush for being loyalists of Idachaba. That I was so labeled was not surprising, but his intention to crush me was something I couldn't understand. I knew right away that it was the handwork of Mzough U'Tiv, who had constituted a major opposition against Idachaba and also orchestrated violence against his administration a number of times. Even more than that, what surprised me was how Gyang, who was not with us during Idachaba's administration, could have been so quickly absorbed in the agitation against Idachaba and the so-called Idachaba boys. I learnt how they hovered round him day and night to put him in their pocket until he was totally consumed in their cause, which I considered very strange for a university professor. Thus, instead of focusing on the mandate of the institution, he had preoccupied himself with such mundane things as ethnicity and the senseless pursuit of Idachaba loyalists, thereby moving towards the path of institutional decay.

As he himself stated at a public function later in his tenure, his priority was to quickly "recover the university from the so-called *ukes* (in contemptuous reference to people from other states of the federation who live in Tiv land), who were perceived as taking the lion share of the 'national cake' the university represents to the people of Benue State particularly Tiv elite" (courtesy of Idachaba in his autobiography, *No Easy Harvest*). Thus, in this mode, a new era had started at UNIAGRIC, one of a distorted value system whereby academic excellence and merit factors were no longer the watchword. Contrary to Idachaba's time, it was one of a parochial, ethnic sentimentalism as a principle of university governance. Indeed, the seed of ethnicity was sown from the outset of Idachaba's appointment as the pioneer VC of the new university in 1988. He was abroad then, and I was the person who sent a telegraph to him in Liberia and the United States, informing him about his appointment. Before he arrived back in the country to assume duty at Makurdi, the Tiv elite had staged a protest against the appointment of an Igala man to head a federal institution in Tiv land, perceiving it as an abomination. Incidentally, the Igala tribe also belonged in the same Benue State as the Tiv tribe at that time, but as the largest tribe, the Tiv people usually claimed exclusive right to leadership positions of government establishments, particularly federal establishments located in the state.

The federal government ignored the protest and had Idachaba assume duty, with heavy security backup for him to settle down in office. When this happened and the local elites failed to stop Idachaba, a number of demonstrations were staged on the campus to further register their hostility against his person. Some of these protests turned violent, during which buildings were torched and burnt, including the university bursary at the temporary site. Apart from the issue of tribe, another excuse given for staging sporadic demonstrations on the campus was to express their opposition to the establishment of a specialized university (of agriculture) in Benue State, indicating preference for the establishment of a general university as their own share of the national cake. All this was mere subterfuge meant to enlist the support of the Idoma (the third most populous tribe) for their goal to unseat Idachaba.

Unfortunately for the Tiv elites, despite the protracted hostility against Idachaba, the man enjoyed the full support of General Babangida, the military president who'd appointed him and given him the benefits of military cover. With the creation of new states in 1991, the Igala ethnic group was excised out of Benue and Kwara to become part of the newly created Kogi State. The implication was that Idachaba was no longer an indigene of Benue State (just like me, who hailed from faraway, Yoruba-speaking Osun State). This development further heightened the hostility of the Benue elites against him. For want of other reasons, the state government decided to establish its own university and chose (rather offensively) to use the same site for the purpose. The site was previously the location of a technical college owned by the state, and it had served as the location of the Makurdi Campus of University of Jos, Plateau State, before serving as the temporary site of UNIAGRIC, pending the completion of the permanent site for occupation.

Fortunately, a permanent site for UNIAGRIC already existed north of Makurdi, where building projects had reached an advanced stage at the instance of the defunct Federal University of Technology, Makurdi, in the early 1980s. By a special clause dealing with perpetual succession of federal establishments, the site and its existing structures had passed onto UNIAGRIC as its permanent site, and so there was no apprehension when the Benue state government made the decision to occupy the temporary site and give Idachaba a few weeks' ultimatum to vacate. As he made moves to comply with this tight ultimatum, the Tiv elites quickly instigated the indigenous population on the site to resist the directive to vacate the land—notwithstanding the fact that federal government had settled all claims and paid them compensation since. The tension had mounted and the drum of war had sounded loud already when the federal troops invaded the site to forcibly drive away the occupants. This heightened hostility against Idachaba, and several agitations followed, including a violent demonstration that threatened his life before he escaped from the irate mob through the backdoor of his lodge.

* * *

When I got the call urging me to stay in the United States following the appointment of Gyang, I simply dismissed it with a wave of my hand. I began to wind down at ISU and planned to return to Nigeria in early October 1996. The worst I imagined was for Gyang to remove me as CEFAS director, which would be good riddance anyway. Idachaba had appointed me to the position in mid-1995, and he had done so based purely on merit considerations in the twilight of his tenure. When he offered me the post, I wondered aloud if he felt the post was good for me at my current stage (a senior lecturer). I told him that his offer was not in consonance with his own model that I had since cherished. He never took up an administrative position, whether headship of department or deanship of faculty or director of anything at the University of Ibadan (UI), until he became a professor. He persuaded me otherwise, saying our circumstances were different and that the position would definitely enhance my intellectual works more than I thought. I obliged him with palpable reluctance.

If a new VC did not want me in that position; I would gladly step down and focus on my primary assignment of teaching and research in the university; that would make me less visible in a hostile administration. Indeed, I had heard through the grapevine about the existence of a hit list that contained my name, and how the shadow cabinet of Gyang planned to remove me as director of CEFAS, to be substituted with Dr P. O. Erhabor, who was a senior colleague in the Department of Agricultural Economics. I also learnt that one Mr Odoemenem, a well-known stalker of mine in CEFAS, had also been jostling to succeed me as director.

To my utter surprise, I arrived at Makurdi and into the warm hands of Professor Gyang, which marveled everybody. The weekend of my arrival coincided with the welcome service held for him by my church, and so we met for the first time at that event. He was a massively built man with a mien that concealed a sinister motive in running the affairs of the institution. After the church service, when I introduced myself to him, he showed a degree of pleasant excitement in greeting me and shaking hands with me. He immediately acknowledged receipt of my letter of congratulation and expressed his happiness about it. He said the letter showed my readiness to work with him—contrary to what some people were telling him.

As we walked shoulder to shoulder to the car park, a number of church members walked behind us and his wife. He said to me that he had heard many good things about me from the registrar and some other people: my diligence at work, intellectual capacity, reform mindedness (an opaque reference to my ongoing efforts to revamp and revitalize CEFAS), and generally my rising academic profile at home and abroad. He said he learnt that my promotion to the rank of professor was due but wondered why Idachaba had not set it in motion before his departure. As he said this, I was in awe of God, wondering how he'd learnt so much about me and so quickly. Who must have briefed him differently outside the realm of Mzough U'Tiv? The answer was quick in coming the next day, Monday.

At last, before he entered his car, he quietly requested that I come with him to his lodge. There was no time to think about it, and I swiftly turned in the direction of my car. Bose and the children were already waiting inside, and I drove out of the car park, following him bumper-to-bumper towards his lodge. I could see the astonishment in the faces of people around us, and I felt a little uncomfortable afterwards. He'd engaged me so far that other people behind us did not have a chance to exchange pleasantries with him, particularly Onyido (who was chairman of the church council) and the chaplain, amongst others.

At his house, we had lunch together with members of our two families, during which I had a chance to offer my hand of fellowship to him. We talked at length. He asked me how my academic visit to the United States had been, and he sought to know more about how I was able to awake the centre from long slumber. Upon seeing how friendly he was, my expectations of him changed, and I offered him my hand in fellowship and hard work. He was delighted to hear that I'd signed two memoranda of understanding with my hosts at ISU; he was also a product of an American university. I illuminated the background of the university to him, and that confirmed my close relationship with Idachaba, who'd sponsored the idea to the government when he'd been a member of the Presidential Advisory Committee during the time of Babangida, the military president. We surveyed the past of the university together, and he solicited my fullest support to make his administration succeed. There and then, I pledged my fullest support and cooperation to help him succeed.

The next day, Monday, Dr Ladele, the acting director during my absence from the centre, briefed me. In the process, he mentioned that it was the turn of CEFAS to brief the new VC that afternoon. I decided to attend the session at the VC's office. Dr Ladele was a visiting lecturer to the centre from the University of Ilorin, at my instance. Unknown to both of us, Odoemenem, who was not yet aware of my resumption from abroad, had planned to double-cross Ladele at the briefing session. When I arrived the venue, I unexpectedly met Mr Odoemenem in a seat at the anteroom of the VC's office, waiting to enter the conference room where the briefing session was taking place. Knowing the man's capacity for mischief, I wondered what he was doing there when he was not the acting director. In palpable shock, he greeted grudgingly, looking askance, which exposed a sinister motive for his being there. Previously, Ladele had told me about Odoemenem's hostile and indecorous attitudes towards him at the centre in my absence. I ignored all that, shook his hand, and then asked him to come with me when it was the turn of CEFAS. I said to him that I had already checked up on him in his office at the centre with the same intention.

As a matter of fact, because the acting VC would not accept my recommendation of Odoemenem to act during my absence, I had invited Dr A. A. Ladele, a senior lecturer at UNILORIN, to CEFAS as part of my preparation to travel abroad for three months. He'd accepted my invitation as a visiting scholar at the centre for the period, and he was the person I assigned to stand in for me when I was away.

During the briefing, Gyang was happy with my presentation, particularly to hear from me that I'd initiated an institutional relationship and project between UNIAGRIC and ISU focusing on CEFAS before coming home, which involved a staff exchange programme and other fascinating project activities. I gave him a copy of the agreement signed with ISU, featuring my signature and that of Professor Stanley Johnson, the provost for extension at ISU.

At the end of briefing that day, Gyang invited me to his office for lunch. I politely declined to join him but took a piece of meat from the plate as he carried it with his two hands towards me across the table. I was a little taken aback when he said, with food in his mouth, that he could now finalise the composition of his cabinet now that I had returned. He said that he was actually waiting for my arrival from the United States before doing so, and that based on what he had heard from me, he wanted me to serve as the head of my department, Agricultural Economics.

Wondering what he wanted to do with CEFAS, I immediately declined. His reason? That he had learnt about the bad situation with my department, particularly the inability of past HODs (Umeh and Erhabor) to produce anyone amongst the first set of postgraduate students since the inception of the university and postgraduate school. Though I knew he had hit the nail on the head about the bad situation of my home department and the negative reference to Umeh as HOD, I did not say a word to corroborate Gyang's point. Truly, our postgraduate programme was in total disarray; the successive sets of students admitted into the programmes abandoned their research after completing course work, frustrated in one way or another.

The simple reason I offered was that I wouldn't want to do firefighting jobs many times in the university. He tried to persuade me, saying that he'd met my department in shambles and would like me to do for the department the type of reconstruction work I did at CEFAS. But that was exactly my point, and I told him frankly that if he would not allow me to continue at the centre, I was prepared to return to my department to concentrate on my primary assignment - teaching and research. At that stage, he stopped the discussion and suggested we continue at his residence later in the evening. I agreed and was at his lodge by 7 p.m.

His wife joined us in the discussion after dinner in support of her husband's offer. I stood my ground. Then he asked me to head both units, the department and the centre, until further notice, when he could get someone from outside the university to head the department. I wondered why he felt so bad about my colleagues in the department that he could not choose any of them as head, even momentarily. The whole university community was bewildered the following day when he published the new officers of the university, and my name appeared in two positions as the head, the only person on the list to be so featured. In particular, the strong members of the Mzough U'Tiv were irked by this development, and my stalkers became more enraged at me. They swore severally and jointly to change that arrangement in no time.

The question on the lips of Mzough U'Tiv members and their sympathisers pertained to how it happened that I'd become a favourite of Gyang in the new dispensation, and how it happened so quickly and against all the calculations of the Benue elite and the consternation of the Tiv elite. As the only one amongst the heads, deans, and directors holding two posts, my academic profile was significantly projected into one of great influence on Gyang, which was what they wished to stop as soon as possible.

Within that period, lasting for probably six months, Gyang and I got on quite well. We became friends, and his family and mine praying together at morning devotion at his lodge a few times. Every now and then, he would call on me to draft papers or speeches for him or to represent him at certain occasions, the exact situation that opened me to envy of my adversaries and my stalkers during the days of Idachaba. Thus, bickering continued unabated amongst my colleagues, who were so much in envy of my productive relationship with Idachaba and of my own contentment in life coupled with my disciplined hard work.

However, Gyang and I did not hobnob for too long before my preexisting stalkers became aggrieved about our friendship, and so they ganged up to sow the seeds of discord between us and brew calculated hostilities between the two of us. That gradually destroyed our relationship till we were no longer on speaking terms, and later it burst into an open clash.

* * *

Quickly Gyang launched a surreptitious investigation of official cars in my custody at the instance of Idachaba. My belief was that the investigation was not targeted at me directly but at my former boss, Idachaba, with a view to finding faults with him retroactively in order to impugn his integrity, destroy his legacy, and subject him to public odium for no just cause. Gyang had surreptitiously investigated Idachaba on a false allegation of "fraudulent purchase of a car that he escaped with together with another vehicle from the university". The enquiry, though targeted at finding fault of financial fraud against Idachaba, would have also roped me in as the person who'd perfected the purchase and arrangement to send the two cars to Idachaba's custody at Ibadan months after he had left the university. However, the investigation was quickly aborted when facts emerged indicating that the car in question was not purchased from university money but from project money (the federal government–funded Rural Infrastructures Survey Project, which had Idachaba as coordinator and me as project officer since our Ibadan days), and that the second car was also a project car (the Federal Ministry of Education sponsored the Middle-level Agricultural Education project), which also had Idachaba as team leader and me as project officer. Both projects had their origin from the University of Ibadan and not UNIAGRIC Makurdi, and activities under them merely continued at Makurdi, where we had moved the cars and other project facilities. As to the newly purchased car, it was found that as the officer who initiated the purchase of the car, I'd followed due process, including the involvement of the purchasing unit and the Works Department whose officers performed the necessary due diligence and the necessary fitness tests in the process.

During Idachaba's time, I acknowledge that these cars were in my custody, projects or no projects, contributing to my high professional profile on campus. I had drawn considerable envy from my colleagues and others who saw possession of vehicles as a status symbol. But unknown to me, some people on campus had ascribed the ownership of the project cars to the university (and more so that they carried official government plate numbers), thereby misconstruing my decision to send two of them to Ibadan as a criminal act of helping Idachaba to escape with government vehicles. The matter was quickly tabled before Gyang and became the subject of a surreptitious enquiry. It was the lot of one Mr A. Ntwenem, a prominent crusader of ethnic agenda in the Mzough U'Tiv group, to conduct the investigation and bring Idachaba to book at all costs. However they found nothing incriminating against Idachaba, and so the allegation of wrongdoing was dropped and everyone involved withdrew to his shell in shame.

They didn't even bother to take any evidence from me before Gyang disbanded the investigating team.

From the outset, in line with the surreptitious plan to tribalise the institution, non-indigenes and other loyalists of Idachaba soon faced intense persecution at the hands of Gyang. Prominent among them were Professor Ikenna Onyido (Ibo-speaking from Anambra State), Dr Olusola Agbede (Yoruba-speaking from Ekiti State), Mr Gbadegesin Adelabu (Yoruba-speaking from Oyo State), Arc Victor Daudu (Ebira from Kogi State), Dr Biyi Shoremi (Yoruba, Ogun State), Dr John Ayoade (Yoruba, Ogun State), and Dr Ayodele Ojo (Yoruba, Osun State. Likewise, many students of the *uke* flock became endangered species at the university, and many other people who abhorred the tense and hostile atmosphere simply decided to flee from the university on their own volition.

Apart from ethnic bigotry and the desperate pursuit of Idachaba, another defining character of administration of the university under Gyang was systemic corruption. Unfortunately for him, in August 1999 a presidential visitation panel was set up by President Olusegun Obasanjo for the university, which gave the opportunity for many people to let off their pent-up steam through petitions against Gyang, bordering on several acts of fraud that opened him up to the public eye as someone presiding over a deeply corrupt system. However, as was widely believed, the panel itself (chaired by a former agriculture minister, Dr Shettima Mustafa) soon had its integrity compromised when its members were alleged of accepting bribes and other corrupt inducements from Gyang and his agents. Little wonder that the report of the panel was manifestly watery in the end and failed to indict Gyang for the several acts of corruption alleged, let alone recommend punitive actions against him for the same.

In order to open the way for unbridled corruption, as it appears, Gyang had hurriedly sent two prominent officers of the university on compulsory leave without any allegation of wrongdoing, in particular the acting bursar, Mr Gbadegesin Adelabu, and the director of physical planning, Arc Victor Daudu. Not a few people smelt a rat in that action, judging from the critical roles of the two officers in the university as principal budget holders, and also the fact that both officers were instrumental in the financial and physical successes of Idachaba's administration. Bursar was the man in charge of funds disbursements, and Daudu was in charge of implementation of major capital projects during the entire period. Even though both officers came back to face further frustrations Gyang put in their ways, they were never allowed to return to their original posts, having been improperly replaced with indigenes from the state while they were away.

Then an era ensued that threw due process to the winds and witnessed wanton corruption through budget padding, kickbacks, and other illicit flow of funds into private pockets—such practices that were unheard off during the tenure of Idachaba. At one instance, Gyang directed a bursary circular to be issued to all budget holders in the university to recommit their cumulative expenditures pending payments in the cash office for a long time before. To me, knowing that the expenditures of my department and centre had previously been entered as spent in the vote book already, this indicated an intention to commit fraud at the instance of Gyang. In order to extricate myself from such intention, I responded to the circular—not to the bursar but to the VC himself—directly asking for confirmation "so as to avoid a fraud". Such a confirmation never came to me, suggesting I was right. Following these and similar developments afterwards, the press soon went agog to focus on the university with stories of corruption through explosive news items and screaming headlines that soon marred the enviable image that the combination of Idachaba and Onyido had built for the institution in the past.

Similarly, the victimisation of non-indigenes was a defining feature of Gyang's administration of the university, which had proceeded unabated; the goal was to pave the way for their replacement by yet-to-be-qualified indigenes, thereby accelerating the delibcrate indigenisation of the institution as mandated by state elites. This policy was quick in changing the staff structure from the previous dominance of competent staff to the preponderance of immature staff in critical posts, such as appointing junior and assistant lecturers as heads of department. A case in point was that of Drs Olusola Agbede and Adeleke Ojo (both Yoruba-speaking by tribe), who were early victims of the aberrant policy. The church service was midway one Sunday morning when Mrs Agbede beckoned to me to come out. She quietly told me that police officers had come to their house and arrested her husband. I had heard before that Dr Agbede had crossed Gyang's path somehow, but no one knew what his offence was, including Agbede himself. I was sure his wife chose me out of the whole congregation for intervention because I was the only person amongst the Yoruba-speaking *ukes* who had some semblance of a close relationship with Gyang. The Agbedes and my family were close enough to elicit my sympathy about his senseless arrest from his house on campus.

I rushed to the police station, where I discovered that another non-indigene, Dr Ojo, had also been picked up by the police and detained like Agbede. Ojo's wife had also contacted Dr Bello in order to secure the release of her husband, and he was there. Bello and I spent many hours before the officer on duty allowed them to see us, saying they were acting on the instructions of the VC to not release both men on bail. When we asked what Gyang's complaint was, we were told that both of them were suspected by Gyang to be "NADECO agents".

"Oh, my God!" I shouted. NADECO stood for the National Democratic Coalition, a body of Nigerian democrats who confronted the federal military government of Sanni Abacha to step down for Chief M. K. O. Abiola, who was believed to have been elected president in 1993, but the election was annulled by President Babangida. The agitation was so intense that Babangida abdicated power for General Abacha to take over, who hunted NADECO members at home and abroad for instant elimination. At that time, anybody found to be related to or associated with NADECO was a living corpse in the hands of secret hitmen, who had already assassinated prominent people in the southwest, including Abiola's wife. The fear of NADECO was the beginning of wisdom all over the country, particularly on university campuses where students or staff could be easily sympathetic and cause troubles.

Bello and I knew that if we did not act fast, our colleagues (both being Yoruba from the south-west) would be whisked away to Abuja by the police or military, and it could be the end of their lives. We started making frantic calls with my Thuraya phone until help came late in the evening for them to be released. I asked myself, *What is that? And what does all this portend for the university?*

To spoil my mood further, the following day when I spoke to Gyang in appeasement about this development and how fears had gripped a section of the people on campus, he didn't care a hoot if the worst happened to non-indigenes who were still around. Unruffled and grandstanding, he simply advised me to warn all *ukes* on campus, including me, to behave properly; otherwise he was ready to deal with them summarily. Ha! How things had changed. People were no longer safe, and the spirit of fear and servitude had suddenly and heavily descended on us all. From this point on, my anger boiled against Gyang, and no one needed to tell me that the friendship between him and me would not last.

Makurdi Varsity:
A Tale of Woes and Corruption

Newswatch

Tales of Tribalism And Corruption

University of Agriculture Makurdi is riddled with allegations of "ethnic cleansing" and monumental fraud

By Nick Odeh

PAGE FOUR   WEDNESDAY, AUGUST 29, 2001

New NIGERIAN

EDITORIAL

ETHNIC JINGOISM

SOME senior employees of the Federal University of Agriculture, Makurdi, Benue State, claiming to be members of a "Tiv Senior Staff Association" are demanding that the Vice-Chancellor of the institution must be, not only an indigene of the state, but of the Tiv tribe. They did not stop there. They are, in the words of their President, "fully prepared to defend, jointly and severally the collective interests" of their members by doing battle with anyone who would stand in the way of their objective. Worse still, they vowed to make the university "unmanageable" should their bid fail.

This threat, in the opinion of the New Nigerian, is mean, uncalled for and at best, tantamount to taking ethnic nationalism too far. First, to insist on a Tiv Vice-Chancellor in a federal university simply because the institution is situated in a state in which the Tiv may be the majority tribe is crass insensitivity, pre-posterous and totally negates the hallowed concept of a university. They reason that as the host community, they deserve to have their own at the very top to defend their interest. But perhaps the Tiv would have earned some sympathy if they had made a case to include the Idoma, Agatu and Itun, who together with the Tiv make up the state.

Second, the fact that three professors recommended by the university council to the Visitor, President Olusegun Obasanjo for appointment as Vice-Chancellor are all Tiv makes the Tiv senior staffers' threat absolutely unnecessary and suspect.

They also alleged that southerners, Igbo, to be specific have cornered 17 of the 34 management positions in the university. Much as we would call for caution here. The danger inherent in pushing a brazen ethnic agenda such as the Tiv's is that the agitators stand the grave risk of being caught on their own petard in the long run.

For instance, by demanding that only a Tiv man be made V.C. of UNIAGRIC in Makurdi, they may dangerously be foreclosing the chances of their qualified kinsmen heading similar institutions in other states. When Professor Daniel Saror, was appointed in 1993/94 as the Vice Chancellor of Federal Government-owned Ahmadu Bello University (ABU), Zaria, his tribe was neither the foremost consideration nor did the indigenes of Kaduna State play the tribe or ethnic card. For this alone, we dismiss the Tiv's threat as politically disingenuous.

Furthermore, we need say that their demand smacks of egregious greed. UNIAGRIC represents a great and remarkable federal presence such. By all means, let a qualified indigene of the state or citizen of Nigeria head the institution but we find the agitators' ground of threat as defeatist, infantile and the language undeservedly confrontational.

The petitioners may have already done an irreparable damage to their cause by making that threat. The Visitor may decide to reject all three nominees and pick a non-Tiv or a non-Benue State indigene for that matter and he will be perfectly legally right to do so. That would be a terrible price to pay for unbridled greed and insensitivity. And the threat, if that happens, to make the university "unmanageable" can only be an inverted way of promoting ethnic nationalism which will definitely leave Benue State infrastructurally poorer.

Tower of Corruption

Erastus Gyang, vice-chancellor of the University of Agriculture, Makurdi, receives knocks and no kudos by all those who appeared before the presidential visitation panel on the institution

By Nick Odeh

THE PRESIDENTIAL visitation panel to the University of Agriculture, Makurdi, UAM, has wound up its public sittings after considering about 80 memoranda and oral testimonies from the public. The visitation panel was set up by President Olusegun Obasanjo last August to look into the activities of the university.

Specifically, it was to look into the financial management of the institution and determine whether it was in compliance with appropriate regulations. It was also required to look into the leadership quality of the university in terms of the roles of the governing council, the vice-chancellor and other principal officers.

Furthermore, the panel was to investigate the application of funds, particularly the special grants and loans meant for specific projects in order to determine the nature of such projects and their relevance for further funding. Other terms of reference included examination of the adequacy of staff and staff development programmes as well as the relationship between the university and the various statutory bodies and other external organs; costs and officers to determine if such relationship accords with the law establishing the university.

From the avalanche of petitions before the panel, Erastus Gyang, the vice-chancellor, received more knocks and hardly any kudos by those who made representations to the panel.

The vice-chancellor was accused of manipulating the UAM approved 1998/99 budget. Thomas Onyido, a professor of chemistry, described as scandalous the N2.5 million and 0.5 million budgeted for running the vice-chancellor's lodge under "administrative and general expenditure" funds (Code 001 item 2053) and "vice-chancellor's office, (Code 607 item 2053) respectively. According to Onyido, these allocations amounts "to ...

Gyang: Under fire for alleged improprieties

... disposed as grants."

Several other discrepancies in the 1998/99 budget were highlighted in another memorandum submitted by R.S. Haruna, a former dean of student affairs in the institution. Haruna stated that apart from the "administration and general expenditure" vote, and that of the "VC's office" there were also votes for the VC's charity fund (N250,000), entertainment (N0.5 million) and hospitality (N0.5 million).

The budget also provides for N1 million security expenses inspite of a separate budget for the security department. By this ...

Newswatch, November 29, 1999

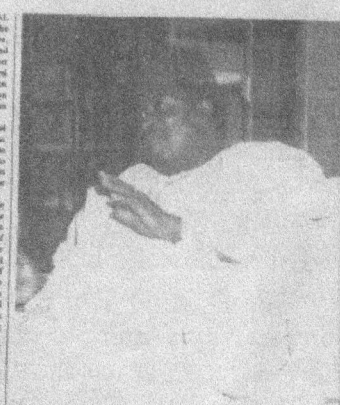

25

How the Hostility Brewed Against me

I was later to learn that my instrumentality in the management of various project funds in the university informed Gyang's decision to remove my name from the hit list in the hope that he would be able to make a deal with me in micromanaging the fund. Though he made a few entreaties in that direction as regards the funds for implementing the RIS project, such deals never materialised because I vehemently disallowed it to happen. Therefore he immediately directed me to move the project's funds away from the university. I hurriedly did so with the concurrence of Idachaba; the project fund was moved to Projects Coordinating Unit of the Federal Ministry of Agriculture that funded it. That action was our very first area of disagreement that dented our relationship. Afterwards, we went on for some time as tongue-in-cheek friends. As a result, he quietly meted some punishment to me by declining approval of my travel claims, even for those trips he had sent me on to represent him before the strain in our relationship had occurred.

Later, another skirmish occurred. This was over another project of mine funded by UNDP at my centre. It was entitled Characterisation of Socioeconomic Activities and Developmental Needs of Rural Poor Women in the Central Zone of Nigeria. The letter of award of this project stipulated that a separate bank account should be opened for the project in the name of the centre rather than using the university-wide account. I began the processing to notify the VC and invite the bursar to act as a signatory to the account, in addition to the finance officer at the centre and me as cosignatories. Gyang told me to lodge the money of the project in the university account instead, but I knew the ulterior motive behind that and strongly declined. Then when he learnt that I had succeeded in opening the account at First Bank, which had the university bursar, Mr Adelabu, and my finance officer at the centre, Mrs Adama, as cosignatories, he directed the registrar to close it down immediately and transfer the money to the university account. This caused me to send a formal appeal to Gyang on the matter. It was dated 19 January 1998.

> Sir, recall my earlier appeal for your kind intervention in this matter; as this threatens the premature termination of the research, I am afraid that the centre may be blacklisted, which does not augur well for future submission of research proposals to UNDP and other international agencies. If this happens, it will be disadvantageous to CEFAS and the university at large against the hope in the future when the centre becomes fully autonomous and can compete for research funds in the international community. Therefore, I count on your usual encouragements in this regard, sir.

He didn't budge. Instead, I received a message from the VC's wife that said I should see her urgently. In the early morning, I rushed to the VC's lodge while wondering what the matter was. As I entered the compound and alighted from the car, she was in front of the building and was about to enter her own car to move out. As soon as she saw me at a short distance, she yelled hysterically, "Ayoola!" loudly enough for the security men at the gate to hear and pay attention to us.

From the short distance, I said, "Good morning, madam."

Then she went on. "I understand you have received some money from UNDP." Holding out her right hand, she said, "Where is my own? N200, 000, upfront"

I was visibly shocked, short of being embarrassed in the full glare of her aides and other domestic staff as well as the gatemen, who were still waiting for her car to move out. Somehow I managed to gather myself and force a grin. "That is true, but it is meant for implementing a project at the centre." I diplomatically added, "However, if you can come formally, I will see what can be done." I turned back towards my car while wondering whether she was satisfied and what the reaction of her husband would be, who knew that like Idachaba, I had zero tolerance for fraud in the system.

Subsequently, Mrs Gyang came formally as advised, through a letter to me as director of CEFAS dated 26 January 1998. It was entitled "Request for Funding to Expand the UNIAGRIC Women Association Makurdi Chapter's Fish Farm Project". I saw this as mere subterfuge and as a damage-control measure at the insistence of Gyang himself. In any case, I refused to be deceived and turned down her request with the maximum politeness and diplomacy I could muster.

> CEFAS as an organ of the university is not a funding agency ... I will contact you as soon as the next tranche of fund is available from the sponsors (UNDP) together with the package of candidate intervention projects to be supported ... It should not be difficult for us to obtain necessary approval of the vice chancellor.

A first manifestation of pent-up anger nursed by Gyang soon came by way of a subtle threat. He sent it to me regarding my contribution at the meeting of deans and directors at which Gyang announced the promotion of Dr S. A. Ikurior to the rank of professor, along with those of other staff. At the meeting. the announcement of Ikurior's promotion quickly appeared to me as fraud. This was because he was not one of those whose publications were sent out to external assessors before Idachaba's tenure had elapsed and which the assessment outcomes were being expected. It was announced in a manner that smacked of favouritism marbled with impunity, too infuriating for me to contain it. It was a breach of the long-standing process leading to the promotion of an associate professor to the rank of full professor let alone a senior lecturer directly to the rank of professor. My sin was the audacity I had, while others looked on, to ask Gyang for an explanation of how it had happened in the case of Ikurior, a fellow Tiv man, an old classmate of his, and the person rumoured to become the deputy VC as ordained by the ethnic caucus. Apparently, he wasn't prepared for that question, and so he could only babble with a phony response.

Incidentally, my case for promotion to the rank of professor came up at the same meeting, so as usual, I was asked to step out when it was to be discussed. As I later understood, the intervention I made on the case of Dr Ikurior almost spoilt my case because the countenance of Gyang appeared to have changed against me. I was told how he tried to stall it by way of unnecessary questions suggestive of deep-seated hostility and anger about me. At last my case succeeded despite all that, and Gyang grudgingly agreed to let it pass—but not without a warning for me. As a fallout of that encounter, the friendship between Ikurior and I waxed progressively cold at the senior staff quarters, where we both lived as next-door neighbours. But, notwithstanding the distance we kept between each other for a long time, which ultimately robbed on our wives, our children remained close friends.

Incidentally, even as innocuous as the report of the Mustafa's visitation panel was, it clearly indicted Gyang on matters of promotions and other irresponsible administrative actions during his era. As if to vindicate me on my previous position on such matters in retrospect, the white paper subsequently issued by the federal government, based on the report, accepted the recommendation of the panel that "All cases of staff appointments, regularisations, promotions, upgrading and discipline including termination, retirement and dismissal since January 1 1996, (i.e. the endpoint of Idachaba's tenure) should be reviewed by the Governing Council when constituted".

And the Bubble Finally Burst at Abuja

Unknown to me, word had reached Abuja on the situation at UNIAGRIC, and several petitions (anonymous or otherwise) alleging Gyang with corruption, nepotism, and gross mismanagement of the institution had been written by affected people.

One day I received a memo from the VC's office, which stated that the supervising minister at the Federal Ministry of Agriculture, Alhaji Malami Buwai, had invited the committee of deans and directors to an emergency meeting at his office in Abuja, the agenda unknown. The meeting was held on 8 May 1998, and a bus was provided on a day trip to Abuja. The bus drove behind the VC's car to the meeting being held in the minister's conference room. In it, the directors of departments in the ministry were sitting opposite the university staff at the conference table, and the VC sat closest to the minister.[1]

---

[1] Attendance at the said meeting was as follows.
- Ministry of Agriculture and Natural Resources: Dr Malami Buwai (Honourable Minister of Agriculture; Chairman), Alhaji Mai M. Jir (Director of Planning, Research, and Statistics), Mr O. A. Edache (Director of Agriculture), Mr L. H. V. Tsumbu (Deputy Director, AUCA; Secretary)
- University of Agriculture, Makurdi: Prof. E. O. Gyang (Vice-Chancellor), Mr E. Kureve (Ag. Registrar), Mr G. B. A. Adelabu (Ag. Bursar), Professor M. C. Njike (Ag. Dean, Postgraduate School), Professor B. A. Kalu (Dean, College of Agronomy), Dr E. I. Kucha (Ag. Dean, College Of Engr. and Engr. Technology), Dr N. G. Ehiobu (Ag. Dean, College of Animal Science and Fisheries), Dr E. P. Ejembi (Ag. Dean, College of Agric. Economics and Extension), Dr O. Amali (Ag. Dean, College of Science, Agric. and Science

The minister opened the meeting without prayers, which was strange according to my knowledge of professional meetings I had held with the same minister before. Getting straight to the point, he asked if we knew the agenda, and the general response was no. He was surprised because according to him, he had directed that each member of the committee should be served the notice of meeting, which indicated that we should all be prepared to frankly and truthfully discuss the issue. But that was not the case because the VC had hidden the actual notice of meeting and directed the registrar to issue a cover-up notice instead. The aim was to prevent us on campus from knowing the specific items on the agenda, which included the issue of petitions about Gyang's maladministration, such as financial corruption, nepotism, and brutality. The minister, after expressing his disappointment about that and slightly castigating the VC, listed the specific topics for discussion. These included the avalanche of petitions, which he said was at a rate that surpassed any other agency under the ministry, with specific reference to allegations of corruption, victimisation of the Idachaba boys, and ethnic cleansing as the most topical, amongst others. The minister then directed that each of us must talk about these allegations as the officers in the top echelon of university management under Gyang. To my astonishment, Buwai said that he had convened the meeting as a last chance for Gyang to change his mode of administration before decisively dealing with the situation. My immediate thought when I heard that was that the story about a forthright minister who returned kickback money allegedly sent to him by Gyang was probably true.

The minister started by asking each of us to introduce ourselves. He went from his left side so that Gyang would be the last to speak. As in the case of Ikurior at the senate meeting, I was bemused while one

---

Education), Dr C. C. Ariahu (Ag. Dean, College off Food Technology), Dr S. O. Awonorin (Ag. Dean of Students), Professor Ikenna Onyido (Director, Center for Agrochemical Technology), Arc. V. S. Daudu (Director, Physical Facilities), Dr D. K. Adedzwa (Ag. Director, CEC), Dr G. B. Ayoola (Ag. Director CEFAS and Head, Dept. of Agricultural Economics), Dr P. O. Erhabor (Ag. Director, UNIAGRIC Consult), Dr S. A. Ikurior (Ag. Director, Academic Planning)

officer after another lied through their teeth by saying that all was well at UNIAGRIC under Gyang—until the turn of Daudu, Onyido, and myself, sitting together in that order. The minister adjusted his sit to hear the truth from the three of us. Daudu stated that he wrote one of the petitions and put his name there, which was about the way he was maltreated out of his office as director of physical planning, how he was sent on compulsory leave without committing any offence, how another person (Mr Ola) was put in his post in his absence, and how he had been sidelined in managing his directorate since he'd resumed duty from an unsolicited leave.

Onyido also spoke frankly. He had not written any petition to the minister before, but he had a letter of appeal in mind bordering on how Gyang was mistreating him in the university as the acting VC who'd handed the university over to him and a deputy VC to Idachaba before then. Gyang had scuttled the smooth running of the Centre for Agrochemical Technology (CAT), which he'd established in the university with funding he'd obtained from CIDA (Canadian International Development Centre). Gyang had lied to security agents that Onyido was making bombs in his laboratory, which caused a visit from the naval authorities to him on the matter. These were just a few of the hardships he'd suffered at the hands of Gyang.

Then it was my turn to speak, and thank God that I spoke my mind with unalloyed honesty and truth, albeit as diplomatically as I could, much to the consternation of everybody present! I said, "My understanding of these three issues is as follows. I have no knowledge of the issue of financial mismanagement. Since I am not involved in the management of finances of the university, I have no evidence against the good office of the vice chancellor. The second allegation, which borders on ethnic cleansing, is only apparent under the administration of Professor Gyang, but it is probably not real. Using myself as an example, I am not an indigene of the state. Yet I hold two administrative posts, and I'm the only person in this room with that privilege. This is what a lot of people have been scrambling for. If the man had the intention of carrying out ethnic cleansing as alleged, would he have favoured me, a non-indigene, with two posts?" I chose my words carefully, though the allegation of ethnic cleansing against the VC couldn't have been more glaring.

"All I can say is that certain things have been happening which are indicative of the ethnic cleansing alleged," I went on. "For instance, there have been recent sackings and suspensions in the university since the VC arrived, and not one of these people was an indigene." Indeed, there were other issues that presented a strong case about the man's ethnic cleansing agenda. A particular incident that came to my mind as I talked was the arrests of Dr Ojo and Dr Agbede. I was in the church when the news of their arrests by police reached me. I had gone with some members of their families to the police station, and we were there all day. None of us knew what their offences were. But when the two lecturers were eventually released, one of the policemen told me that the VC had come to report the two lecturers as NADECO members. NADECO was a forbidden word during Abacha's self-succession plan, and anyone suspected of belonging to the coalition was in for a lot of trouble.

I decided not to bring up the incident directly. "If there were such things as ethnic cleansing in the university, I am the wrong person to ask because it has not affected me in any way. As for the last issue, which is the victimisation of Idachaba boys, I can categorically say there is no evidence to substantiate that. Again, I'd use myself as an example. If there is anyone who comes close to being called an Idachaba boy, I qualify more than anyone in the university for being so closely associated with Idachaba before, during, and after his tenure as VC of the university. But this has still not deterred Professor Gyang from giving me two posts under his cabinet. It's hardly what one expects from anyone with an agenda against the so-called Idachaba boys. Therefore I really don't think he hates Idachaba or believes in the existence of his boys on campus." However, I went on, the issue of the senseless use of the phrase *Idachaba boys* cannot be controverted. The issue has to be viewed within its historical context. The phrase predates the vice chancellor; therefore, the man has nothing to do with it."

To substantiate my point here, I pointed at Professor Njike. "This man sitting across the room coined the phrase when he stormed into my office one day during Idachaba's administration. He had been having this running battle with the former vice chancellor, and when the vice chancellor went on his terminal leave before the end of his first term in 1991, it had been widely thought he would not be coming back. So Professor Njike entered my office, ostensibly to provoke me. He said, 'All of you Idachaba boys, when he does not get his second term— we will make sure he does not get it—we will see where you will go. We will personally carry your loads and dump them inside the River Benue.' I must point out that I am a victim of transferred aggression from Professor Njike, who was a senior member of my faculty at that time." We were using faculty then when we were still restructuring the school. "The man has been oppressing me ever since the former VC refused to give him a post under his cabinet, when they fell out over the issue of his promotion. Professor Njike has especially targeted me because of my perceived closeness to the former VC. It was this continuous oppression that made me resign my membership of a committee he chaired in 1993.

"Sir, the new VC came in 1996; this is 1998. People are saying he is victimising Idachaba boys; I don't believe this. The victimisation started before he came. However, if the vice chancellor gives these perpetrators of the victimisation of Idachaba boys room to continue with their nefarious agenda, then I think the petitions against the vice chancellor will continue. I remember taking up this issue of victimisation of Idachaba boys with the vice chancellor, and I advised him to stop people like Njike. The vice chancellor is here, and he can attest to that."

Professor Onyido's statement at the meeting clearly corroborated mine. He stated that he did not write any petitions but expressed surprise that the state security service had interrogated him at the instance of Gyang, which was based on wrongful accusations, from being the head of a cult group on campus to making bombs in his laboratory as a chemist and breaching national security by receiving scientific equipment from Canadian International Development Agency (CIDA) under his project. Corroborating the allegation of ethnic cleansing agenda of Gyang's administration, he stated that he too had appealed to the VC to accept all his staff and treat them equally. He was motivated to attend this meeting as an opportunity for him to appeal to the honourable minister to talk to the VC in order to provide an environment conducive for effective teaching and research in the university.

After everyone else had talked, the minister said to the VC, "What do you have to say?"

"Well ..." Professor Gyang's voice cracked with an emotion that I couldn't fathom. "As Dr Ayoola has spoken, if I had any ethnic cleansing agenda, I wouldn't have given him two posts under my cabinet. The allegation of victimisation of Idachaba boys is a non-issue. I have adopted an open-door policy in my running of the university, where everybody has been given equal opportunity to excel. As you can see, nobody here has said anything contrary to this."

"OK, fine." The minister's voice was gentler now. "Thank you very much for honouring my invitation. The purpose of this meeting, as I said earlier, is not to apportion blame on any of you, but to address the complaints that have been raised in the various petitions addressed to me." He looked at the VC. "You should further investigate these complaints and look for ways to address them ... to foster peaceful co-existence among all members of staff. There should be regular flow of communication between the ministry and your institution to eliminate the mistrust among staff.

"You should all endeavour to live in peace and not allow yourselves to be summoned to a similar meeting. Go back and put your house in order. Then come back and give me feedback."

The meeting ended on that note, or at least, so I thought. Outside, clouds gathered on the horizon, accentuating the silence that hung heavily on us as we departed for Makurdi. Everyone was preoccupied with his thoughts, oblivious to the hasty departure of the VC, who had already gone ahead with his driver. In my estimation, I had done what needed to be done. Even though so many had hedged around the main issues, I had brought to the fore the problems besetting the university. In truth, it worried me greatly that things had degenerated to such an extent. The recent brain drain from the university was alarming, the atmosphere of fear the new administration had engendered was worrying, and staff spirits had been crushed. No, there was no way I would simply fold my arms and watch an institution I'd helped build go to ruin on ethnical whims or whatnots. It was imperative that someone spoke up to arrest further deterioration of the situation.

There was no doubt the minister was ready to terminate the VC's appointment. His statement for us to go back and put our house in order was a warning rattle before a more drastic decision would be taken, if situations remained unchanged. This fact was very much confirmed when I later heard the minister had initially made up his mind to remove the VC. But it was the former registrar, Mr Lawrence Tsumbu, who had an office in the ministry, who waded in by enlisting the help of some close friends of the minister to prevail on the man to rescind his decision. The minimum he could do was to summon us deans and directors to a meeting, as he did.

Ideally, no minister has the power to remove the vice chancellor of a university. But a supervising ministry serves as a channel for the flow of information between the office of the president and the university. It also helps in the regulation of affairs, especially in the absence of a governing council, which had been the case since Professor Gyang had arrived. In any case, it was the period of the military, where impunity was the order of the day; paradoxically, the VC's excesses needed some reining in.

Unfortunately, soon after the Abuja meeting with the minister, a cabinet reshuffle took place in the federal government, and the agriculture minister, Malami Buwai, was changed to another person, Alh. Sani Zango Daura. Then Gyang, breathing an air of relief from the pressure from Abuja, quickly convened another deans and directors meeting on 18 May 1998, and he tongue-lashed me about my contribution at the Abuja meeting. He howled and raged at me. I managed to keep my cool till the end, watching the eyes of Dr Segun Awonorin across the table urging me to remain calm. When Gyang lost control of himself in anger, the meeting came to an abrupt end. As he rose to go, fuming and beating his chest and boasting, he said that he had gotten all it would take to nail me down, and he swore he would do so at all costs. He said he and I had stepped into the same trousers (I didn't know how that was possible) and that he would show me he was a son of the soil, which I was not. I quietly followed him, and some officers present at the meeting followed to pacify him in the long corridor between the council chambers and the VC's office. He kept bragging and promising the fire and brimstone he would hurl at me in due course. I walked behind him and others by his side. Midway, he looked back and saw me, stopped suddenly, and raged at me for a moment as if to throw a punch, but I was too far away to take it. My intention was to follow him to his office and tender an apology to him, but some of my colleagues advised me against this, and so I turned back to go home.

Downstairs, I noticed his car pulling out from the garage and asked my driver, David, to follow him to the lodge. He probably noticed I was the one behind him, and so he instructed the gatemen to shut the gate before I reached it. One of them walked to my car and bent down to pass the instruction of VC to me that I should not be allowed into the lodge. I asked my driver to pull back towards my residence within the same staff quarters. I went straight to my study, turned on the computer, and typed out a letter of apology for what had happened. I gave it to David to deliver it by hand to VC's lodge. I wrote in complete sobriety.

Professor E. O. Gyang,
Vice Chancellor,
University of Agriculture Makurdi

Before the sun sets, sir, I must apologize profusely for embarrassing you at the Abuja meeting as revealed to me earlier today. But God knows, that was the exact opposite of my objective at the meeting; so I feel an urgent need for quick clarifications.

I had reasoned that, given the premise established by the Hon. Minister that the university administration had been variously accused through petitions, it seemed somewhat unnecessary at that stage to say that issues of ethnic divide did not exist with us; after all they did also exist with the past administration(s) and elsewhere in the civil service. I thought that what was important at that point in time under the mood of the ministry was to show that the university administration did not mastermind such issues and had nothing to do with them; that was exactly what I tried to do that I have now been totally misunderstood. I ventured to be empirical about my submission, citing the case of myself under your administration.

As to my citing of Professor M. C. Njike in my statement, merely to drive home the point, when you are kind to grant me an audience I will express how I feel.

I am really sorry that my short contribution at Abuja in the way I did has now produced an unintended consequence, and I hope you will overlook the impolitic referencing to Professor Njike and other aspects that made you so angry with me on the issue.

Thank you, sir.

G. B. Ayoola.

18/5/98

Then I gave the day's encounter a thought for a moment and shut my mind to it, expecting the very worst to happen. For the next two months or so, I lived in fear of Gyang, not knowing what he would do to me in due course, as he has promised. Later, in association with my fellow endangered people on campus—specifically Agbede, Onyido, and Daudu—a formal complaint was submitted to the new minister, Daura. The letter, titled "The Bizarre Situation at University of Agriculture Makurdi", was an audit of Gyang's maladministration in its different aspects and dimensions, but it was not acknowledged, let alone acted upon by the minister.

Meanwhile, a period of uneasy calm ensued between Gyang and me, during which I expected something bad to happen to me. Sometimes I had a moment of quiet monologue. How was this war between Gyang, as head of the institution, and me, a simple-minded university teacher, going to be fought, won, and lost? Sometimes I had a moment of quiet soliloquy. Sure, my days were numbered in the offices I held, but that didn't bother me a hoot. I was convinced of towing the right path and doing the right thing all along. I insisted on accountability and transparency in managing public funds under my watch for research and general administration of my centre and department, I had spoken up in senate and other official meetings against the application of non-merit criteria for appointment or promotion of university staff, affecting my colleagues and friends. I'd said the truth with maximum diplomacy at the extraordinary meeting with the minister at Abuja on issues bordering on maladministration, particularly the adoption of tribalism, nepotism, and corruption as deliberate policies in running a university. Thinking about these things in retrospect, there was no regret whatsoever. But how did I move forward in my present situation, when the VC had openly declared a war against me? I simply overruled myself and began to move out of the institution in my mind. It was something of a restraint. What about my pending promotion to the rank of professor, which the process had commenced and my publications were sent to external assessors? All the same, I should get out of the university before it was too late.

From the outset of the looming crisis, I felt the need to turn to God, even as revelations came indicating that I could win the war only on my knees. First, at the instance of Onyido, the four families in focus organised a constant prayer meeting on every Friday, specifically to table our matters as things unfolded. Next, some brethren raised themselves into prayer warriors for us specifically and the generally bad atmosphere on campus, as what became known as "Thursday Watchers", in order to continually intercede for us in prayer on a weekly basis. Onyido was part of it from the start, and I subsequently joined Wilson Asawanta, Biyi Oluremi, Friday Ugbenyo, Joel Adaji, and Sola Solomon, to whose family homes the "Ark of God" moved from one week to the next as venues for intensive prayers. Furthermore, I mobilised for prayer from home, especially at the Christ Apostolic Church, in which my father-in-law was a pastor. But for this diligent prosecution of the Gyang war, I am sure the story would have been different for the four of us, and we would have been totally consumed.

My Three Stalkers

Dr J. C. Umeh

He and I were postgraduate students in the department of agricultural economics at the University of Ibadan in the 1980s, where we were not particularly close. At that time, he was a PhD student under Professor Idachaba, and I was an MSc and PhD student under Professor A. O. Falusi. I became a research assistant to Idachaba on his famous Rural Infrastructures Survey (RIS) project, thereby becoming a career staff of his, and my profile rose with his when he became the head of the Federal Agricultural Coordinating Unit (FACU) and later the VC of UNIAGRIC, Makurdi. I was instrumental to Umeh's appointment as a senior lecturer at UNIAGRIC.

Following an initial vacancy announcement, Idachaba told me to scout for qualified staff for our new department, I travelled to various universities in the country to invite qualified agricultural economists to join our brand-new department. At that time, Umeh was occupying a Lecturer I position at the University of Ilorin, Kwara State, as was I. He jumped at the invitation, which he saw as an opportunity to not only move a step up on the academic ladder but also move closer to his home state in the southeast. When I told him that Nsukka was to be my next port of call, he requested I took a letter along to his wife at that place, which I gladly accepted to do, and indeed I did. I believed it contained the topic of our discussion. I urged Umeh to respond to the vacancy announcement and promised him I would discuss his demand for a higher position with Idachaba as an incentive for him to do so. Even though Idachaba's disposition to Umeh's coming was not so enthusiastic, which I understood in the context of Umeh's recalcitrant behaviour as a student under his supervision at Ibadan, it was possible for university authorities to offer him a senior lecturer position as he desired.

However, to my surprise, no sooner had Umeh assumed duty in my department than he developed a deep-seated contempt for me at UNIAGRIC, at first by grandstanding about such petty things as my calling him, now a senior colleague, by his first name. Later, when he became head of department, he stalked me incessantly, in envy of my closer relationship with Idachaba. In any case, I also gained promotion to the rank of senior lecturer, and soon afterwards I was subsequently appointed as director of the prestigious Centre for Food and Agricultural Strategy (CEFAS), a development that substantially deflated Umeh's ego.

When Gyang came on as the new VC, it was quite obvious to me and everybody else that Umeh felt particularly bitter about the way Gyang had dropped him as the HOD and appointed me to that post instead, especially because I was still retained on the post as director of CEFAS. As his HOD, our no-love-lost relationship notwithstanding, I held out my hand in friendship, to no avail. I made sure I carried myself lowly with him and did not want the palpable strain between us to escalate during my two-year tenure as HOD. Yet he gave me so much pressure from behind to stalk me all the way.

A couple of weeks into my headship, Mr Victor Ehigiator, a postgraduate student, reported his frustrations with Umeh as his major supervisor. When my appeal to Umeh to forgive the man for whatever offence committed against him failed, the student formally submitted a written petition. The petition, dated 1 April 1997, was submitted two months after his verbal report and my discrete intervention in the matter had failed to yield positive results. The student claimed that Umeh deliberately failed four of them in his research methodology course for refusing to travel to Katsina Ala to collect data for Umeh on a different research project of his. Subsequently, Umeh had abandoned Ehigiator's thesis work for the same reason after he had come back from the field and produced the draft, which Umeh had read and corrected before the trouble broke out between them in 1994. Umeh had blamed the refusal of the four students to collect data for him on Ehigiator, who as a devout Christian excused himself from undertaking the journey because of "a dream of blood" he'd had overnight. Unfortunately for Ehigiator, Umeh was his supervisor, and Umeh decided to pay the student back in the same coin by failing him and the three others who'd joined, as well as by refusing to read the draft thesis any further, thereby denying Ehigiator the benefit of a post-field seminar or a chance to complete his MSc programme. As a result, Ehigiator had abandoned the programme for about four years (1994) till that time with me as HOD in 1997.

Meanwhile, the frustrations that postgraduate students faced during the time of Umeh as HOD were a major reason why Gyang removed Umeh as HOD and appointed me instead. Thus, I had embarked on the resuscitation of abandoned students' programmes, as directed by Gyang, based on several petitions from students to him as the new VC. Indeed, Gyang, as evidence of leadership failure in my department, specifically cited the case of Ehigiator, and this prompted the senate of the university to issue an ultimatum of only one semester of grace for such students to complete their programmes under me as HOD. I made several appeals to Umeh to forgive the student, without success. I also sent brethren to him to do the same, to no avail. Realising that the deadline of the university senate was fast approaching, I decided to serve Umeh a query on the matter, not only to have something concrete to report on the matter but also as the basis to withdraw Ehigiator from Umeh and make me his major supervisor for the balance of his thesis. Umeh was angered by my decision and petitioned against it to postgraduate school, where he gained support from the dean, Professor M. C. Njike. It failed at the level of senate, making Umeh even bitterer in his subsequent relationship with me.

Thus, it did not come as a surprise that Umeh was later to act as a principal hatchet man for Gyang in the latter's bid to nail me down. Umeh was particularly vulnerable to playing this role given his sad state of mind about his promotion to the associate professor position, which had failed at the stage of external assessment of his publication for the position during the time of Idachaba. Gyang capitalised upon this and found Umeh useful against me at the peak of the hullabaloo.

Mr I. U. Odoemenem

The origin of Odoemenem's hostility dates back to the period just before I was appointed as director of CEFAS. He was on ground at the centre as a research fellow since 1989 or so, when he joined the centre, till the time I came in mid-1995. As a non-PhD holder in agricultural economics, he could not secure promotion to the senior research fellow position, going by a special rule governing promotion of academic staff in the university system at that time. For that reason, he was constantly at loggerheads with Professor Martins Ijere, the elder statesman who, upon retirement at University of Nigeria Nzukka, came to UNIAGRIC as director at the centre for a period of two years. At that time, Professor Ijere enjoyed my intimacy and contributions to progress at the centre.

For about two years after the departure of Ijere, Idachaba did not find Odoemenem fit for appointment, notwithstanding that he was the most senior amongst the staff of the centre and the de facto director during the period. Sometime in 1995, I applied for an official vehicle to attend a conference to represent the VC, and the transport officer withdrew the CEFAS car for my use, as it was sometimes the practice during the time of Ijere. Odomenemen had grudgingly complied to release the car for the journey, which I returned that weekend. On Monday, Odoemenmen came to my department to howl at me, complaining at the top of his voice that the car was returned to the pool without washing it. I apologised on behalf of the driver, and he stormed out in anger.

Fortuitously, that same day, a letter was issued to me from VC's office stating that I had been appointed as the new director of CEFAS. Mr Odoemenem's spirit sagged, and he was very bitter about this development for two reasons. One, he ought to have been appointed instead, as the person holding down the fort Professor Ijere had left about two years before. Two, I was not a member of the centre but a staff of the college in the agricultural economics department, which he saw as an indictment of him for unsatisfactory performance. He rejected me as his boss from the outset and refused to cooperate with me throughout my tenure from June 1995 to December 1998.

Irked by his negative disposition towards me, Odoemenem's colleagues in the centre freely offered me information about some issues I could use to nail him down and get him out of my way as quickly as I wished. One such issue was an allegation against him during the time of my predecessor, Prof Martins Ijere, about the authenticity of the man's master's degree in agricultural economics, which he claimed to have been obtained in the USA. Another issue was about an expensive camera purchased for the Centre under the World Bank-assisted project but which Odoemenem had converted to his own. However, I never wished to take him up criminally on these and other allegations against him predating my arrival at the Centre, in order to avoid unnecessary distractions.

Instead, in an attempt to appease Odoemenem, I wrote a passionate memo to him within the first six months of my leadership at CEFAS. My memo of displeasure, dated 23 January 1996, was titled "Towards a Better Working Relationship and More Productive Centre", and I structured it in four sections to illustrate Odoemenem's unruly conduct in various ways: unfriendliness and disregard; gossip, backbiting, and loose talk; unproductivity, unenthusiasm, and complacency; and official blackmail and unadministrability. I concluded the letter with the following words.

> I am requesting you to examine the above matters thoughtfully and come up for a discussion of them for clarifications on both sides. I am practically unable to admit that these highlights represent your natural behaviour and natural attitude to work. I want to see a complete change of attitude upon which this Centre's successful administration could be based to achieve its mission statement."
>
> Therefore I hereby invite you to a discussion of these observations on Friday 20th January 1996 at 11 a.m. Honestly I am open to be convinced against any of them

that is exaggerated misunderstood or misconceived. But the onus of proof rests clearly on you because I have my facts to substantiate all observations being made, albeit without ill feelings whatsoever.

My letter failed totally. Odoemenem simply ignored it and continued in his ways.

It soon became clear to me that, having irreversibly fallen out of Gyang's favour, he would soon be looking for a suitable person in the centre, someone unfriendly to me—someone like Umeh who was desperate for promotion and could be baited with a promise of that—for enlistment as an instrument to witch-hunt me, either then or after leaving the office as director. My vulnerability in that regard was imminent, and so it crossed my mind to do a comprehensive report of such a person before leaving office. Hence my memo dated 25 August 1998 and addressed to Gyang.

> I am finally compelled to file a formal report on the official conduct of someone in the Centre for Food and Agricultural Strategy (CEFAS) …
>
> My experience is that this person is practically ungovernable within the established limits of the authority vested in the office of Director. He has refused to give recognition and regard to successive officers holding that office over the years. All appeals and advice have failed to make any change in the negative attitude and poor official conduct of the staff. Lately his posture has graduated into seemingly violent tendencies and perfidy, which continuously sets the Centre backwards in the conduct of its mandate activities.
>
> Therefore I have produced a summary sheet (attached) of issues in the files to show the general picture of the conduct of this staff, predating my period as Director of the centre. The following elements are discernible therefrom in addition to my general knowledge of him under my leadership:

i. Gross insubordination.
ii. Absolute disrespect to constituted authority.
iii. Blunt refusal to take instructions
iv. Abdication and non-performance of assigned duties.
v. Unsatisfactory productivity.
vi. Inciting other staff.
vii. Violent tendencies.
viii. Open insults and physical assaults.
ix. Official blackmail and lying.
x. Unbecoming practice of Academic fraud and sharp practices.

The most plausible among the theories that explain the negative attitudes and behaviour of this person is his expressed bitterness for the administration's refusal to appoint him to fill the vacancy as Director of the centre in the past. In this connection he had gone to ASUU in 1996 to generate reaction against the administration. He has also embarked on holding meetings to incite hitherto peaceful staff of CEFAS against decisions of the administration about payment of academic allowances and involvement in research projects based on flimsy grounds.

These observations could be verified using information available in the files together with oral evidence from staff in the centre and the university at large. For instance, the leadership of the College of Agricultural Economics and Extension also has record of this person in terms of trouble shooting such as a pending case of academic fraud in collusion with other people, payment of SIWES allowance, to mention a few.

As the summary sheet shows, several queries had been raised over the long time of this person's poor conduct, a number of which, together with his responses, had been copied to the establishment officer. In addition I had indicated the poor conduct and performance as a staff in my comment inside the annual appraisal form in the past.

Action Sought: At this stage, I would like to advise that a full-scale investigation be conducted into the official conduct of this person as honestly observed and highlighted above.

Professor M. C. Njike

At the inception of UNIAGRIC in 1988, Dr Njike was on ground as head of the animal production department of the erstwhile Makrurdi campus of the University of Jos, located in Plateau State. I was employed in the crop production department in the same faculty as he, the then faculty of agriculture. Njike and Idachaba initially related well, sometimes serving as acting VC for Idachaba when the latter was away from campus, until the issue of Njike's promotion emerged. They parted ways for the balance of Idachaba's time in office.

It was then that Njike developed a pathological hatred for me as the foremost Idachaba boy to pay for the sin of the VC in opposing his promotion to the rank of professor by the University of Jos. The bone of contention between them was whether that promotion was appropriate, as announced by the governing council of University of Jos when Njike had become a staff of the new university UNIAGRIC, and a new governing council was already in place for the latter as well. Although Njike saw nothing wrong about it, Idachaba saw an administrative snarl there and initially refused to recognise it until the governing council of UNIAGRIC waded in and found a way to resolve the matter.

Meanwhile, I had suffered at the hands of Njike, who transferred his anger to me and stalked me in the faculty till the collegiate system commenced, a new College of Agricultural Economics and Extension Communication was created, and I was separated from Njike. Even at that, he continued to harass me at the slightest opportunity, to the extent that I had to write a letter to his HOD complaining about the foul language that Njike had used towards me. I also withdrew my membership from a proposal-writing committee that he chaired. He derided my relationship with the VC and at one occasion promised to throw "all such loyalists of Idachaba into River Benue" if Idachaba failed to secure a second term as VC.

Part Two
Onslaughts

♪
And when I think that God, His Son not sparing
Sent Him to die, I scarce can take it in.
That on the cross, my burden gladly bearing
He bled and died to take away my sin."

> *"The world will not be destroyed by those who do evil, but by those who watch them without doing anything."*
> —*Albert Einstein*

The balance of 1998 after the Abuja encounter was a most uncertain period for me, when my fate hung in the balance. I didn't know what Gyang would do to nail me down at all costs, as he had sworn to do. As I conjectured about his immediate actions towards me, his first move was to strip me of my loyal officers at the centre. He transferred my competent administrative secretary, Mr J. A. Idah; my dutiful finance officer, Mrs Mariam Adama; and my faithful driver, David Adamu. They were hurriedly posted out of CEFAs to other units of the university. In particular, I took a special notice of the posting of David to the VC's lodge, ostensibly to extract information from him in order to track my coordinates in time and space with precision. I imagine his mindset about David as his best recruit for that purpose, given how close he had been to me as my driver for several years.

Soon afterwards, Kureve, the acting registrar of the university, quietly called for all the files we kept in the centre for scrutiny at his north core office. (CEFAS was located at the central core.) The purpose of this was to comb through them and harvest any conceivable faults that could be found and launched at me in my role as director of the centre. The strategic significance of CEFAS as the focus of Gyang in pursuit of me officially was that he was my immediate supervisor; he did not need the cooperation of an officer between him and me before he could unleash any havoc on me. Also, I noticed that Odoemenem had been recruited, as a mole in the centre to help Gyang in witch-hunting me from within the centre, and later Umeh was a mole in the department for the same dirty job. I doff my cap for Gyang as a strategist in planning evil against me, knowing fully well that the duo of Odoemenem and Umeh were sworn adversaries of mine at my two duty posts. There was no message of evildoing he could send them that they would bat an eyelid at. This, plus the pathological bitterness of Njike against me, made the trio a perfect strategy for Gyang to nail me down as quickly as he wished.

Human beings will always forget to factor into their plans, when enraged against fellow human beings, the disapproval of God to allow them to succeed in their evil. Given that I was still in post, both as the boss of Odoemenem in the centre and the boss of Umeh in the department, I also noticed that the promotion papers of both of them soon began to fly past my tables. This sensitised me to the irresistible bait for both of them to play the traitor, like a Shakespearian Brutus, in delivering me to Gyang.

Odoemenem, in his desperate quest for promotion, was the first amongst my stalkers to fire a salvo towards me. In a surface-scratching effort, he secretly wrote a petition to the acting registrar, Kureve, which was obviously induced by the VC in his desperate bid to nail me down. Odoemenem had trumped up certain wrongdoings against me. Kureve, himself a stooge of Gyang's, invited me for discussion about Odoemenmem's allegations. It turned out to be an intense, private inquisition into my leadership in the centre. The inquisition took place on 24–25 August 1998 while I was still in post at the centre. I subsequently documented our discussion as file notes, which I later forwarded to the VC and Ag. Registrar. Excerpts from my file notes in reaction to specific aspects are as follows.

1. That I did not involve others in the UNDP Project except Mr J. M. Ogbonnaya, Youth Corper, and my wife. This is not true. All members of staff were involved. For instance, we held meetings together, at which I highlighted future roles of individuals. I assigned Mr Ogbonnaya specifically as implementation task manager for the project. All members of CEFAS academic staff were involved to write papers for the planning workshop, and

each of them received honorarium for that purpose. The youth Corper was involved to pre-test the data collection instrument prior to mass production and fieldwork. Dr A. A. Ladele, Mr Ogbonnaya, and I jointly produced the draft instrument with the participation and input of Mrs J. B. Ayoola (her ongoing PhD research was related; she had commenced her own research for about one and a half years prior to this UNDP project). Specifically we borrowed ideas from her questionnaire to produce one for the UNDP project. Mr Odoemenem presented a muddled-up questionnaire to Ag. Registrar at the meeting to implicate my wife. I made clarifications to the effect that her questionnaire was different from the two sets of UNDP questionnaires. I showed the correct versions of these to Ag. Registrar at the meeting.

2. That I withdrew money (N400, 000) at once from the project money. I reacted that I am the coordinator of the UNDP project. The initiative and actions for the research proposal came from me, with practically no role performed by Mr Odoemenem. I withdrew money for implementing the project as proposed to the sponsors, and records were kept and progress reports were submitted to sponsors as approved. I disclosed that greater amounts of money for implementing several projects in the university had been managed by me as coordinator in the past. I also said that the amount of money in reference was not the highest amongst project monies of many other academic staff as coordinators of other research projects in the university. I made reference to another person in the university who also won the same UNDP project as mine, at the same time, and for the same amount (N700,000). He was not facing problems because he was probably wiser by not lodging the money in his department in the university. I probably pulled down the ants that bit me because I gave the project, which had emanated from me, an institutional outlook within the university and invited popular participation of staff under me. Mr Odoemenern was one of such staff who now turned around to challenge my own sense of project execution.

When asked by the Ag. Registrar what research proposal he had won in the past, Mr Odoemenem could not mention any. Rather, as a subterfuge to save his face, he said I killed the only (research) proposal he pursued in the past. How? He circumlocuted extensively without showing exactly how I'd killed it. According to him, I did not approve money for him to travel to Abuja more than once. I submitted to Ag. Registrar that there was no fund in the centre's budget to give staff in pursuit of research proposals. In my several years of academic practice, I had never enjoyed any HOD or dean giving me money, even once, to travel for following up proposals. This appeared to me as intellectual indolence, or naivety at best. The fact was that this man could not write a proposal to convince the dumbest funding agency, let alone successfully implement a project.

3. That academic staff in the centre were not involved in the activities of the centre other than Mr J. M. Ogbnnaya. I submitted that there were only four academics in CEFAS besides me: Mr I. U. Odoemenem (agricultural economist, like me), Mr D. C. Aniekwe (agricultural engineer), Mr J. M. Ogbonnaya (agricultural engineer on a PhD programme), and Mr E. S. Attah (agronomist on a PhD programme). I had illustrated the unfavourable disposition of Mr Odoemenem to work herein and how he had co-opted hitherto peaceful staff (Mr Aniekwe and Mr Attah) to organised opposition. I declared that in this circumstance, the person I found most useful, most hardworking, and most loyal was Mr Ogbonnaya: He had evidently performed his assignments very effectively and successfully. On the other hand, Mr Odoemenem, and by association Mr Aniekwe and Attah, had not produced definite output in their various assignments. See the programme directive file for copious evidence of definite job assignments.

   a. Mr Odoernenern: Coordinator of research; newsletter editor. Poor job performance on all counts.

b. Mr Aniekwe: Task manager for training activities; coordinator of seminars. This man could not even produce a training manual till the due date, let alone take initiative to organise any short-term training. I had recently assigned him as task manager for the ongoing UNIAGRIC/MANR collaborative project—tongue in cheek, of course. Besides, Mr Aniekwe was implicitly dishonest and ungrateful; there was an allegation that in two periods of time, he had kept a parallel job along with his employment in the university.

c. Mr Ogbonnaya: Task manager for Makurdi annual lectures; task manager for implementing the UNDP project. The successive success of the two Makurdi annual lectures was there for everybody in the university to see. Despite the stiff opposition of his colleagues and other problems in regard to the UNDP project, Mr Ogbonnaya was performing according to my expectations. I was in the best position to know that a considerable portion of the enhanced limelight status of CEFAS locally and internationally under my leadership in the centre over the past three years was due to the high sense of duty and disciplined hard work of Mr J. M. Ogbonnaya. He, like me at the helm of affairs, had shown no time for frivolities in the process of pursuing the mission and mandate of CEFAS.

d. Mr E. S. Attah: Task manager, resource development.

4. That the Ag. Registrar should ask me where I have kept the N50, 000 approved for the UNIAGRIC/MANR collaborative project. I am sure he was simply being mischievous here. He knew that Mr Aniekwe was the person I put in charge of the project and had a clear picture of the status of its implementation to date. There was practically no problem with the implementation except some delay of certain actions arising from the ministry's end and the university's end. The money was approved by the vice chancellor in my name, and I was officially

accountable. I could not imagine such a mean question from a senior research fellow worth his salt. He did not actually allege anything in particular. Probably he wished to make certain allegation, but on realising it could not be sensibly justified, he stopped short of saying anything further along that line. I wished he had come out clearly to engender a definite reaction from me. The money in question was being spent for the purpose assigned.

5. That I made wrong use of facilities, with particular reference to the computer. The issue of the computer had been attended to adequately in my comments on the petition. Mr Odoemenem could not substantiate the wild allegations made. I had my own computer and so didn't even compete with my staff for use of theirs. He failed specifically to say or show that I prevented him from the use of secretarial facilities, including the computer. He expressed a few problems he had with computer operators in the past, but he did not cite any problem with the typist or typewriters. Such problems pertained to availability of paper or ribbon for printing, but that did not constitute lack of access. Apparently for his failure to make a case along this line, he spent much time on the use of the computer by others. He referred to somebody from BNARDA whom nobody knew, as well as Mr Matthew Itodo, who was my technical staff in the department. He avoided the allegation that my wife spoilt the computer of the centre as contained in their petition, apparently because this had been established not to be so in the centre. On the whole, I observed that Mr Odoemenem was trumping up the allegations in his extreme bitterness as usual, and the onus was on him to prove that they were so.

Generally, I permitted liberal use of the computer by the staff, but not by outsiders. I had organised in-house training for all staff (secretarial and academic) to become computer literate. In particular, I wanted the academic staff to be able to input and analyse their scholarly works themselves, thereby reducing pressure of work on only one operator. I installed my personally owned software packages for this purpose.

I promised to pay overtime allowance to the operator for staying after office hours to train staff for one or two hours. I approved a timetable for this purpose. But Mr Odoemenem was not ready to learn; he said the operator was too junior to train him. Other staff, specifically Mr Aniekwe, said they wanted me to pay overtime money for them as well. That is, I should pay them to learn computers. The training programme was frustrated to this date. This was the stuff of academics in my staff.

Concluding Remarks

It was plausible to explain Mr Odoemenem's poor official conduct in terms of the action of the university administration not to appoint him as director of CEFAS in two or three successions. In addition, I found him most professionally inept as an academic staff in the centre, which was corroborated by evidence from the people who knew him well within the larger university community and by his former colleagues at the University of Nigeria, Nsukka. Meanwhile, his activities in the centre, as enunciated in these file notes, had the effect of incessantly setting this centre backwards. There was an urgent need for definite inquisition into his general conduct and professional capabilities in relation to his qualifications. I also felt that a comprehensive staff audit of CEFAS was very necessary at this stage.

* * *

As the hatchet men delayed cooking the next story, Kureve nose-dived directly into the arena of conflict by posting Mtwenem to CEFAS as administrative secretary of the centre. This was the same Ntwenem who'd conducted the surreptitious investigation about cars back in 1996. Obviously, this move was to plant him as a mole in the centre in order to spy on me in-house and find a more tangible fault against me than Odoemenem could. I was manifestly rattled by this move, knowing how lethal the man could be as a kingpin of the Mzough U'Tiv, the sociocultural or ethno-linguistic group that Gyang rode on its back to become the VC. After Mtswenem finished the surreptitious investigation about cars and failed to nail Idachaba down, he was given the post of transport officer to replace Mr Ajogu, of the same Igala descent as Idachaba. I became curious about his clandestine mission to CEFAS. By instinct, I realised that this posting was a ploy, and so for Ntwenemen to be allowed to play a sniffer dog in my centre was akin to putting fire in the roof of the house and going to sleep. I decided to counter the move before it was too late.

Even though Ntwenem was allowed to burrow through the files in the hope of finding something incriminating against me, I was confident that he'd end up with nothing, I did not like the idea of Gyang's mole snooping around in the centre. Therefore I thought of a way of having Ntwenem reposted. He was a favourite of Gyang, and I had to shoot him down and fast. I noticed he had displayed sheer dereliction of duty by not resuming at his new post weeks after his posting, thereby creating a gap in the office. On this I wrote a memo to the registrar rejecting his posting and requesting another person. But the registrar quickly intervened, appealing to me to be patient with Ntwenem, who was carrying out an assignment for him and would report to duty shortly.

Further, I knew that Ntwenem would not last with me, given his antecedents as a loyalist of Gyang's. Conscious of this about him, I baited him with a juicy assignment as soon as he reported to my centre, and much like a hungry fish, he rushed at it. I gave him an assignment to organise the budget symposium at the centre. As soon as I approved the fund for Ntwenem and he collected it, he vanished into thin air for a long time, thereby putting the symposium in jeopardy. By the time he appeared, rather than spending the money for the purpose meant, he had apparently embezzled it, thereby playing into my hands. I queried him for this and associated other offences, and a panel was set up for the purpose and found him allegedly guilty of fraud.

Without any delay, I forwarded the report on the investigation panel to Gyang, asking that appropriate disciplinary action be taken against Ntwenem. Apparently destabilised and recognising this development as a spanner in the wheel of progress to implement his plan to nail me down, Gyang made some overtures to me to get Ntwenem off the hook, which I repeatedly rebuffed. I understood Ntwenem had other issues hanging on his head at that time with the administration, and this one would throw things aboard for him. Eventually Gyang, probably acting under a moral pressure, and mindful of the obvious nature of this particular case as a scandalous one, he quietly eased him out of the university to avoid an open scandal, tactfully putting him on suspension. He was never to return to the university, let alone serve as administrative officer at the centre under me.

I did not delude myself about the little victory in the case of Ntswenem. I knew the battle had only just begun. By the time Gyang publicly declared an all-out war against me, the trio of Umeh, Odoemenem, and Njike had forged an unholy alliance, spurred by their common hatred of me. The head of the hate group, Njike, had begun to strategically link Odoemenem with both the acting registrar, and he'd reconciled Umeh with Gyang, who previously had pathological hatred for him. Subsequently, I learnt that Gyang had secretly recruited Njike, Umeh, and Odoemenem as part of his next strategy to nail me down at any cost. Their different instrumentalities were quite obvious to me: Njike, as the dean of postgraduate school, to help him find fault against me within my assignment as a supervisor of postgraduate students' theses; Odoemenem, at the CEFAS, to probe my actions in office as director of the centre for the past four years; and Umeh, at the college, to help Gyang find fault against me within the context of my academic work in the department. Each time I examined that strategy, I developed goose pimples, and I further doffed my cap for the deftness of Gyang as a despot and an evil genius in the administration of the university.

* * *

Next, Umeh and Odoemenem joined forces and acted in criminal alliance to fire another shot at me, which got me rattled a bit. I cleverly deflected it in a back-to-sender tactic. Sometime in the past, not long after I'd assumed the headship of the department, there was an instance whereby two sophisticated cameras were stolen from a cabinet in the HOD office as an inside job. When it'd happened, I'd privately mentioned it to only Umeh (as my predecessor during whose time those cameras were acquired for the department through a World Bank project), so as not to jeopardise the efforts I was making to recover the stolen item. For the same reason, I did not tell him the details of how I was going about recovering it (through the police and other means). But now imbued with mischievous intents, Umeh, not knowing that I had since recovered the stolen cameras in the department with the help of police, told Odoemenem about the story. Odoemenem jumped at it as a possible angle to strike me. Odoemenem in turn notified Gyang about it, and Gyang hurriedly directed the chief security officer of the university to investigate the matter so that Gyang could subject me to disciplinary action.

I received a memo dated 23 February 1998 from the security coordinator of the university, Mr D. A. Kombo, that said he had received a report of "loss of two (2) Cameras belonging to the Centre for Food and Agricultural Strategy (CEFAS)" under my watch, and that I should confirm to him "if the report is true or false". Shocked, I recognised this memo as a planned move to incriminate me officially so that Gyang could nail me down, as he had vowed to do. By instinct, I noticed how they had goofed in the memo; the cameras were missing in the department, not the centre, and that mistake was probably due to incomplete knowledge on the part of Odoemenem. Remembering the information about the centre's camera that Odoemenem had purportedly annexed to become his own, I thought I could latch on to that by pretext. Thus, baiting him on the subject matter, I minuted on the security coordinator's memo to Odoemenem for him to "Comment in respect of the CEFAS camera" in his possession.

Playing into my hands, and in his habitual arrogance, he minuted back to me, "I do not know what you are talking about." This formed the basis of my response to the security coordinator's memo, with the aim of diverting attention away from the department to the centre, and from myself to Odoemenem. My minute read thus: "Record shows that CEFAS has only one camera (not two), which Mr Odoemenem is in possession of. But he is not willing to cooperate with information required to confirm it lost or not. I hereby hand over Mr Odoemenem to Security for him to produce the item without delay, please." It worked, at least to shift their attention from me to Odoemenem as the wrongdoer. Acting innocently as a pawn in the game, Mr Kombo compelled him to return the camera of CEFAS in his possession, which he complied with through me in palpable embarrassment. Even though he returned a rickety camera to me, I overlooked the need to conduct an investigation any further that could subject Odoemenem for trial for theft of the centre's property.

Soon afterwards, Gyang deployed another instrument for my continued witch-hunt. Having noticed the mistaken information he'd earlier received about missing cameras, he launched directly at the department to investigate the matter further. His approach this time was to order the stores unit to conduct an inventory of store items in the department. Unfortunately for them, by this time the police had helped recover both cameras, and they had been put back in the cabinet. To the astonishment of the trio in conspiracy against me, the two electronic cameras of the department were found firmly in place, with the same serial numbers. Confused, they dropped the matter of missing cameras like a hot potato and looked for other ways to nail me down.

* * *

Soon another trouble brewed for me in the department, this time with Umeh playing the traitor. Dr P. O. Erhabor, who was the most senior person in the department but at that time was holding an office in Gyang's administration in the north core as director of consultancy, had an office next to Njike's. He walked into my office in the department to inform me about the trouble brewing. He said that Njike had handed over the thesis of my master's degree student, Patrick Magit, awaiting senate approval of his oral examination results, to Umeh to help critique it and to find fault in me as the supervisor. Marveled about this, I shouted, "A thesis that has passed before an external examiner? With the same Umeh, a member of the oral examination panel that passed the thesis?" Ehrabor calmed me down and said that was why he had come: to ask me to convene a departmental postgraduate meeting, of which the three of us were the only members, to talk to Umeh so he would decline such an ignoble assignment. I did so immediately, and Umeh rather shamefully confessed to Ehrabor and me that it was true. He promised that he would no longer carry out the assignment.

In slow, measured cadence, I chipped in, "You profess to be a Christian, Dr Umeh. What type of job is this? Do you want to tell me you didn't know that the purpose has been to destroy me? If you are not aware, I am the one they are looking for. You were once a HOD, and you also supervised students. This kind of assignment cannot produce anything constructive for our department. I want to use this opportunity to implore you to turn down this assignment, as you have just promised to do. Please do not stir up any issue that would bring this department to disrepute; it is unheard of that a thesis previously passed before a departmental oral examination panel (subject to minor corrections), and before an external examiner for that matter (the highly respected Professor James Olukosi from ABU, Zaria), is no longer so and should be destroyed by you, a member of the panel. You did not disagree with the verdict of the panel. That would be treacherous against me, the supervisor; Magit, the student; and our department, the organiser of the oral examination."

Somehow, my words of reproach seemed to hit a raw nerve in Umeh. He solemnly apologised and promised to discontinue with the evil assignment handed over to him to critique Magit's thesis, which had passed at the departmental level. But Umeh's apology was not genuine, and he went back and changed his mind to destroy the thesis in a senseless critique. He lied through his teeth professionally and engaged in academic dishonesty to achieve his devilish intention.

At the senate meeting to discuss and approve pending postgraduate theses, Njike, as dean of the school, presented the case of Magit for consideration. What first stuck me was that the dean's report of Magit's oral examination panel was not put in my folder as a member of senate. *Why?* I quietly asked myself. I reached out to the senate secretariat staff to obtain a copy while the discussion was going on. Suddenly I noticed a discrepancy on the results sheet between what I'd submitted to postgraduate school as the head of department and what Njike had brought to senate for approval! He had reproduced the results sheet I'd submitted and cleverly changed the decision of the examination panel from option B, which meant "That the thesis be accepted and degree awarded subject to (minor) corrections to be certified as may be determined by the panel", to option C, which meant "That the thesis is referred for amendments to be certified by the External Examiner". Njike had achieved this by retyping and cyclostyling the result sheet instead of simply photocopying it. In the process, he made the alteration on the results sheet, which now made it appear as if the oral examination panel had failed in the first instance. Njike had altered the result sheet, thereby outrightly deceiving the senate. At that stage, there was nothing to suggest to me that Umeh had gone ahead with the evil assignment of writing a critique of the thesis, but I had a premonition that he might have armed Njike with a technical justification of the alteration.

By instinct, I rose to complain to Gyang, who was chairman at the meeting, about the anomaly I observed. To my embarrassment, in a loud voice he bullied me to sit down. Yet I had managed to express my surprise and asked the case of Magit be stood down for me to produce the authentic result of his examination as it had originated from my department. After the senate meeting, I drove straight to the department to search for my copy of Magit's result sheet, which I found. There it was, with the signatures of the external examiner from Ahmadu Bello University, Professor James Olukosi, and other panel members, indicating option B and not C, contrary to Njike's version distributed at the senate. Obviously, a crime had been committed, and I swore to pursue it to its logical conclusion.

The next day, I wrote a memo to Gyang complaining that Njike had altered the examination result and should be punished for doing so. I acted as if I did not know that he was acting on Gyang's script. I understood their game plan immediately: reject the thesis first as a ploy to raise an allegation of professional negligence against me as Magit's supervisor, punish the student, and dismiss me from the university. The student could be pardoned later. However, my protest was completely ignored, and the matter was put in abeyance until later, when I had vacated my two offices and ceased to be a member of the senate.

From this point on, through Gyang's actions, he soon declared me a persona non grata. He stopped inviting me to meetings of the several decision-making committees that I belonged as director or HOD. The few ones I attended, where he was handicapped and I had to attend because of my role (such as issues bordering on presentation of examination results of my department), he responded violently to any contributions I made. One of the tactics he employed was to give orders to not serve me notices of meetings until the meetings had ended. While my colleagues were attending meetings, I was in the dark. I'd only hear about a meeting after it had taken place. Later, I consulted with my friends and started attending meetings even without getting invitations. This was my statutory responsibility, because the same people who did not extend the invitations to me could use my non-attendance against me.

I ploughed on until November, when my term as HOD ended. As expected, the option of renewal would not arise. I was already looking forward to when I'd be free from working directly with the VC. It was obvious Gyang and I could no longer work together. Either he terminated my appointment or I resigned altogether. My two-year term as HOD elapsed in November 1998. I thought of the need to apply for my accumulated annual leave of three hundred days, which I did. The establishment officer innocently approved it, but when it came to Gyang's knowledge, he realised that I was probably trying to run away. He hurriedly ordered the withdrawal of the approval. Such an application would not be granted until the vacancies were filled. I had targeted this period as my getaway from the university because I had been teetering on an emotional precipice since the war had started. I needed to get away from Gyang's seething cauldron of victimisation in order to salve my anxiety and emotional heartache. I intended to be away for a year, starting with the Christmas break. I was also due for sabbatical leave, which I had applied for in expectation of the expiration of my tenure as HOD, but this was also turned down. It was obvious Gyang wanted me around while the heat was being cranked up on me. The most worrying aspect was that I didn't know from which angle they would strike.

As for the centre, the registrar's inquisition had indicated they were ready to go to any length to destroy me. Was it from the case of Patrick Magit or from that of Victor Ehigiator? I could imagine what their game plan would be at this stage. They'd probably get me out of the administrative offices I held so that I would not be eligible to attend the high-level meetings at which critical decisions would be taken to use these students' matters to get at me. Alternatively, they could keep me in these positions so that Gyang could easily find fault with me directly, as my immediate boss, instead of capitalising on the instrumentality of my stalkers for that the purpose. Either way, I saw trouble ahead of me that would hatch in 1999, and so I thought the best way was to exit from the university altogether; in which case the options on the table for me were just two: exit by taking a leave, or exit by seeking appointment elsewhere. Neither was feasible, and so I was resigned to my fate, ready to fight it out. I counted the years that remained for Gyang to finish his term in September 2001. Three long years of trouble ahead!

Deeply troubled, I reached for a lawyer who could help me threaten my stalkers to desist from their collusion to help Gyang nail me down at all costs. I found a bright one with blessed memory in Eche Ada, who wrote a punchy letter to Njike and Umeh on my behalf.

C. Eche Adah & Co.
(Ihotu Chambers)
Legal Practitioners and Consultants

Professor M. C. Njike,

No. 14 Staff Quarters,

University of Agriculture, Mnkurdi.

Dear Sir,

<u>RE: DEFAMATORY STATEMENTS AND CONDUCT AGAINST DR G. B. AYOOLA</u>

We are Counsel to Dr G.B. Ayoola, (hereinafter referred to as 'our client'), on whose behalf and instruction we write you this letter.

Our client's instructions are as follows:

1. That he is the Head of the Department of Agricultural Economics and the Acting Director of CEFAS at the University of Agriculture, Makurdi.

2. That on August 27, 1998, you presented to the Senate of the University, the report of the examination panel in respect of P.D. Magit, a Post graduate Student in the Department of Agricultural Economics for ratification; the said report was reproduced by you from the original copy that emanated from the said Department. And it was based on the oral examination of the candidate on November 10, 1997. In your position as Dean of Postgraduate School, you had unsuccessfully attempted to stop the oral examination from holding. When this failed, you were determined to prevent the results from being adopted by the relevant university authorities;

3. It was observed that the copy of the examination report you presented had been altered. Specifically, your own copy of the report contained an insertion that introduced a new dimension to the decision of the oral examination panel. While it was not the decision of the oral examination panel that the external examiner should certify the thesis after corrections, your report indicated so;

4. Our client in his capacity vigorously sought to correct this impression to no avail. To the contrary due to the said deliberation and dubious insertion by you, our client was subjected to serious harassment and embarrassment inter alia a liar and dishonest person for no just cause. All thanks to you.

5. Subsequently, our client took the risk and expended a lot of resources to obtain, the attestation of the external examiner as demanded from him by University Senate;

6. Furthermore, at the next meeting of University Senate, you submitted a memorandum on the same thesis to the effect that there was professional fraud on the part of our client as the major supervisor of the candidate in quest ion. Your submission indicated that data was "cooked" by our client, thereby wrongfully subjecting; our client to ridicule and casting serious aspersion on his professional competence, honesty and probity;

7. It was observed that your memorandum bordered on technical issues in the Agricultural Economics profession that you do not belong to. However, it was clear that you were aided and abetted in your defaming mission by Dr J.C. Umeh, of Department of Agricultural Economics.

Our further instructions are that the said Umeh who has his own axe to grind with our client is your co-conspirator, and has generally carried on various other defamatory attacks on our client including writing memorandum containing wild and unfounded allegations relating to mismanagement of funds and that of public property,

Our instructions are that our client is most upset that you and Dr Umeh seem to have joined in an unholy wedlock to destroy our client's hard earned name, reputation and position, for' no other reason than professional jealousy and bare-faced malice.

We have therefore, been instructed to demand that within two (2) weeks of this letter you and Dr Umeh are to write a letter of apology to our client, through this office: you are also to pay the sum of #500, 000 being damages to our client within the same period.

TAKE NOTICE that your failure to comply with the above, will leave us no other option than to follow our full instructions which include seeking redress against you in the law courts WITHOUT FURTHER NOTICE to you.

TAKE NOTICE that on the event of perfecting our instructions by proceeding to court, we shall be claiming aggravated damages among other things.

A stitch in time saves nine

Yours Faithfully,

* * *

Year 1—1999

After the break, I resumed to the news that the VC had reconstituted his cabinet to take effect from 1 January 1999. That was not unexpected because his current cabinet, including me, had spent the statutory two years in office since November. In the new cabinet, Gyang appointed Erhabor as the new HOD, and so soon afterwards, he was appointed as the secretary to government of his home state, Edo. Even at that, Gyang remained skeptical about appointing Umeh, an associate professor, to the post. He found it more comfortable to appoint Achamber, a Lecturer II staff, as acting HOD instead. The skepticism reflected Gyang's negative mindset against Umeh from outset, which he had shared with me previously; whereof he attributed the state of entropy he met our department to the ineptitude on the part of Umeh as the HOD at that time. When the newly reconstituted cabinet was officially published, unlike the other posts, which carried the names of officers occupying them, CEFAS was left blank. I welcomed the news of my replacement as HOD in the department, though I was angry that no definitive decision had been taken over my headship of CEFAS. I had waited anxiously for the past few months to be relieved of both posts since mid-year when things fell apart between Gyang and me irreversibly. My appointment as director of CEFAS was indeterminate—the appointment read "until further notice", but I no longer had the inclination towards working there.

The next morning, I went to see the CEFAS staff to bid them farewell. I also went to the department to do the same thing. Gyang tried to make issue out of these actions of mine that suggested it was good riddance for me to leave these positions and get off his hooks. Indeed it was, and even more than that. Unknown to him, I was waiting and praying for this to happen so that I could gradually disappear from his administrative radar; this was my prayer heard. I clearly recognised my vulnerability in these positions that situated Gyang as my direct supervisor, which meant that he was the one to approve my travels and expenditures in running the affairs of these units, as well as other memos for official actions. It was these positions that opened me to sporadic punches from him, and once I could vacate them and become a single-minded lecturer back in the department, it would become impossible for him to pursue me as he was presently doing.

I considered this development as good for me. It implied that I was taken out of his viewing range, meaning that he could no longer act directly as my administrative head. Now that I was no longer holding any administrative position, he would find it more difficult to reach me and find fault with me. At the least, he needed the cooperation of my head of department or the dean of college before he could cook up or sustain any allegation against me. Luckily at that time, friendly people who were also sympathetic to my course occupied the two positions: Dr E. P. Ejembi as the dean of college, and Mr N. I. Achamber as the acting HOD. I felt somewhat comfortable about the administrative situation at the college and department. But the situation in CEFAS was not similar. The senior person, Odoemenem, had been hostile throughout my tenure at the centre, and he was stalking me all the way.

By this time, I had seen the handwriting on the wall. Though I heaved a heavy sigh about leaving these offices, it struck me that I needed to look outwards, and I began to think of a plan to not only leave UNIAGRIC for some time but also leave the country and get a breath of a different air for a year or two before coming back, by which time tension would have reduced. Towards this end, I quickly secured a placement for sabbatical leave at the University of Cape Coast, Ghana. Gyang, sensing that I was trying to run away from him, immediately refused my application. I didn't know he would deny me that opportunity, so I had even paid a reconnaissance visit to the institution in Ghana, during which my office had been identified and the research work was discussed. I had met with the VC of Cape Coast University at a conference in South Africa and shared my situation with him. He was quite sympathetic towards me and was willing to offer me "refugee status" as a visiting professor at his university.

The thoughts of my three stalkers regarding their potency to help Gyang nail me down remained worrisome to me. Meanwhile, Odoemenem was already poised for action, gallivanting about in bravado to malign me in town. He had also helped Gyang with a list of trumped-up charges against me that led to my inquisition by Kureve, the acting registrar of the university. At this stage, I considered the need to consult a lawyer, and on the advice of Professor Onyido, I visited the chambers of Eche Ada and Company to discuss the matter. Eche Ada, himself a university lecturer, quickly realised the dangers ahead of me at UNIAGRIC and convinced me about the need for him to write a preemptive letter to them ahead of any evil acts they might be planning.

Sporadic Offensives

In January 1999, just a couple of weeks after I vacated my two administrative offices, the act of deliberate faultfinding against me began in earnest and soon snowballed into an open war with Gyang and his hatchet men. It was the deliberate action of Gyang to first get me out of the way administratively so that I would lose the opportunities open at meetings and the post to defend myself from his allegations before he could take action. Thus, it was to be a tough year for me, and as it turned out, it was most traumatic. Beyond that, though Gyang had served two years already, I was very apprehensive that he still had sufficient time for him to hatch his evil plans against me and nail me down as he wished. Banking on the joint or sole instrumentalities of my stalkers on his side, he had several angles to strike me from, particularly the many issues on the ground that had previously brewed to maturity at the end of December 1998—namely, the matters of Patrick Magit and Victor Ehigiator, let alone the many others waiting to be hatched against me with the help of my stalkers. Moreover, in January 1999, a devastating student rampage occurred in the university. Going by the magnitude of destruction caused, including the residences of Gyang and Njike, which were completely razed to the ground, a more fertile ground had presented itself for them to plant and harvest new allegations against me, and they fired new shots towards me. In the following pages, I'd like to present the sporadic offenses launched against me in chronological sequence.

I. First Onslaught

I received a letter early in the year (7 January 1999) that summoned me to appear before a one-man panel (Njike) to try me for a fictitious allegation against me, specifically "to investigate the circumstances of the query" that I'd issued to Dr J. C. Umeh when I was the HOD "in respect of Mr Ehigiator's thesis corrections". As stated in the memo, written by Njike himself, "The purpose of this letter is to inform you that the full investigation of the matter will begin on 14th January, 1999 at 10.00 am in my office." The meeting was held, and the witch-hunting goal became real.

The date for the second meeting was fixed but did not hold, as the adjourned date coincided with a devastating student rampage that occurred on 24–25 January 1999 and badly affected Njike, with his and Gyang's house being two of the three that were burnt down by rampaging students. The third house belonged to Dean of Student Affairs I. D. Yakugh. All three were relocated to town, and I joined other people to pay sympathy visits to them at their new abodes, notwithstanding our strained relationships. Subsequently, I also wrote a letter of sympathy to Gyang in which I extricated myself from the actions of the students.

February 15, 1999

Professor E. O. Gyang,
The Vice Chancellor,
University of Agriculture Makurdi.

Dear Professor Gyang,

Letter of Sympathy

My wife and I would like to sympathise with you in the present situation of the university following the heedless destruction of property and threat to security of life and property on campus, occasioned by the recent students rampage. In particular, we would like to share with you and your family the trauma of the sudden dislocation and personal loss consequent upon the unfortunate event.

Our prayer is for God's Grace for you to fully regain the physical, mental and emotional strength to the level required to handle the situation successfully. As we can imagine the shock that this situation presents to Mrs Gyang and children as well as other members of your household, our wish is that God shall grant them quick recovery and replenish them manifold.

Permit me, please, to state categorically that there is absolutely no truth in any thought that I, and anybody I know of, have a hand in this act of the devil to use students in this negative mode to set our university back at this stage of its development. In this difficult circumstance, I can only pray that God almighty shall reveal the truth behind it all and grant you the wisdom to manage the situation.

Please accept our sympathy.

Signed:

Dr G. B. Ayoola

During the interregnum, I resorted to playing defensive tactics by writing a letter to Gyang (copied to Njike) regarding the several concerns I nursed about the one-man Njike panel. In this, I raised a serious objection against that move, showing why Njike was not competent to investigate me on such a ludicrous, trumped-up offence against me. The kernel of my memo, entitled "Investigation of Query—Preliminary Objections", was as such.

> I hereby humbly raise preliminary objections based on concrete grounds as follows:
>
> 1. Professor Njike has been party to the whole issue involving the postgraduate student (Mr Victor Ehigiator) whose registration dates back to 1991 as a member of the very first set of students. He (i.e. Professor Njike) has demonstrated substantial vested interest in close association with Dr Umeh from the outset and is instrumental to the official wrongdoings of Dr Umeh that form the basis of the queries. I would like to cite certain instances that the Vice Chancellor

is familiar with - (a) Professor Njike was vehemently opposed to my withdrawing the student from Dr Umeh as the original major supervisor until he lost the case on the floor of the university senate which ordered the oral examination to hold immediately; (b) in apparent vengeance Professor Njike caused delay of the oral examination of the student for one year after it was ordered by the senate; Professor Njike aided Dr Umeh to attempt to scuttle the oral examination and subsequently launched written and verbal attack on the student including threatening him after he has successfully defended his thesis by a unanimous decision of the oral examination panel.

Sir, it is the same issues that Professor Njike has been so deeply involved and partisan about that are before him to investigate now.

2. The focus of the trial appears to be misplaced as it is sharply put on me to defend my actions in office rather than the erring Dr Umeh to purge himself of the allegations properly levied against him in the queries issued to him. If I have found it necessary to query a staff under me, how can the focus of investigation be on me again as is presently the case judging from the discussion at the meeting? I had thought that I should only give testimony in the trial of Dr Umeh, at best.

3. The opening remarks of Professor Njike at the meeting were very tendentious. He said that his civil service experience had shown that "when a boss issues a query to an officer under him he (the boss) himself could run into trouble and be subjected to disciplinary measures instead of the erring officer". Based on this statement, I venture to suspect that the implicit motive of Professor Njike is to merely hang a charge on my neck after (my) leaving office.

4. Professor Njike has carefully excluded Professor P. O. Erhabor from the investigation process as the person that has succeeded me in office as the new Head of the Agricultural Economics Department, which is not

proper. When I drew his attention to this procedural omission, he swore that Professor Erhabor would not be invited. I had argued that as the (new) HOD, Professor Erhabor is the person to attend to issues emanating from queries raised by former HOD to a staff; I also reasoned that he is the person to draw inputs from me in the course of attending to such issues, while I have lost official strength to be so directly responsible particularly in terms of access to relevant file on the matter at the present time.

5. There is a parallel investigation of the same matter being undertaken by the Dean of the College of Agricultural Economics and Extension, Dr E. P. Ejembi as earlier assigned by the administration. When I sought to determine if Professor Njike was aware of this parallel effort, he was highly sensitive in his response, challenging the basis and authority for Dr Ejernbi to have been so assigned. My feeling is that Professor Njike together with Dr Umeh has shown preference against the Dr Ejembi's investigations for obvious reasons.

6. I have given instructions to my lawyer to commence legal action against Professor Njike and Dr Umeh in connection with other matters (Attachment 1) that are separate from this. As such, I am afraid that the task for Professor Njike to handle the queries issued by me to Dr Umeh in fair and just manner is not feasible in the circumstance.

Thank you, sir.

Dr G.B. Ayoola

15/2/1999

Gyang completely ignored my two letters, and worse still, he was not impressed by my show of sympathy. Rather, in his embattled mind, he saw the student rampage as a better opportunity for him to nail me down faster than the lame offensive of Njike's panel. Meanwhile, as a sequel to the rampage by students, the university had been shut down and students were sent home. The university staff was advised to take annual leave.

According to a public statement made by the student body to rationalise the motive behind the protest, the numerous grouses against Gyang's administration bordered on (in their own words) the "Carryover-repeat policy introduced, whereby whoever failed even a course must repeat an academic year; Removal of florescent tubes for small bulbs not used for reading". In conclusion, the student body wrote,

The problem in this University will be solved if:

i). The Vice Chancellor is removed outrightly
ii). Total reorganisation is done among principal officers of the University.
iii). The Dean of Students Affairs is removed on the ground of his zero experience in human training. He is a student in the University and therefore should be over-engulfed with series of activities. We know they will never accept non-indigene. We even want a Tiv man who is not an amateur in human management.

II. Second Onslaught

I received an invitation to appear before the student rampage panel, chaired by Professor Ikurior, the deputy VC. When the university was shut down because of the student rampage, the academic staff was advised to proceed on annual or accumulated leave. While I was on leave at Ibadan and trying to seek employment elsewhere, the two sister universities of agriculture invited me for interviews at different times: the University of Agriculture, Abeokuta (UNAAB), in Ogun State, and Michael Okpara University of Agriculture Umudike (MOUA), in Abia State. Both of them invited me to interview for the post of professor, and I succeeded in both cases. But something astonishing happened at the UNAAB interview. As soon as I sat down, the chairman of the panel and VC of UNAAB, Professor Julius Okojie, asked me an embarrassing question: whether I had cleared myself from certain allegations of criminal wrongdoing in Makurdi, particularly with respect to a recent student rampage that had caused tremendous damage to university property—and whether I was trying to escape punishment or seek refuge at UNAAB! I was visibly rattled and denied any wrongdoing. I almost asked to terminate the interview when Professor Akinwumi, the consultant on the panel and my lecturer at Ibadan, intervened to calm me down and persuade me to continue the interview. As I later learnt, Gyang had phoned Okojie the night before the interview, when he'd learnt I was invited, to poison his mind against me and to stop Okojie from appointing me as a staff of UNAAB, saying that I was instrumental to the student rampage.

Despite all this, UNAAB wrote a letter to me (as did Umudike) saying that the interviews were successful and I should deposit my publications for external assessment. I declined to do so in both cases. At that stage, I had seen the inevitability of the war; Gyang really meant trouble. The blackmail meant that he was ready to crush me at all costs, even if this required him to impugn my character or damage my personal and professional integrity.

Later, a letter came from the panel that I should appear before it on 1 April 1999, which I complied. (The memo was dated 30 March 1999). On the journey back to Makurdi, I braced myself, having found myself poised between two stools: either staying on at Makurdi to fight back, or running away and leaving my name behind. I chose the former! I nursed the feelings that Ikurior, whose relationship with me had been strained because of the contribution I'd made at the senate about his promotion, would like to seize the opportunity of a student rampage to settle scores with me and take his own pound of flesh. Therefore he would easily do Gyang's bidding to nail me down through the work of his panel. However, when I appeared, the interaction that I had with panel members left no sign for me to anticipate trouble. Neither was there any allegation of complicity levelled against me, nor an insinuation made to incriminate me in the matter throughout the interaction.

But in spite of that, as I learnt through the grapevine, the panel had labelled the four of us—Onyido, Agbede, Daudu, and me—as "aggrieved persons", and they roped us into a matter we knew nothing about, recommending us for outright dismissal from the university. There was no governing council in place that had the statutory powers to dismiss us like that, and so Gyang had taken the report of the panel to the minister of agriculture for endorsement, which I learned about through my friends in the ministry. As soon as our informants helped us with a copy of the panel's report, we rushed to court to seek an ex parte order to stop the process, pending the determination of our substantive suit challenging the outcome of the panel's work. We secured this from the federal high court in Jos and caused it to be served immediately to Gyang, which shocked him to the bones.

III. Third Onslaught

I received a letter dated 4 February 1999 from the security coordinator, Dr T. Avav, an academic in the College of Agronomy. I was accused of "harbouring students other than direct children" in my house, contrary to the directive of the administration after the student rampage. This was another attempt at scratching the surface at the instance of none other than Gyang. This time he sought to frame me for having breached the security arrangements put in place after the student rampage. At least as the VC, he could use that to declare me a security risk and open a new channel of administrative trial, which could lead to my summary dismissal from the university. The letter read in part:

> Reports have indicated that contrary to the circular ... you have continued to harbour one Moses Joseph Olufemi, a 300 level, Civil Engineering in your house. So also is your female relation. This note is to remind you of that order and to record that you have breached same.

Noticing how he had goofed severally in this letter, and how he had betrayed himself as an apologist of Gyang's vow to nail me down at all costs, I charged back at him with harsh words. First I noticed that they were trying to get at my brother-in-law, whose name was Obafemi Adio (not Moses Joseph Olufemi), and who was truly a final year student in civil engineering and lived with me. Obafemi had only escaped a guilty verdict when his student identity card was allegedly found at the crime scene, a story which the investigation panel had cooked up on Gyang's orders as evidence to punish Femi for the damage caused by rampaging students. Of course, Gyang would be very glad to scapegoat any member of my household if he couldn't nail me down as quickly as he had wished. Unfortunately for the panel members, facts soon emerged during the investigation indicating that Gyang's niece was in the company of Femi and other colleagues of theirs somewhere else at the time of the rampage and she willingly volunteered to testify to that effect before the panel. Therefore Femi was eventually let off the hook, to the sadness of Gyang, who could not sacrifice his niece to secure his burning desire to punish my relative.

Next, I noticed that they were also trying to get at my niece, Tunrayo. They didn't know her name and simply referred to her as "a female relation". Armed with these inaccuracies, I gave a reply that stopped them from pursuing me in that direction.

> With reference ... there is no such person by name Moses, Joseph Olufemi ... in my house as you claim; also I don't know the meaning of female relation as applied in your memo wherein you failed to state whether daughter or wife or other relation...
>
> However, I am surprised about your allegations that I have breached an order in connection with the implementation of the circular. I consider it grossly over-reaching for you as security coordinator to pre-determine the structure and composition of my family without prior contacts with me; the result of this is false specification of the members of my family as reflected in your memo as well as the wrong conclusion and allegation consequent thereupon.
>
> Therefore, given the bad situation we are already in, in terms of the lack of peace of mind and budding uncertainties that are already affecting our normal lives and sagging our morale at work as members of this University community, I would like to advise that facts of the issues be properly established before accusing us as contributors to the bad security environment prevailing at the moment.

IV. Fourth Onslaught

Gyang had appointed Odoemenem to the position of CEFAS director, and it was something he'd dragged his feet on for about three months longer than the time he had filled all other posts since December 1998. He wrote a letter to levy another allegation against me.

> Our records show that you sent 400 copies (four hundred copies) of CEFAS publication titled "Commodity Boards in Decentralized Economy" to Professor M. O. Ijere in 1996 on request for sale at N200 per copy ... Could you please keep me posted on the status of the sale and proceeds.

I saw where he was coming from and where he was going—just another scratching of the surface. I was quick to nip it in the bud and stop them from going any further on the matter.

> As you know, Professor M. O. Ijere was the former Director of CEFAS that I succeeded in the office in June 1995; he is presently Director of a similar Centre at the Federal University of Agriculture, Umudike. He had organised the workshop and processed the book of proceedings for publication in 1994 before the end of his term, including editorial works and printing. Incidentally, you are the officer I assigned to make payments and take delivery of 1000 copies of the book from the publisher in Nsukka in late 1995/early 1996.
>
> Subsequently, the Professor kindly agreed to undertake distribution of the books to certain parts of the country and oversees consistent with the policy to put CEFAS in circulation at home and abroad. When he suggested that the book be put on sale as cost recovery measure for our university, I did not authorize that for the absence of necessary clearance from the administration; as you, as well as other staff members of CEFAS knew, all the copies of the book in question and other publications of the Centre during my time distributed through the staff and other means were definitely not for sale as a matter of my administrative policy.

Therefore, you probably want to get in touch with Professor Ijere for further information or updating.

At this stage, I quickly revisited the letter of my lawyer to Odoemenem and his friends from last December, and I took a preemptive action to file a libel suit against the trio in the high court of Benue State. Odoemenem simply shrugged it off and dared me to institute any case in court against him, if I liked. Information also reached me that he cursed, saying that the damages I was claiming in the libel suit would be deposited on his grave.

V. Fifth Onslaught

Regarding the instrumentality of Odoemenem as the new CEFAS director, Gyang quickly resumed action on the probe of my tenure as director of CEFAS, which Kureve had started before but soon dropped while I was still at the helm of affairs at the centre. A letter came from central administration that Mr Zhizhi, the executive assistant to Gyang—not Kureve this time—had been assigned by Gyang as a one-man panel of inquiry to probe my tenure of office at the centre. The allegations, as induced by Gyang and at the instance of Odoemenem, included the following: that I took sixty-six books from the centre; that I was in possession of a stabiliser of the centre's at my house when I had ceased being the director; that the computer of the centre that went for repairs was not returned to the centre; that I paid university money to the computer company in full for the repair of printer that had not been completed; and more. Zhizhi invited me to the centre to give evidence, and he'd visit my residence to conduct a search for books in my private library and examine my household items in search of the stabiliser or other items belonging to the centre.

I made a written submission to Zhizhi in defence of myself on all counts, dated 3 March 1999. In the end, as the fine Christian that Zhizhi was, he submitted an honest report to Gyang, saying that all the allegations against me were totally untrue and that it was all fictitious. He was thoroughly dressed down by Gyang for saying the truth.

By this time, Onyido, Daudu, Agbede, and I had harboured palpable trepidation in our minds and families, which prompted us to write a "save our souls" letter to the new agriculture minister as soon as Obasanjo formed his cabinet. Unfortunately, it produced no results to change our situation for the better.

July 19, 1999

Alhaji Sani Zango Daura
The Honourable Minister
Federal Ministry of Agriculture
and Rural Development Area 11 Garki, Abuja

Dear Honourable Minister,

The Bizarre Situation at University of Agriculture Makurdi

We the under-listed members of staff of the University of Agriculture, Makurdi, would like to congratulate you on assumption of duty as Honourable Minister of Agriculture and Rural Development. We are also delighted to identify ourselves with the cardinal principles of your new administration of the ministry consistent with those of the new federal government, particularly the tenets of public probity, accountability, rule of law and respect for fundamental human rights of every Nigerian to freely live and work anywhere in' the country.

Sir, against the background of the present political air of freedom, justice and fair play, we are constrained to draw your attention to the bizarre situation existing at the University since the inception of the administration of Professor E. O. Gyang as the Vice Chancellor in September 1996. The situation we are reporting to you now had earlier overwhelmed the former Minister of Agriculture and Natural Resources, Dr Malami Buwai, to the extent that he summoned the Vice Chancellor and key functionaries of the university as well as extremely afflicted members of staff to an urgent meeting with him (minister) on Friday May 8, 1998. The outcome of that meeting was the directive of the Minister for the Vice Chancellor to urgently take certain steps to redress the situation. However, the Vice Chancellor not only wasted the opportunity the occasion presented, but regressed to intensification of a reign of terror, executive victimisation and witch-hunting in spite of the several representations made to your predecessor, Dr Jonah Madugu, with whom he appeared to have developed a disquieting personal relationship. The situation has now reached a crescendo epitomised by extreme suffering by the University community, and specifically characterised by arbitrary sacking of staff, as well as a sagging of staff morale and correspondingly abysmally low staff productivity. It is not far-fetched to state that the unfortunate students rampage of 24 and 26 January 1999, in which property worth over N50 million was destroyed, is a direct consequence of Professor Gyang's misrule. In addition, numerous court litigation (about twenty at the last count) have been instituted against the University and the Ministry for the abuse to which Professor Gyang has subjected this University, on which colossal amounts of public funds and valuable man-hours are being wasted. Specific elements of the situation on ground that need your kind and urgent intervention are as follows:

1. Orchestrated agenda of ethnic cleansing to frustrate and flush out non-indigenes members of staff who have put in the most productive period of their career to develop the University from the scratch to an enviable international status inherited by Professor Gyang;

2. Frustration of academic initiatives, collapse of academic programming and total relegation of research and other intellectual endeavours, aimed at institution building.

3. Unorthodox and arbitrary management of capital projects as reflected in complete jettisoning of due process and proper procedure, complete disregard for transparency, probity and accountability in spite of the specific directive by the federal government;

4. Lack of regard for rule of law and statutes including decree 48 that established the university;

5. Demonstration of intense hatred for the previous Idachaba-led administration, its achievements over eight years and anyone who had tangible role to play during that period;

6. Institutionalisation of a management policy and style that has engendered untold misery, deprivation and hardship of University staff in contrast to overt favouritism of the Vice Chancellor's sycophants, all those who kowtow for him particularly those belonging to his ethnic group.

7. Institutionalisation of the use of extra-University machinery such as ethnic caucuses, rumours and petty gossips as a basis and instruments of governance;

8. The use of security system to turn the university to a police state;

9. Poor management of the recent students' devastating rampage and follow-up orchestrated attempt to use a panel's report to victimise innocent staff who had been originally classified as enemies of the Vice Chancellor.

10. Predilection of verbal violence, which runs short of the minimum expectation of a person occupying the high office of a Vice Chancellor.

The undersigned would feel privileged and honoured in the service to our country if the Honourable Minister would avail us an opportunity to substantiate, expatiate and prove beyond reasonable doubts the issues raised herein. In addition, we wish to draw the attention of the Honourable minister to numerous petitions and complaints existing in the ministry about these issues.

Thank you sir as we anticipate your kind and urgent action to salvage the modest contribution of honest and hard working Nigerians in this University and the task of nation building from dilapidation and total collapse.

Yours faithfully,

Signed:

Dr 0.0. Agbede
Professor I. Onyido
Arc. V. S. Daudu
Dr G. B. Ayoola
CC: The Honourable Minister of State for Agriculture and Rural Development

VI. Sixth Onslaught

Dissatisfied by Zhizhi's report, Gyang constituted another panel to conduct further investigations into my tenure as director of CEFAS, going more in-depth than Zhizhi's exercise, which failed to meet Gyang's need (letter dated 7 July 1999, dubiously titled as "Invitation to Appear Before the Administrative Committee on CEFAS"). The same issues or allegations as those of Zhizhi's panel were raised: sixty-two missing books; computer monitor; Nulec stabiliser, and more. The membership of the committee was comprised as follows.

1. Professor Friday Anugwa—head, Department of Animal Production
2. Dr D. K. Adedzwa—acting director, Cooperative Extension Centre
3. Mr J. I Moughsha—deputy bursar, Internal Audit Department
4. Dr R. H. Sha-ato—acting head, Department of Chemistry
5. Mr P. T. Amando—administrative secretary, CEC

In response to its invitation dated 7 July 1999, I appeared before the committee. My request to tape-record the proceedings was turned down, and the information I volunteered at the meeting, that the matter was seemingly subjudice, was equally discountenanced. Therefore I articulated my notes on paper and forwarded the same to the committee, in order to put the records of my appearance straight.

Highlights of My Reactions to Issues Being Investigated by the Executive Committee on CEFAS

The existence of an Administrative Committee on CEFAS was rather strange, judging from my knowledge of the organogram of the centre as Director for over three and a half years; I observed that the nomenclature of the committee was a misnomer and wondered why the intention of the exercise was not reflected explicitly which was to investigate my stewardship as Director between June 1 1995 and December 1999, based on the allegations of the incumbent Director!

I observed that the mode of delivery of the memo by dropping it in front of my residence was probably intended to make it impossible for me to appear before the panel so an offence could be hanged on me similar to that of Dr O. O. Agbede.

I expressed the opinion that I have been under siege in the university based on the series of investigations and frivolous allegations against me so soon after vacating my former offices as Director and HOD; I felt being witch-hunted and victimized and discriminated against and disfavored and hated for no just course.

I informed the committee that the issues raised for discussion constituted key elements of a legal case that I have instituted to the knowledge of the university administration already.

Background to Allegations:

(i) I was Director of the centre for three years and seven months and took over directly from Mr I.U. Odoemenem (the incumbent Director) who refused till the end of my term to hand over the centre to me at all.

(ii) Mr Odoemenem was very hostile under my leadership at that time to the extent that I could not attribute any positive contribution to the modest success we attained. I had occasions to make reports of his. Poor official conduct to the university administration but no action was taken.

(iii) I established that I used to relate well officially and privately with the Vice Chancellor from the outset of his tenure to the effect that I was the only officer under his administration saddled with the tedious responsibility to direct a centre and head an academic department contemporaneously; however the situation changed when Professor M.C. Njike was subsequently appointed Dean of Postgraduate School and he quickly succeeded to insinuate himself into favour with the VC and established a wedge of hate with me in relation to the overall administration; by the way, (Professor Njike had grudges with me since 1988 punctuated with concrete events up till date). Within this context the Vice Chancellor had demonstrated intense hatred and hostility towards me on a number of occasion; I gave examples of harassments and battering and ridicule at official meetings including when he said he would "nail me down" on the floor of senate in the context of the case of a postgraduate student, and that he would "deal with me" in the context of my contribution at a meeting with the Honourable Minister of Agriculture and Natural Resources at Abuja in May 1998. Therefore I expressed the feeling that all acts of investigations and allegations against me before and after my tenure of office as Director and HOD are consistent with the desperate intent to "nail me down" and to "deal with me".

(iv) I expressed that my understanding of the strategy to "nail me down" and "deal with me" has three people as principal instruments namely, Professor M.C. Njike (Dean of Postgraduate school who had grudges with me from a long time ago), Dr J.C. Umeh (who has been very bitter that I was appointed to replace him as Head of Department and was visibly antagonistic and uncooperative as staff under me throughout the period of my leadership), and Mr I.U. Odoemenem (who was very bitter about the decision of the university administration to appoint me as Director of CEFAS from the Department instead of him as the then senior-most officer and person in charge of the centre at the time). Therefore I expressed my hope that the current "Administrative Committee on CEFAS" would not be another mode to "nail me down" and to "deal with me".

(v) I stated that the circumstances surrounding the appointment of Mr I.U. Odoemenem as Director of the centre to succeed me directly is very suspect to me, given the amount of hostility he had demonstrated and the fact that I had submitted several reports of official misconduct about him to the university administration without any action; I suspected it was specifically for the primary purpose to consciously exhume any previous actions of mine in the files as former Director that could be used to "nail me down" and to "deal with me" as originally desired.

Reactions to the Allegations:

- 62 missing books: I referred to my previous statement before the Zhizhi panel to the effect that I did not make away with any 62 books. I confirmed that I personally procured the books for the centre at my own costs in the first instance and would not destroy my own handwork as it were. I showed some cartons and parcels that I procured for myself also from abroad at the same time indicating how I personally addressed them in the USA to myself at CEFAS, UNIAGRIC, Nigeria. I urged the committee members to clarify at the mail office how these items arrived over the time and I paid personally for their collection; it would appear that Mr Odoemenem had wrongly believed that the materials as I took them home belonged to CEFAS. In any case those belonging to the centre were properly treated for shelving in the Resource Room. We undertook a casual inspection of the cabinets in the Resource Room (incidentally the venue of meeting) and a member of the committee discovered one book that appeared on the list of the missing books.

- Computer monitor: I referred to my statement before the Zhizhi panel to the effect that computer monitor is not missing; as decided by Mr Zhizhi, administration is continuous so the incumbent Director should retrieve the item from the workshop where it was taken by the technician for repairs under my approval; the normal official process for repair and movement of items in and out of the university was followed. For the avoidance of doubts records show the name and address of the company and liabilities involved.

- Nulec Stabiliser: I referred to my statement before the Zhizhi panel to the effect that the stabilizer is not missing. I was allocated a stabiliser for use in my residence at that time as was the practice of university administration (to provide certain facilities to deans and directors). The computer officer (Mr Tony Oochi) obtained my permission to exchange it with that of the computer room in order to verify the course of an electrical problem that was slowing a job down; in the process stabilizers were exchanged between my residence and CEFAS computer room. The decision of Mr Zhizhi was that the same officer should reverse the exchange but that had not been carried out till date, I understand under the instruction of incumbent Director. A new allegation surfaced about the actual number of stabilizers supplied to CEFAS at that time; (Chairman made reference to my memo requesting three rather than two); I submitted that only two stabilizers were provided and the supplier was Messrs. G. Matins in Makurdi so the committee could verify from the company and stores records/Bursary Department.

"Loose End Issues"

Committee raised the issues of "sale of CEFAS Publications" in reference to an earlier memo of CEFAS Director to me. I submitted that I did not authorize sale of any CEFAS publications as a matter of policy during my time. I referred to my earlier response to the memo in question to the effect that I gave the books as shown in the file records to Professor M. O. Ijere, former Director of the Centre who actually executed the project to publish the book during his term as Director of the centre, only as a channel to distribute the books at home and abroad, free of charge. I urged the panel to establish contacts with professor Ijere for necessary clarifications.

Committee raised the issue of UNDP project in terms of the allegation that I did not involve staff of the centre as well as management of the fund. I established how I involved staff; A member was specifically assigned as officer in charge; all members played specific roles at the planning workshop of the project declared open by the Vice Chancellor and all participants received specified payments for their roles. However, Mr Odoemenem was inpatient with the sequence of stages of the project to the next stage that would involve him before he spearheaded a petition to the Vice Chancellor in which he wandered about to employ falsehood to justify the frivolity of their complaints. I have since sent my detailed comments to the VC about the matter in addition to verbal defense of my actions. Subsequently the administration closed the project account till date, claiming it was not authorized, when the Bursar, CEFAS Finance Officer and myself are signatories and when I wrote memo to inform VC about the project and its conditions including the requirement to open a separate account and the fact that several other projects exists in the university operating separate accounts. It appears, with benefit of hind sight, that I actually pulled the ants that bite me down on myself by institutionalising the project account in the name of the centre in the spirit of good leadership; otherwise, why is it that a similar project funded by the same UNDP and granted at the same time to Dr C. P. Obinne on similar topic has not received such a frustration? Is it because he was wiser by making the project account external to the university? Or (though I forgot to ask at the meeting) because Mrs. Gyang made two separate requests for part of the money and I was unable to grant them? I expressed further reservations on the matter of this UNDP project because of some embarrassments I suffered from the university administration through certain

> correspondences including my several appeals to VC that failed. Meanwhile the project had suffered extreme time delays and truncation of implementation in my hand till date.
>
> The UNIAGRIC-MANR collaborative project was raised as an issue by the committee. I submitted that the fund provided had been spent to implement the project including the aspects of organising a planning workshop (declared open by VC and Director-General of Ministry), preparations of the data collection instruments and publishing of the proceedings of the workshop. I have since retired it to the bursary.
>
> Dr G. B. Ayoola

The committee finished its work and submitted its report to the VC, of which I was able to obtain a copy. The report did not indict me anywhere; rather, it vindicated me here and there, particularly the finding that "the present/incumbent Director [i.e., Odoemenem] never really accepted the headship of Dr G. B. Ayoola as Director of CEFAS". Also, "He and some other staff of CEFAS regarded Dr G. B. Ayoola as an imposition on staff of CEFAS." Rather surprisingly, I received a reprimand from Gyang based on the committee's work in the form of a "warning". Seeing that as one step towards sacking me from my job, I rejected it in its entirety and went to court in a case of fundamental rights enforcement. I submitted a formal protest to the Minister of Agriculture as well, who was acting as a supervisory body in the absence of governing council at that time (my protest letter dated 17 November 1999).

Not only was the court judgment in my favour, in which both the letter of warning was totally quashed, but also the VC was lampooned and expressly castigated in strong terms. Specifically Gyang was characterized in the judgment as a despot by the judge.

> Even though we have many despots here and there in the country it is the collective will of Nigerians that they be governed by Rule of Law and not that of the despots. ... Where a people who are supposed to be civilized behave as

if they are not, they have to be shown the correct thing to do and they should not be encouraged in their misconduct.

VII. Seventh Onslaught

Satisfied that I was no longer a member of senate and so could not defend myself and nip issues in the bud as before, Gyang reopened the matter of my postgraduate student Patrick Magit. The student received a letter notifying him that he had been dismissed from the university and that his thesis was rejected. It was unmistakable whose handwork this was: the duo of Umeh and Njike. As I recalled, the verdict of the oral examination panel was signed by all members, including Umeh himself, and also me as the HOD and major supervisor. We had passed the thesis with option B, "thesis accepted subject to corrections to be certified as may be determined by the panel". The report also stated. "Thesis is concise and appropriate. The literature review, problem statement and justification for the study are very well written. The conceptual framework is clearly stated."

The panel suggested certain corrections to improve the thesis, which involved the need to run other functional forms in addition to the Cobb-Douglas. The student carried out the corrections to the satisfaction of the external examiner (Professor James Olukosi for Ahmadu Bello University Zaria), who certified it on item-by-item basis in strong terms.

a) Each chapter in the table of contents has been given a title.
b) The abstract has been reduced as suggested.
c) The objectives have been corrected as appropriate.
d) Chapter two has been correctly titled as "Literature Review"
e) With reference to p. 35, different functional forms have been tried. Even though the Cobb-Douglas function appeared to give the best fit, the MVP for potato seed is no longer negative due to better redefinition of the variables. The interpretations of the results are now adequate and acceptable".
f) The references have been rewritten in standard form.

The external examiner concluded thus: "As was discussed in March 1998 with Dr Ayoola, HOD, Agricultural Economics, I gave him the go ahead to approve the thesis based on the satisfactory completion of the thesis corrections as stated above."

To the contrary, Umeh's secret write-up, which formed the basis of rejection of the thesis and dismissal of the student by senate, maliciously characterised the thesis as follows.

- a. That "the re-run function in the corrected thesis had produced a result which is radically different from the original one";
- b. that "the data used in the analysis of the original thesis were not the ones used in the analysis of the corrected thesis, and that two sets of data were used";
- c. that "The radical changes in the Cobb-Douglas functions in both the draft and corrected theses are worrisome. It is either that the two sets of data were used or the estimates were cooked up or both"; and
- d. that, the thesis employed "unacademic means" and engaged in "academic dishonesty" in arriving at the results

One mischief concealed in Umeh's write-up was that it was the oral examination panel that "suggested" Magit should fit other functional forms and choose a form that would return a positive parameter estimate for the seed variable, which was hitherto negative. Indeed, as the student explained to the panel, the negative sign of the seed parameter estimate in the Cobb-Douglas function, though not consistent with a priori expectation (as sometimes the case in agricultural economics research), could be due to diminishing returns to seed in potato production enterprise in the study area. Nonetheless, it was the preference of the external examiner for him to try his hand in a set of functional forms apart from the Cobb-Douglas that he had fitted before. In the final analysis, option B was chosen by the panel, which implied that the thesis had passed subject to those minor corrections, the advice to fit new functional forms notwithstanding.

But in his mischievous write-up, Umeh, who had agreed with the panel's decision as a member, had turned around to capitalise on the same decision to shoot down the thesis.

Another mischief concealed in Umeh's write-up was that he knew even with the same set of data, fitting different functional forms would normally return different values of the parameter estimates associated with variables without necessarily "cooking the data". This was the case with Magit's econometric rerun, whereby the previous estimate of the parameter associated with land changed from a negative value to a positive for some of the newly fitted functional forms. The third mischief in Umeh's submission on Magit's thesis was that the panel did not consider it as a major correction; otherwise, the panel would have chosen option C for him, which would have implied that the thesis had failed and would have to be re-examined.

In any case, the damage had been done. What mattered going forward was how to stop them from reaching me for punishment, which as I knew was their real goal. The game plan, as I understood them, was to shoot down the thesis as the basis to punish me as the supervisor, and to feign a pardon of the student afterwards. It seemed to me the only option available for me was court. I entered the magistrate court on the matter in a case of criminal prosecution against Njike, as well as the high court to file a civil suit on the same matter with the student, Patrick Magit, as the sole plaintiff. Also, the need arose to checkmate my stalkers together—Umeh, Njike, and Odoemenem—by filing yet another suit against them jointly at the state's high court.

The criminal case, with the summons was dated 14 June 1999, raised the most dust in Gyang's camp as a case of direct criminal prosecution of Njike for forgery, injurious falsehood, and framing incorrect evidence. If established, it carried a jail term of seven to fourteen years. My courage to file the case charged up the whole university population beyond expectation, but it enraged Gyang even more against me. Indeed, judging from the way the case commenced and progressed in court, my first counsel on that case, Barrister Okpale, from the law firm of Eche Ada & Co., was cocksure that he would secure the conviction against Njike in the criminal case—up to fourteen years in jail without the option of fine, he said. His opinion was based on the counter-affidavit in which Njike arrogantly admitted that he'd made the alterations in the oral examination result sheet as I alleged, but only as part of his job in processing it for senate consideration! As a gimmick to prevent Njike's arraignment, the defence lawyer came by way of preliminary objection to Njike being prosecuted for the offence based on that and other grounds. The grounds of objection were fiercely agued by my lawyer, and the magistrate eventually ruled in our favour. Following that, Njike was formally arraigned and docked, thereby suffering the first defeat in court. As the case formally opened and Njike was docked already in order to take his plea, he looked visibly jittery and practically lost; supposedly wondering about the possibility of going to jail, which now loomed large upon him.

During the trial, Njike suffered humiliation a couple of times, especially when he failed to come to court. Each time this happened, my counsel considered Njike failing to abide with his bail conditions, which formed the basis to press for his arrest and commitment to prison. On one occasion he was arrested to be taken to prison custody, but for the frantic efforts of Gyang to prevail on police authorities to keep him in police custody instead, at which he slept on a narrow bench till next day, when he was produced in court. The magistrate pardoned him and grudgingly resumed his bail.

At this stage, realising that the criminal offence for which Njike was arraigned bordered on the examination of malpractices law, I wrote a letter, dated 17 August, 1999 to notify the Minister of Education about the pendency of the case, with a view to causing the minister to interdict Njike and take up his prosecution from me, due to Njike having been arraigned for a criminal offence bordering on forgery of student examination result. However, the ministry was not sensitive to this development, and so no action was taken except a belated acknowledgement of my letter sent by surface mail and dated 1 November 1999, signed by one Kobani Bere for the minister, tacitly saying, "I have instruction of the Honourable Minister of Education to acknowledge receipt of your letter of 17 August 1999 and to inform you that the issues raised are being looked into. You will be reached in due time.", but which time is not due till date.

Strange Illness

Under the intense physical, mental and emotional pressure, I suddenly took ill, and another hour would have been too late for me without an emergency medical attention. I was rushed to Madona Hospital in Markudi town thanks to the brethren, who stopped by after the service when I was not present in church on that fateful Sunday. One of them was Dr Omeche Onoja, the medical officer at the university clinic, who had treated me for malaria fever a couple of days before and was constantly following me up. When Dr Isaac Amuta, the Medical Director of the university noticed such a fast deterioration of my health he hurriedly decided to refer me to a private hospital, at which I was revived. There I lay prostate at the hospital till I was discharged twenty-eight days later, having lost ten kilogrammes of my body weight.

By the time I arrived at the hospital, I could no longer recognise the brethren who accompanied me, not even my wife, who had already been sobbing before we'd left the house. As she later told me, before I entered the vehicle that took me to hospital, I took her to my wardrobe area and showed her where I kept the key to our Ibadan house. She understood that to mean I was bidding her my final farewell on earth. On arrival at the hospital and after receiving the first round of injections, the last thing I noticed happening at my bedside was the intense prayers of brethren, biding and casting out the devil with vigour. I fell asleep and went straight into a prolonged trance with astonishing clarity.

In my dream, the same brethren marched after me on a beautiful road on my way to heaven! I was so elated to be on the right-hand side of a dual carriageway moving towards a quiet gate in front. On the other side was a noisy gate swinging forth and back as many people rushed through it. Wondering why the gate on my side was so quiet, I decided in the spirit to cross to the other side so I could pass through as well. I attempted to jump across the aisles of beautiful flowers separating both lanes of the dual carriageway. The brethren held me back by force, saying that side of the road was not meant for me to pass through. As I struggled a bit with them, a fight broke out between us and a group of people passing on the other side, and I saw myself in armour against them fighting hard.

I came face-to-face with Njike as he fired an arrow that flew past me, and from nowhere during the melee that ensued, someone else's arrow hit him in the back. He felt flat, face down and gasping for breadth, to the jubilation of brethren who spontaneously transformed with me into a congregation of praise singers in a stadium setting. As clearly imprinted in my spirit, the leader of the choir was an unrecognised lady in a blue suit, and the victory song rendered by the band was Francis Adjei's famous "God, You're so Good".

> God, You're Good,
> God You're kind
> Lord You're wonderful
> my Lord You're excellent
> Excellent is thy name
> Excellent is thy might
> Lord You're are Wonderful
> my Lord You're excellent …

I woke up with this song in my mouth. I felt a deep sense of relief and heaved a heavy sigh, cocksure in my spirit that the battle of Makurdi had been fought, won, and lost. Dr Oluremi was the first to pay me a visit in the morning and I shared the dream with him. Later in the day, I was told that two men appeared in the ward, when prayer was going on the previous day and I had fallen asleep. According to the story, one of them wore dark glasses and kept his hands in his pocket, and the other was recognised as a former driver at UNIAGRIC. They stood still while prayer was still going on and then turned back to go out of the hospital. The story had it that they'd come in a small, unnumbered red car and that the one man did not remove his hand from his pockets until they entered the car and zoomed away. The conclusion was reached that the man was likely an hired assassin, but he did not find the environment conducive to carry out the assignment. Fear gripped me, and that added to my sickness. Based on the advice of brethren, I contacted my lawyer, who immediately decided to write a letter to inform the commissioner of police about the danger posed to my life, citing some of my observations about Professor Njike before I'd fallen sick and other circumstantial evidence that had formed part of the story I'd received while on my sick bed. The contents of the letter, dated 26 August 1999, included the following excerpts.

- That Mr I. U. Odoemenem had openly told our client "the damages you are claiming from us will be put on your grave".
- That immediately before and after the ruling wherein the courts ruled that Prof. Njike had a case to answer with respect to the criminal charge against him, the said Prof Njike had relocated from his postgraduate school office to that at the (building housing) the Department of Agricultural Economics near our client. And since then our client has been noticing some strange movement around his person, office and residential premises. All these apparently are attempts at finding ways and means to silence and or deal with our client in a way and manner that he will not be able to successfully prosecute the numerous cases he has against the herein before mentioned persons and the university of agriculture.
- That these suspicious and apparently dangerous movements aimed at our clients' life came to the open when our client suddenly fell ill and was taken to the Madonna hospital, Makurdi. Two men in an unmarked security car followed our client to the hospital room in dark glasses with both their hands in their pockets and stood there for about ten minutes without saying anything. However, when they were about going one of the two whom our client recognized as a retrenched driver with the university said "Dr we have not

been noticing you at the office for some days now, so we checked at your house and have to follow you here".
- What strikes our client immediately the above quoted statement was uttered, the said retrenched staff has not been friendly with our client, while in the employment of the university and he has been retrenched long ago. How come he was able to know that our client has not been going to the office? It is our client's suspicion that from the surrounding circumstances as stated in the preceding paragraphs the two men were set against our client by some people to silence him, and for the herein before stated reasons. Our client was lucky, very lucky they could not carry out their mission that night at Madonna Hospital in the presence of people that were with him. They said, "We shall come back".
- It is in the light of the above surrounding circumstances that our client fears threat to his life and is therefore seeking police protection. Our client is a law-abiding citizen and who has consistently followed administrative procedure in his dealings. It was only when the university administration refused, neglected and or failed to take actions that our client has gone to the law courts to seek justice and redress.
- That indeed the forgery complained of herein and which was admitted by the said Prof. Njike before the court in his own affidavit, has frustrated the educational career of Mr Patrick Magit, who had spent over six years to pursue a course that would ordinarily have taken him two years. Now he is neither here nor there.
- It is in the light of the above that our clients seeks and pleads that you use your good office to intervene and safeguard his life and that of his family before the worse happens.

Not a few people believed that Gyang and his hatchet men desired me to die for daring to put up a fight against them in the court generally, and subjecting Njike to criminal prosecution specifically. Sometime before I took ill, I had heard that they or their sympathisers had resorted to fetish practices to eliminate me from the surface of the earth. Some of these stories might appear incredible, but sometimes they could not be totally discounted. For example, someone told me that a cow had been buried alive somewhere in my image, that someone was sponsored to take his birth with a pot of things on his head at the bank of River Benue, and that someone had climbed a tree naked somewhere to attack my spirit by saying incantations and sorcery in a bid to end my life.

I remained unperturbed till I was discharged on my twenty-sixth day in hospital. Incidentally, while looking through the car that took me back home that day, I saw Gyang and some officers of the university probably carrying out an inspection of the signpost under construction at the junction of the road leading to the university. As our eyes met, he stood still, completely lost, as my car passed. Obviously, he was in awe of me because I had come out of hospital alive.

At home I learnt that the twins had come home on holiday from secondary school and a domestic accident had happened, whereby Taiwo mysteriously stepped on a needle that stood on its head and it disappeared into her flesh completely, right in the living room. She was rushed to the clinic at which doctors decided on a surgical operation for quick removal of the needle before it entered into her bloodstream and traveled to her heart! For obvious reasons, the doctors chose another hospital different from that where I was still on admission. I suddenly became emotional as I listened to such a strange story. Then, cuddling me on both sides, the twins began to pray, not ordinarily this time, but to my big surprise, also in tongues. Afterwards, seeing how surprised I was to hear them praying like that for the first time, Kehinde looked up to me and subconsciously manufactured a wonderful reassurance I needed at that moment, saying: "don't worry dad, they don't know yet the son of whom they are fighting against".

After I was discharged from the hospital, the spiritual enmity against me became more intense, with a number of strange objects finding their way into my office, either stuck to my chair for me to sit on, tucked between the maze of papers for me to step on, or hidden on my table in order to do me some spiritual harm. Sometimes I picked up such substances at my residence, such as dead ducks with black rings in the mouth, and I witnessed occasions when owls and snakes found their way into my bedroom. However, one after another they failed to achieve their devilish intentions.

A breather came when I was able to negotiate sick leave upon a referral I obtained from the chief medical officer to the University College Hospital, Ibadan, for a comprehensive review of my health situation.

Year 2—2000

VIII. Eighth Onslaught

Notwithstanding the pendency of the case of Magit at the High Court of Benue, the VC swung into action to subject me to disciplinary action (in a letter dated 7 July 2000). He had quickly caused the disciplinary committee of governing council to be reconstituted, which had Professor Njike as a member. They charged me with an offence of "academic dishonesty" before the committee. Furthermore, before the matter was tabled, the disciplinary committee's punishment was meted out to me by way of suspension from postgraduate supervision. I rejected this punishment in my submission that follows.

> 21 July 2000
>
> The Vice Chancellor,
> University or Agriculture. Makurdi.
>
> **Objection to Punishment**
>
> I write with reference to the letter of 7th July 2000 (Ref: UNIAGRIC/ACA/COM/04/Y) written by Acting Registrar. According to the content of this letter, senate considered the thesis of my student, which had been successfully defended and duly certified. This is the thesis of Mr P. D. Magit, which was submitted for appointment of external examiner on 20 October 1997, and the oral examination took place on 10 November 1997. The student passed before the oral examination panel (of experts) and the final version of the thesis was forwarded for award of degree on 6 April 1998.

The present letter from Registrar (dated 7th July 2000) indicates that senate raised an issue against the thesis about the corrections carried out by the student, which the External Examiner and I (as the legitimate experts involved) had certified as properly carried out. Subsequently senate did an "analysis of the circumstances" without me (and without the student concerned) and concluded that I did not supervise the student's work properly and that was the reason the student employed "unacademic means" in the thesis. Senate views my role as "academic dishonesty" and directs that I should be suspended from supervision of postgraduate students until further notice. Furthermore, senate had, by concurrent action, rejected the thesis and expelled the student from the university.

I would like to raise an objection against the above scenario based on the following grounds:

1. The issue raised borders on Production Function Analysis and Econometrics, which are highly specialized areas of our own discipline (Agricultural Economics). Therefore senate cannot raise and determine issues in these areas without the panel of experts which the student successfully defended the thesis before it.

2. Senate cannot delve into the scientific content of the thesis, as it did, with no reference to me as the supervisor (and even the student) at all before inflicting injurious punishments on me (as well as the student) by rejecting the thesis, expelling the student and punishing me by suspension!

3. The allegation of academic dishonesty against me is totally unfounded in both logic and reason and I hereby deny it without any reservation. The allegation was sponsored by Professor M. C. Njike, Dean of Postgraduate School, in deep-pocketed hostility against me, and for the sole aim of spoiling my personal and professional image at all costs; that hostility dates back

to 1989/90 and has been demonstrated and celebrated on many occasions to the full knowledge of senate and approval of the Vice Chancellor for reasons other than my professional competence and ability to perform in office. Lest senate forgets, I was in office as the Head of Department when the thesis in question was submitted, defended, processed and forwarded for award of degree; simultaneously I was also in office for 3 1/2 years as tile Director of the Centre for Food and Agricultural Strategy (CEFAS) in the university.

4. Senate considered and determined the issue raised in complete difference to the need for fairness and justice, against its full knowledge of the specific antecedents of the case. For instance, senate is aware that this is *the same thesis* that the same Professor Njike had struggled very hard to destroy at earlier stages. Also, senate knows that Professor Njike is standing criminal trial at the Chief Magistrate Court for an offence pertaining to the alteration he made on the report of the oral examination panel in an earlier (desperate) attempt to destroy the <u>same thesis</u> at all costs. Yet senate was so easily "convinced" when *the same Professor Njike* raked up another (false) issue against *the same thesis* to the extent that it accused, tried and judged the supervisor (and student) behind their back.

5. The observation of senate was wrong, that the student did not address the issues as suggested by the oral examination panel. The student painstakingly carried out all the corrections including No. 5 as conveyed by the attestations of supervisor (myself) and the external examiner (Professor James Olukosi from Ahmadu Bello University, Zaria), both of which were placed before senate.

6. Senate was utterly wrong to evaluate my supervision job performance as it did, after the successful oral examination of the candidate and initial approval of the thesis. The appropriate point to evaluate supervision job performance is at the oral examination when the external examiner is available to examine the student

and observe the professional competence of the major supervisor vis-a- vis the thesis under focus. In this regard, I am happy to tell senate that throughout my HOD/Supervision experience none of the postgraduate students of mine, including the eleven (11 No.) MSc students that I have presented so far have failed at the oral examination stage. Rather, lest senate does not know, the only two failed theses in my department till date were supervised by the current HOD, Dr J. C. Umeh who has produced only four MSc students till date (ref: referred theses of Ivlr. Tsavua and Mr Ogebe).

7. It cannot be correct that a re-run of the Cobb-Douglas function should produce the same results after the re-run, given the fact that the oral examination panel directed the student to reconsider the underlying model and data in certain ways. Indeed.' the oral examination panel expects such possible changes to take place particularly in respect of one variable that its estimated coefficient initially did not follow the *a priori* expectation.

8. Senate was explicitly biased when it ignored the important fact that the report by Professor Njike that formed the basis of the allegation against the thesis was unsolicited and it came to the floor of senate only after the initial approval of the thesis on an earlier date. The report in question bordered on issues of agricultural economics and econometrics and was secretly supplied by Dr J. C. Umeh who is in that area. Dr Umeh did so against the fact that he was a member of the oral examination panel that unanimously passed the student in the first instance; also he subsequently gave his approval of the corrections carried out by the student prior to forwarding of the thesis for award of degree. If senate has been balanced enough in its approach to interrogate this set of facts, it would have been able to unearth the bad faith implicit in the report and conclude differently.

9. Senate had in the circumstances plunged into an arena of professional conflict that it lacks inherent capacity

to sustain. It is unfortunate for senate to reduce itself to such a laughable position in the eyes of any expert in Agricultural Economics who might come across its opinion on the matter; let alone the punishments meted to the innocent student and me as well as the insults it represents to the professional competence and integrity ·of the external examiner originally appointed by senate.

10. I stand firm by my decision to certify the corrections in all aspects including the microeconomics and econometrics of the work. I would like to invite anybody in my discipline (not Professor Njike, who is a poultry expert as a branch of animal production) to challenge me in the open (not at my back) on behalf of senate anywhere any day, any place and any time for us to demonstrate our knowledge of the subject matter with respect to the specific issue in question. Senate may wish to organise an open scientific inquisition on the matter if it so wishes, to be witnessed and resolved by other experts and representatives of the Nigerian Association of Agricultural Economists (NAAE), and not people who cannot even appreciate the relevance of technical coefficients in econometrics or elasticity parameters in agricultural production economics.

Action Sought

Based on the above grounds, I am unable to accept the sanction against me and the letter is hereby rejected. Therefore I humbly seek the action of the Vice Chancellor to cause the letter to be withdrawn and declare its entire content ineffectual and inconsequential.

Thank You, Sir.

Dr G. B. Ayoola
Senior Lecturer

In the end, we lost the case in court—not on the propriety of university's actions but on the restriction the court placed on itself to not interfere in the process of awarding degrees in the university. And notwithstanding our notice of appeal, filed immediately at the Federal Court of Appeal, Abuja, the disciplinary committee made the much-awaited move to invite me to appear before it to defend the charges levelled against me by the university administration (in a letter of invitation dated 3 October 2000).

I found it totally objectionable that Njike was a member of the committee, given that he was a principal character in the many cases I had filed against the university. Even though I saw this as a suitable basis for me to not appear before the disciplinary committee unless Njike recused himself, my lawyer advised otherwise. Also, even though there was obvious risk of contempt of court on their part for subjecting me to disciplinary measures on a matter still pending in court, and though I realised that an order of court for contempt proceeding against Gyang could easily be obtained, in this particular case my lawyer preferred that I act in obedience to the governing council as my employer.

The charge against me before the committee, termed "academic dishonesty", pertained to my official role as the supervisor of the thesis submitted by the postgraduate student Magit—a thesis that had previously passed before an external examination panel! However, prior to my appearance on the date fixed, my lawyer, Okutepa, had sent a legal threat to Gyang through the defense lawyer in Magit's cases, S. P. Ejale, deploying pungent words, as shown hereunder.

> Please refer to the above cases pending in Courts and which your Chambers is handling for the defendants and the accused person therein respectively at the instance of the University of Agriculture Makurdi's Administration and the proceedings of 9/10/2000... We have instruction and it has come to our notice that while these cases are (still) pending in the Courts the University administration has set up a disciplinary committee on 10/10/2000 ... While we concede that the University administration is not a party to the proceedings in the two cases, there is no doubt that the University administration/authorities and agents are aware of these case, as they were the one who briefed your firm to defend the defendants and the accused

person in the cases above. (Therefore) We write this letter to draw your attention and request you to use your sound knowledge of law to advise the University accordingly, as we hold the legal view that it will amount to contempt and usurpation of the functions of the Court, for the disciplinary committee to proceed to trying our client while he is in courts challenging the basis of what the committee is inviting him to defend.

That correspondence stopped the work of the disciplinary committee, as the venue was empty when I showed up for trial on the appointed date. Then I reduced my defence to a memo I sent to Gyang, with the following excerpts (from paragraph 2.2 to the end).

Particulars of Defence:

The kernel of the allegation is contained in the paper for senate presented by Professor M. C. Njike, as mentioned earlier. In the paper in question, after first confirming that truly the student fitted other functional forms "as expected of him" he went on to allege that "he did not give any guide on the choice of his lead function using econometric criteria"; he then made the spurious finding that "we are still not sure which function (or model) fitted his data best". I would like to submit that this is completely farce and it reveals the ignorance of a poultry person diving head-on into murky waters of agricultural economics. The fact is that the student did an extensive theoretical exposition earlier in the thesis whereby he clearly provided the basis for selecting a lead equation. Subsequently he chose the Cobb-Douglas as the lead equation for direct use in computing the necessary economic parameters required. He then showed wisdom to present all the functional forms in the appendix for verification purposes. I was perfectly satisfied about this approach adopted by the student and I remain so till date. There is no law or rule in agricultural economics research that compels the researcher to situate information (of secondary nature of this kind) in a particular place. If Professor Njike and his secrete backers (of course Umeh in the same discipline as I) are not sure as claimed it must be that it is because they are ignorant of the issues involved and aberrant, as it were, in knowledge with respect to the subject matter as obviously Professor Njike is.

Secondly Professor Njike criticized the thesis for the fact that "re-running Cobb-Douglas has produced a result which is radically different from the original one in the draft thesis in very many ways". Further he (Umeh masquerading as Njike) made a rather lame statement "that the radical changes in the estimates of Cobb-Douglas functions in both the draft and corrected theses are worrisome" and emerged at a distant end of the fraudulent reasoning to conclude that "it is either that the two different sets of data were used or the estimates were cooked ...". In the final analysis he delivered a most callous ruling against the thesis as follows: "Whichever is the case, it is unacademic and unacceptable". This is where the administration anchored its intellectual mischief for the purpose of nailing me down professionally at all costs. But it only shows the scarcity of intellect in the system to interrogate the nature of the academic issues involved properly (which borders on the subject matter of econometrics).

In evaluating the issue here I take cognizance of the fact that no member of the disciplinary committee is an agricultural economist and, so, would be able to appreciate the technical issues to the extent desired by me. Nevertheless, I will adopt a pedagogic approach to deal with the issue for your consumption. Let us adopt the definition of econometrics as in David Pearce ed. (1986)— The Dictionary of Modern Economics: Econometrics is a branch of statistics concerned with the testing of economic hypotheses and the estimation of economic parameters, mainly through the use of multiple regression techniques. The same source defines regression as follows: An analysis involving the fitting of regression equation (or mathematical relationship) to a set of data points. From these definitions we note that econometrics is exclusively an economist's business and basically an estimation process, i.e. estimation of parameter values associated with an economic equation or relationship of specified functional form. The raw material required to perform the estimation is a set of data. So, what Professor Njike who is not an expert in econometrics (but a poultry scientist only) is saying in the allegation, is that if you run a regression of the Cob-Douglas form on computer once using a given set of data, you cannot rerun the regression of the *same form* and with the *same data* to obtain different results in terms of the estimates of parameter values. It is my humble submission that this view is absolutely incorrect to hold.

First, to say that the output of a regression analysis before and after rerun cannot be different even when data had been altered is opposite to ordinary common sense. It is like asking why the characteristics of a product have changed after reconstituting the inputs used in the production process. Such a question is manifestly illogical, mischievous and intellectually deficient. As the supervisor and the authorized expert in the matter of this thesis, I was and am still satisfied with what the student did. I approved his explanation for the change in the values of regression coefficients as provided. I quote him expressly herewith: "Six functional forms including the semi-log were tried, after the required transformation as directed by the panel of examiners". You can see, sir that the panel directed the student to transform the variables, which he did in obedience and showed the documentary evidence of doing so at the computer centre of the University of Jos. Transformation of data or variable is legitimate in agricultural economics research. The most distinguished authority in econometrics is Jan Kmenta, author of Elements of Econometrics. In this textbook (copy available herewith) the theory of variable transformation is extensively treated within the context of special regression models including the type employed in the thesis in question (see pp: 409–). According to the theory, transformation of data is an inevitable step in the process of subjecting a non-linear functional form to linear regression analysis. Also a variable may also be transformed from one form to another in terms of its redefinition, re-specification or re-limiting. I submit that there is no way any of these legitimate things can be done without changing the outcomes of regression analysis even when the data and functional form of model remain the same. I have another authority with me here to show the committee members; this is Regression Diagnostics by David Belsley and others, wherein the theory of variable/data transformation is also treated extensively (see pp: 177-185). So how can an animal science person with no demonstrated expertise in quantitative analysis in his field, let alone in my own field, be telling us that regression coefficients can only change when data is cooked (admittedly such a person is as econometrically dumb as his backer, Umeh). That is heresy and should not be believed.

Let me submit therefore that there are many legitimate ways of re-running regression equation to yield different parameter values without necessarily using a different set of data or "cooking data" up. I am prepared to challenge Professor Njike or Dr Umeh or any faceless expert reviewer of the thesis to an open inquisition on the issue where experts in agricultural economics (not animal science) will be invited. Meanwhile, I am the expert to be believed at this point as supported by the external examiner who is a well-respected member of the profession (and myself now a distinguished fellow of Nigerian Association of Agricultural Economists).

Concluding Remark

In conclusion, I would like to submit that the allegation of academic deceit or dishonesty leveled against me should not be sustained. The allegation as can be evaluated based on the foregoing account, is malicious, anomalous, illegal and indeed contemptuous, speculative as well as technically deficient. Also it has been tabled before you without following due process. Therefore it should be completely discountenanced and I should be discharged unconditionally.

Finally, sir, I would like to draw the attention of this committee to the numerous injuries that I have suffered in the process of intense official hostility against me, as listed in my letter to chairman of council. These include financial, emotional, physical, and personal among other injuries.

The real motive of the administration is to destroy me personally and professionally because I had the gut to speak truthfully and frankly at Abuja. But I know that God is not going to allow that to happen because I had served this institution with disciplined hard work and unflinching loyalty. I was responsible for revitalising a moribund centre and later revamping a department that was literally dead in action under Dr J. C. Umeh This Dr J.C. Umeh was in charge of department when no single postgraduate student was produced between 1991 when the program commence and 1997 when I took over from him following a special request by the VC (Professor E.O Gyang). In my two years of headship 22 finished including 14 that successfully defended their thesis and the others awaiting oral examination. It is ironical that it is that same success framework from which a grievous allegation of this nature will be brought out.

I served the VC faithfully prior to the Abuja saga; writing papers for him, accompanying him to important academic functions and backstopping him intellectually all along using my professional knowledge. My wife and I also joined him at his residence a number of times to hold morning devotion and pray for him and his family to succeed. In misplaced excitement I sent letter of heart-felt congratulations and advice to him from the USA when he was appointed as VC in 1996. Yet he must take a pound of flesh at all costs. I sympathized with him and his family when students burned down his official residence in January 1999, but he didn't send even a get well card when I was hospitalized for 28 days when I took ill in August/September 1999.

As you can see in my case, sir, the present administration is good at identifying suitable characters as instruments of oppression and repression of honest staff. In my case, the goal was to run me down as somebody who is professionally incompetent, using Professor Njike, Dr Umeh and Mr Odoemenem as instruments. There was a period of time when Professor Njike was running a viscous campaign of calumny on the academic block corridor to convince colleagues that I was not professionally competent in his bid to make Dr Umeh win deanship election in my college board. The man lost against my ghost at voting with a result of 4 for him versus 12 for me, despite the frantic effort of administration to back him up with brute official force.

If a charge of unethical professional misconduct is to be preferred against somebody in this university that person is Professor Njike. He was the person who smuggled eleven articles of his into successive issues of his society's journal when he was Editor in Chief; if those papers were removed from his CV his assessment for professorship would fail badly, even today. Professor Njike he is who never published other than the work he did at the National Veterinary Research Institute, Vom to become Professor of University of Agriculture, Makurdi. Professor Njike he is who had never been major supervisor of any postgraduate student (MSc or Ph.D.) but became Professor and was appointed Dean of postgraduate school; what an oddity? Professor Njike he was who was indicted by a council committee to have deliberately altered the date of official letter in the process of evaluating his promotion to professor, similar to the way result of oral examination of Mr Magit has been falsified. That is the same Professor Njike who today is member of governing council and member of disciplinary committee?

As to whether I am professionally sound or not, that is for well-meaning-members of academic society to judge. But at the maximum risk of sounding immodest, I can do a rough score of my small self. By the special grace of God if I become VC or DVC of this university or any university in this country tomorrow, the students' body would not publish my school certificate results to exhibit aggregate 35 or fail in physics and/or mathematics (as recently done for Gyang and Ikurior respectively). I passed my school certificate examination in Grade One and I never knew what a second position looked like in my class from beginning to the end of my secondary school education, let alone failing mathematics or physics or English Language in the certificate. At UNIFE of old (not OAU) I was a "National Scholar" from inception to the end of my program; that was the highest academic award for brilliant students in the whole university system at that time. And since I have been practicing this enviable profession of Agricultural Economics, God has blessed my little effort with recognition at home and abroad: I have been an *economic adviser to Minister* of Agriculture since 1990 (barely two years after my doctoral graduation) till date. What's more the International Bibliographic Centre at Cambridge has honoured me as one of the "2000 Outstanding Intellectuals in the 20th Century", based on my work as an academic.

Therefore I refuse to accept the castigation of idle people and busy bodies to portray me in bad professional light. I can only wish the disciplinary committee the wisdom to discern the trend of events in this university and salvage the vestiges of its old self from sinking permanently into the oblivion. In this regard, the content of page 40 of yesterday's issue of the Punch newspaper is most helpful to the success of the disciplinary committee.

Kindest personal respect Sirs.

Dr, G. B. Ayoola.

IX. Ninth Onslaught

Next, Gyang turned his attention to another case in waiting, that of student Victor Ehigiator, who had also brewed in Umeh's pot of troubles with me. In the same mode as Magit, Dr Umeh had jumped at an evil demand from Njike to write another critique against the thesis of Ehigiator, to which he readily acceded. Again in his write-up, Umeh raised econometric issues as he had before, but it was different from the issue of sample size that was raised by him (and addressed) during the oral examination. Also, playing a similar script to Magit's own, a paper for the senate was generated and presented by Njike, following which a kangaroo panel was set up to investigate the matter (and of course to work to the answer) for the student to be punished so that an allegation of negligence could be leveled against me. Like the former case, the panel, chaired by Professor B. A. Kalu. an agronomist, agreed to play ball. Most preposterously, the only evidence taken by the panel was that of the accuser, Umeh, who presented a computer printout of Ehigiator's to him as the former supervisor—after craftily removing a crucial page from it. No member of the panel—the membership was comprised of another agronomist, Professor E. O. Ogunwolu, and Dr C. C. Ariahu, a food scientist—was knowledgeable in econometrics, and so that criminal act of Umeh's was not observed. Without inviting either the student Ehigiator or his supervisor (me), a verdict of guilty was passed by the panel and reported back to senate, thereby providing the fertile ground desired for Njike to make his foolish sweeping recommendations, as follows.

1. That the thesis be rejected in its entirety
2. That supervisor's (Dr Ayoola's) role in the conduct and execution of the student's research left much to be desired. The (Postgraduate) Board concluded that it was Dr Ayoola's negligence as a supervisor that caused the wide manipulation of data and forgery that was evident throughout the thesis. The Board considered the action of Dr Ayoola despicable and a breach of academic ethics and gross academic misconduct. The Board therefore recommends that:
    a. The action of Dr Ayoola be referred to the University Administration for appropriate disciplinary action; and
    b. Dr Ayoola should not be allowed to supervise and teach postgraduate students.

How can that be? What an artful witch-hunt of me! Even Assuming without conceding that the student had cheated in writing the thesis or in the examination of the thesis, how can the major supervisor be held responsible and culpable? They had also totally forgotten that Umeh, the accuser, was also the minor supervisor of the student in this case. Neither did they know (or remember) the background of Umeh's hatred of the student, so as to consider the possibility of bias in his attestation of the student's thesis after external examiner had passed it. Only a dumb university senate, like the one that Gyang presided over, could debate and approve such a callous academic witch-hunt of a student by the combination of Njike and Gyang.

In any case, considering the full weight of this report on my personal and professional integrity, it was clear to me that Njike had succeeded in passing the ball easily for Gyang to score a goal against me in the game to nail me down. But unfortunately for them, as soon as the senate approved Njike's recommendation, my informant in the senate sneaked a copy of the committee's report, together with the recommendations, into my hand that same day. In trepidation I rushed to court for an order to stop Gyang before he could act on the senate's decision on the matter. I entered court to file two cases for adjudication, one filed for the criminal prosecution of Njike and Umeh as conspirators at the Magistrate Court Makurdi, and the other a suit filed at the High Court of Benue State in Ehigiator's name and mine as the plaintiffs against the university senate and its accessories. Then I secured an ex parte order of the court stopping Gyang from carrying out any action on the matter, pending the determination of the case. By that action of mine, I locked Gyang in and beat Njike to it, thereby winning the match for the time being.

X.   Tenth Onslaught

The witch-hunt continued unabated by instituting a probe into select postgraduate courses in my department, with the sole aim of discrediting me professionally and subjecting me to disciplinary action by any means. Based on Njike's instrumentality, a "Senate Investigation Committee on the Teaching and Examination of AEC 701, 703, & 705" occurred, and all these were courses taught in my department. Again, I knew where they were coming from and that I was the real focus of that investigation, in order to further explore another opportunity to nail me down professionally.

Gyang had just removed Mr N. I. Achamber as HOD of my department and appointed Umeh instead. In trepidation, both Achamber and I recognised the purpose (which was to witch-hunt us), and we petitioned Gyang himself to raise certain concerns. Our joint memo is below.

Concern against the Recent Appointment of Dr J. C. Umeh as Head of Department of Agricultural Economics:

We the undersigned staff of the above named department wish to refer to the recent appointment of Dr J. C. Umeh as Head of Department.

Preamble:
We wish to declare as follows:

1. That we are responsible and peace-loving citizens of the Federal Republic of Nigeria and will continue to obey the laws of the land.

2. That we pledge our loyalty and support to the administration of the University of Agriculture Makurdi and will do everything to promote peace and unity in the University Community.

3. That this concern of ours is in good faith and is not based on malice or prejudice against anybody.

4. That we are the most senior and longest-serving members of staff of the department at present after Dr Umeh, and have occupied the post of Head of Department at different times in the past. Therefore we are in a vantage position to make factual statements concerning Dr Umeh as a member of the Department.

Grounds of Concern

1. Dr J. C. Umeh was the acting Head/Dean up to 1996. Records have shown that this period was characterized by lack of academic progress, and peace among other vices. In fact this period (Dr Umeh's previous era) is largely responsible for some of the most embarrassing academic and management problems that the department is still struggling with to date. For example not a single postgraduates (M.Sc.) student graduated

from inception of the programme in 1991 up to the time he left office in 1996. It was also during this time that the Postgraduate Diploma (PGD) programme in Agricultural Risk Management (a very popular programme of the department) had to be suspended midstream by Senate, causing untold hardship to students and embarrassment to the college. At a point the whole of our PGD programme was threatened and the students had to write a "save our soul" (SOS) letter to Senate. Therefore, Dr J. C. Umeh had failed in the past to show effective academic leadership and administrative competence, leading to stagnation of the department for a long time.

2. The relationship between Dr Umeh and the generality of staff is not cordial, as revealed through numerous queries, victimisation, vengeance, acrimony and mutual suspicion. Past records also show his bad relationship with Senior colleagues particularly Professor P. O. Erhabor and Professor Aja Okorie. Drs Ejembi and Ayoola never considered to request him (Dr Umeh) to hold brief for them in office despite his senior position. Presently Dr Umeh had taken some staff members and students to the police alleging that they wanted to kill him, namely Dr E. P. Ejembi, Dr G. B. Ayoola, Mal. S. I. Audu, Mr G. A. Abu, Mr A. Tsavwua, Mr E. V. Ehigiator, Mr P. O. Magit; the case is still pending with police till date.

3. This curious appointment of Dr J. C. Umeh, spontaneously after he was overwhelmingly rejected as Dean at the recent college Deanship election, is a potential source of danger to members of the department. It should be noted that staff of the Agricultural Economics Department constitute well over two-third (2/3) internal membership of the college Board that rejected Dr Umeh as Dean even when no candidate contested with him (4 for "YES", 12 for "NO"). The implication of this is that the same staff of the department who rejected Dr J.C. Umeh en-mass as Dean are now being forced, by virtue of

this appointment, to have him as their leader (Head of Department); this amounts to imposition by other means, which is very unlikely to work.

4. Dr J. C. Umeh has been consistently rejected as leader at the department and college levels in the past; for example he was overwhelmingly rejected in two previous elections to choose the college representative in Senate. Also he was rejected in two previous elections to choose the Dean of the college.

5. The Official conduct of Dr Umeh is a matter of concern as reflected in official reports on him by previous HODs and Deans; there are issues of insubordination, non-cooperation etc., leading to pending recommendations of disciplinary action till date.

6. Dr Umeh secretly wrote the malicious reports to destroy the theses of two M.Sc. students who had successfully defended in this department. Both students have taken the University to court for violation of their fundamental rights following the decision of the administration to reject the theses and expel the students.

7. The University administration is consistently aware and conscious of the limitations of Dr Umeh as leader when:

   (a) He was removed in 1996 as Head of Department; instead Dr Ayoola who was Director of a centre was appointed to also double as Head of Department between 1996 and 1988.

   (b) He was refused the same appointment in 1998; instead Prof. P. O. Erhabor was brought from his post as Director of University Consultancy to take up headship of the department.

   (c) He was again refused the same appointment when Dr Erhabor left the services of the university in

1999; rather Mr N. I. Achamber, a Lecturer II staff member, was appointed as Head of Department by the same University administration. Given this scenario, we now wonder when Dr J.C. Umeh suddenly becomes "born-again" in the eyes of the Administration to merit this appointment.

Action Sought

(d) Based on the above grounds, we strongly believe that the present appointment of Dr J. C. Umeh as Head of Department is not in the best interest of the department, college, and the University. Therefore we humbly request the Vice Chancellor to reconsider and withdraw the appointment of Dr Umeh in the overall interest of progress and good health of the system.

Thank you.

Dr G. B. Ayoola (Senior Lecturer)
Mr N. I. Achamber (Lecturer II)

The courses in question were taught to only one student at the PhD level, Mrs. Lawal, who happened to be Umeh's candidate as the major supervisor of her research. By the way, the premature removal of Achamber was Gyang's punishment of the man for daring to depose to an affidavit in my favour in one of the ongoing cases against the university at that time. Achamber was Gyang's fellow tribe's man in the Lecturer II position in my department, who was appointed as HOD at the expiration of my tenure, even when Umeh, an associate professor, was available, but not in the good books of Gyang yet. Thus the appointment of Achamber itself was to further spite Umeh at that time when Gyang had not enlisted Umeh, though very disgruntled against me, yet as a hatchet man. But Gyang was practically disappointed in Achamber not only because the man ventured to support my case in court with an affidavit but also because he had refused to be used against me in Gyang's bid to nail me down when he was HOD. On the contrary, Umeh, in his desire to be quickly promoted to the rank of full professor, had jumped at the offer of appointment as HOD, of course with the terms to help Gyang nail me down at all cost—an evil assignment that Achamber, as a friend of mine, had refused to carry out all this while.

Thus with Umeh now in post as HOD, the postgraduate courses I had taught or administered in the past when I was HOD became handy for Njike to explore in finding fault against me at all costs. Njike quickly asked senate to investigate the circumstances in which Mrs Lawal was awarded an F grade by Professor Ehrabor in two of those courses, and to determine the role of HOD (i.e., me) in the matter; by which time the lecturer, Ehrabor, had left the university to become secretary to government in Edo State.

An F grade awarded by Ehrabor, which was the right thing to do, came about when the student, Mrs. Lawal, refused to turn up for examination in the courses, citing her fear of victimisation by Ehrabor, whom she alleged was in enmity with her in the past during his tenure as dean of the college. On the same basis, she had come with her husband to me at home, when we were family friends, to request that I should not allocate her courses to Professor Ehrabor. Unsatisfactorily to both of them, I declined.

At issue now, a couple of years on in the bid to nail me down for Gyang, was what my role was as HOD in sustaining the F grade for Mrs. Lawal. That is, why, in my judgment of the case as HOD, did I not upturn the grade to record it as absent for her instead, in order to avail her of the opportunity to re-register afresh in the course next time? Doing so would violate the rule that absence of a candidate in an examination of a course registered for, without permission of the appropriate authority (this time the senate), should carry the penalty of an F grade. But now, totally impervious to reason, a dean of the postgraduate school who wanted to nail me down for the VC would accuse me of injustice against the student rather than commend me for strict compliance with university rules.

The probe was launched, and the panel beat about the bush before proceeding to investigate me for proficiency in my teaching assignments. Just in case it might form the basis for another litigation,

I did put up a strong defence, tendering my lecture notes, which in uncommon diligence indicated the start and stop dates I delivered my lectures. I also gave photocopies of my assignments submitted by the students, amongst other pieces of evidence that could vindicate me. The panel collected a sample of students' notes as well, in order to correlate them with my lecture own notes by content and dates, which turned out to correspond very well. The students who testified before the panel attested to my diligent teaching of the courses, and they seized the same opportunity to lampoon Umeh as a wicked teacher, demonstrating how he did not teach the two courses that Mrs. Lawal failed when he took them over from Ehrabor; he simply awarded marks to her in them. Based on students' testimonies, I was expressly vindicated and Umeh was roundly castigated, which meant that Njike and Gyang, who'd moved to nail me down in that direction, had shot themselves in the foot. The report of the panel did not see the light of the day in order to shield Umeh from trouble. Specifically, Umeh was embarrassed about the findings of the panel, which confirmed his sadistic character as a victimiser of students in the department. Indeed, he'd victimised Patrick Magit and Victor Ehigiator through his malicious write-ups targeted at me as their major supervisor. This aberrant behavior of a lecturer had deteriorated the user experiences of the affected students as consumers of educational services in the university.

XI.   Eleventh Onslaught

By the second half of 2000, the penultimate year of Gyang in office as the VC, he had become very anxious about what to do to nail me down at all costs. Then a memo came from the chief security officer of the university inviting me to "appear for his interview on Monday 15th May, 2000 at 10.00 hours prompt", which according to the memo was "to enable him discuss a very vital and urgent Security matter with you". I wouldn't know what that invitation was all about, but I hoped Gyang had not wound a security issue around me as a measure of retaliation for my criminal prosecution of Njike. My reply, dated 13 May 2000, was simply to turn down the invitation.

The purpose of this letter is to say that, based on the deep sense of insecurity and fear, which I feel under the university administration at present, I am not in a position to walk blindly into a meeting that its agenda is not stated. Therefore I request you to declare the topic to be discussed at the interview before the time (in order) to enable me prepare for the discussion adequately.

Surprisingly, the matter died there.

How Umeh Lost the Deanship Election to My Ghost

The narrative of this event is better captured through my communication with my lawyer on "Update on Litigations", which I wrote on 2 February 2000, and the subsequent communications with him on the subject matter.

1. **Background:** The Deanship Election of my college (and two other colleges) became due at the expiration of terms of the incumbent late last year. I have since received several representations from many sections of the University community trying to persuade me to vie for the post as one of the three eligible candidates. I had persistently refused to vie as variously advised. The University administration (apparently upon conviction that I would not participate) issued circular to announce date of election, consistent with the requirement for two weeks' notice as contained in the relevant guidelines. It happened within that period that I succumbed to the pressure and agreed to participate. As soon as the University administration received the nomination of my name, they decided to postpone the election indefinitely two days before the event as scheduled. This action reflects the preference of the administration against me to become Dean of my college, given the high probability of that happening in the present situation in the college."

> **"Motives:** I understand strategies were being designed to discredit and disqualify me before the election could hold. One of these is that the case of Magit be invoked. The VC informed the subsequent senate meeting that the thesis of Mr Magit (which is a subject of a criminal case at the Chief Magistrate Court, and a civil suit at the Makurdi High Court) has been sent to another external examiner. The usual prank is to produce a doctored report as basis to hang an offence on my neck and subject me to undeserved disciplinary process; then they would say (as in the case of Dr. Ayoade and Dr Shoremi) that a disciplinary matter was pending as basis of disqualification for election, and also for stalling promotion matters, to mention a few.

On receiving my nomination, Gyang's camp was in turmoil, noting that I was a more popular candidate and fearing that Ayoola, as dean of his college, portended more troubles for Gyang in central administration. Gyang ordered the electoral committee to move against me by all means. A day before the election was initially scheduled to hold a college board meeting, Uzer issued a circular, dated 6 June 2000, entitled "Nomination for the Election of the Deanship of the College of Agricultural Economics and Extension", wherein he stated "that, at the end of the deadline only two nominations were submitted, Dr J. C. Umeh and Dr G. B. Ayoola" and that:

> In view of the fact that Dr Ayoola has a number of cases in various courts against the University Authorities, and in view of the fact that the kernel of some of these cases touches on his professional ability or disability, and in view of the fact that these cases have not yet been disposed of, it is the candid view of the administration that it will be improper for him to be fielded as a Deanship candidate until these cases have been disposed of... The Deanship election is now scheduled for Thursday 8th June 2000 at 10am in Block A Conference Roam.

I immediately called on my lawyer, Okutepa, to show him the letter and share the contents of another circular I had produced to counter

Uzer's. In anger (as usual), Okutepa quickly wrote his own letter to Uzer, wherein he said,

> Having carefully studied your (circular) letter addressed to those who are by law regarded as electorates for the election, and the biased, prejudiced and contemptuous contents therein, we hold the legal view that:
>
> i. You have stepped into the arena of the alleged conflicts between the University Administration and our client and therefore not qualified to be the electoral officer for the election as you have by the contents of the letter, have your vision beclouded by the dust of the encounter between our client and the University Administration.
> ii. You have by the contents of the said letter assumed position of a campaign manager of the other candidate for the post of Deanship and you; therefore lack the acceptable qualification and competency of an unbiased umpire to effectively referee the election as an electoral officer in the election.

Okutepa concluded as follows.

> Consequently, we have the instruction of our client to demand and we do so accordingly that:
>
> i. You honourably disqualify yourself and resign your position as the Electoral Officer of the election as your continued stay in office as the electoral officer is undemocratic but illegal and uncivilized as well as unacceptable to our client:
> ii. You cause your letter aforesaid to be withdrawn immediately, failing which, you will be cited for contempt of court, as your letter constitutes an undue interference in the administration of justice.

My own circular, dated 7 June 2000 was posted on notice boards in the college building and other places in both the south core and north core of the university. In the circular, I made a number of observations bordering on several aspects of Uzer's circular that I found offensive enough: that it was an abnormality for an electoral umpire to issue such a circular, that my fundamental right to go to court was incontrovertible, that my professional ability was not in doubt by any means, and more. Then I enjoined the members of the College Board to vote according to their conscience and "to refuse to be influenced by the unsolicited view of the Gyang's administration as conveyed by the electoral officer. I am sure if truly I have issues of professional disability the administration would have clearly said so without alluding to cases in court and proceeded to take appropriate actions". Further, I said, "The fact of the matter is that there is plenty of shadow boxing going on, which should not be related to the deanship election in the college wherein, by the special grace of God, I am presently the longest-serving member of the staff, academic and non-academic combined." Therefore,

> In sum, I humbly declare that I am still available for the election tomorrow as nominated, and still request your vote as previously discussed. On my side, I can only pledge my disciplined hard work to pursue a serious intellectual enterprise in the college with a view to improving its limelight status as a legitimate organ of UNIAGRIC.

On Election Day, I could read the determination of College Board members on their faces as we met one another on the way to the meeting. The meeting started, and I raised my hand to speak. Uzer, as the electoral officer, innocently allowed it. It was sore in its mouth when the kernel of my speech was to move a vote of no confidence against him as electoral officer and his principal, Gyang, as VC. My motion, as typed and distributed at the meeting, was titled "Motion of No Confidence in the Electoral Officer and University Administration as Regards Their Role in the Deanship Election of the College of Agricultural Economics and Extension, 8 June 2000". It read as follows.

Preamble

There are three letters in circulation that are germane to this electoral process:

My Days in Court

1. Circular letter ref: R/UNIAGRIC/ACA/COM.51/Vol. V dated 6 June 2000 written by the Electoral Officer, addressed to all members of the College Board.
2. Circular letter dated 7 June 2000 written by Dr G.B Ayoola, addressed to all members of the College Board and copied to ASUU Chairman and the Electoral Officer.
3. Letter written by solicitors, J.S. Okutepa (Esq) to the Electoral Officer on behalf of Dr G.B. Ayoola.

I have the copies of these letters to read at this meeting of the College Board as they form the basis of the motion of no confidence.

Motion:

- Whereas the post of Dean of this College has been vacant for a long time now,
- Whereas the University Administration had fixed an earlier date (19 January 2000) for the election of another Dean, which was subsequently postponed indefinitely.
- Whereas another date (today, 8 June 2000) has been newly fixed for the election to hold.
- Whereas the Electoral Officer has issued a statement at the instance of Administration in disfavor of one of the candidates.
- Whereas the candidate involved has issued a statement to negate the view of the Administration.
- Whereas the solicitor to the candidate has corresponded with the Electoral Officer.
- Therefore, the basis for free and fair election has been totally destroyed.
- I hereby move a motion of NO CONFIDENCE in the Electoral Officer and Administration as regard their roles in the electoral process.

Respectfully moved by me

"Dr G. B. Ayoola

The electoral officer, Uzer declined to entertain the motion to be seconded or discussed. Rather, he chose to proceed with the sole item on the agenda, the election. He resumed action to say that the only candidate approved by administration was Umeh and therefore returned him as having won unopposed. Then the members cried foul. A motion was moved by a member and seconded that even at that, a yes or no vote should be carried out. Uzer had no choice to decide otherwise. But when voting was done by secret ballot, Umeh lost the election to my ghost, with 4 votes for him and 12 against—a result that not only revealed the general bad light in which the reasonable members of the university community viewed Umeh as a person but also demonstrated the possibility of "guilty as charged" to be pronounced on Umeh in the court cases I'd filed against him and his principal.

The Coming of Seven Gunmen

On Wednesday 25 October 2000 late at night, seven gunmen besieged my residence, looking to wipe me out from existence, outright and completely. This happened at a time I'd embarked on a research on indigenous vegetables in collaboration with Rudy Schippers, a scientist based at Natural Resources Institute, Chatham Maritime, United Kingdom. In the penultimate week, Rudy had travelled down for fieldwork in a sample of states, one each from three agro-ecological zones of the country: northwest, Jigawa State; central zone, Benue State; and southwest, Ekiti State. Rudy had arrived in the country through the Kano Airport, where I had obtained travel authorisation to join him from Makurdi for the commencement of the fieldwork in nearby Jigawa State. Rudy and I proceeded on road to Makurdi for the weekend in the hope of carrying out the survey of Benue State the following week. Next on our schedule was travelling to Ekiti to work there for another week before his departure back to UK via Lagos.

Prior to my journey to join Rudy, as administratively required of me, I had filed the standard form for travel authorisation and submitted the same through the HOD, Umeh, and to the VC, Gyang, in line with the schedule of fieldwork agreed with Rudy. Thus, for the gunmen to have struck during the week I should be home indicated to me that they had information about my movements, and the responsibility for their plan to kill me should be found on the doorsteps of Gyang and Umeh, working together based on their full knowledge of my travel authorisation form. Indeed, the information that Gyang was planning to assassinate me had filled the air for some time following an incident in the past when Professor Onyido and I were returning from town one evening. At a blind spot on the rough road to campus, gunshots were fired at us, which both of us heard, but they did not hit our car in motion. That is, the coming of seven gunmen for me at my residence was very likely a follow-up move in the same direction. Unfortunately for them, and much to their surprise, my wife and I were not at home that night, having travelled at different times earlier in the week.

How did that happen? Arriving at Makurdi from Jigawa on a Friday, I took Rudy straight to a hotel in town to settle down. I planned to hold a review meeting with him the next day. However, I met Rudy in a bad mood on Saturday, which was based on news he had received from UK that his aged father had slumped and fainted in a foster home, though he was not dead yet. Therefore we decided to terminate the ongoing survey work to allow Rudy travel back to London earlier than planned. We agreed to skip Benue State and to pass through Ekiti State to make new arrangements with our contact persons, on the way to Lagos to catch his flight. So unknown to Gyang and Umeh I would not be operating from Makurdi in that week anymore so they could seamlessly hatch their plan to murder me in cold blood.

On that Wednesday, Rudy and I passed the night at UI Hotels, Ibadan. The next morning, prior to setting out to Lagos Airport, we were at the front desk checking out when I instinctively felt the need to place a phone call to my father-in-law, who lived at Ile-Ife. The old man shouted at the other end, asking where I was. He had just received a phone call in that morning from my lawyer, Okutepa, who informed him about the coming of seven gunmen to my house the previous night! I froze up at first but managed to tell him I was in Ibadan. Later, my brain resumed, and I called Okutepa, my lawyer, who narrated the story of how they'd come and had molested my children. I asked, "What about my wife?" He said she had also travelled, which was totally a surprise to me because I hadn't expected her to do so. I'd worried that the gunmen had killed her, in my place.

It was obvious to Rudy that I wouldn't be following him to Lagos anymore. We parted ways, and I returned to Makurdi from Ibadan, with a stop over at Ile-Ife to see my father-in-law. There I met my wife sitting beside him. Fortuitously, she had travelled out of Makurdi Wednesday afternoon on a last-minute decision to attend the burial of her late friend's mother, which was fixed for Thursday. Because she'd started late in the day, she'd broken her journey to pass Wednesday night at Akure. At the time I was speaking to her father, she was on the road to Ile-Ife, and the gunmen did not meet her in Makurdi.

I arrived back in Makurdi and went straight into hiding in a hotel in town, Bandiko Hotel, for a couple of days. During that time, Okutepa, my lawyer, held private sessions with me for a full briefing. He had reported the matter to police already, having found enough reason to believe that Gyang, in conspiracy with Umeh, was the person who'd organised to kill me in cold blood. On 30 October 2000, he and I met with the police commissioner, who approved two police guards as bodyguards for me from the stock of policemen on campus. Later he added to them a plainclothes policeman directly from state headquarters.

Meanwhile, I had received a fuller briefing from my children and wards, as well as the different interpretations of how my wife and I had vanished into the thin air. A couple of days later, I did a memo to formally report the incident to Gyang. He sent a tongue-in-cheek sympathy letter to me on the incident, and a belated one at that. (The memo by Zhizhi was dated 16 November 2000). On the part of Umeh, I sat down bemused as my other colleagues in the department and college stopped by my office in solidarity or sympathy visits—but not Umeh. Instead, like someone out of his mind, Umeh wrote a nauseating sympathy letter accompanied with a memo entitled "An Advice". The latter bordered on issuing a query for my absence during the week that the gunmen had come! His innate concern was that the travel authorisation I'd taken did not cover that particular week (which was probably why their mission to kill me had failed). I simply ignored him, but the question came propping up in my head as to whether truly Umeh could be so bitter against me as to be instrumental to a plot to kill me.

This question resonated in my mind again afterwards, when my father died the following year, and Umeh did the same thing. On this occasion, again like someone out of his mind, Umeh wrote an insipid condolence letter to me accompanied with a query for travelling home for that purpose without permission. As usual, the allegation was untrue. I filled the relevant form, which passed through HOD to Registrar and was acknowledged by the latter even before I travelled out of town. But this time I couldn't stomach it, and so hurriedly replied to him. My memo, dated 7 August 2001, was copied to the pro-chancellor, the vice chancellor, registrar, the chairman of ASUU, and Barrister J. S. Okutepa. Excerpts:

Response to Memos on Condolence and Travel without Authorisation

I have received your two memos stapled together and at the same time. The first one dated 18 July 2001, was titled Letter of Condolence (i.e. in respect of the death of my father, which had occurred on 13 July 2001). The second memo is titled Travel without Authorisation (also in respect of my emergency journey home in response to the distress call from Ibadan following deterioration of my father's health that I undertook on Sunday 15 July 2001). I am to observe that the bad faith of the second memo had nullified any good intention of the first memo, which leads me to the unreserved rejection of the first one while I attend to the issues raised in the second one. There is absolutely no need for any pretenses or smoke screen to trivialize the official query that the second memo represents while appearing at the same time as if we have a humane system in place that understands the proper meaning and importance of someone's father dying. I would rather accept the genuine condolences of other people in the department and elsewhere who have or had fathers that they appreciate in life or in death, and thus are able to put one's father's death in the proper physiological, emotional and psychological contexts it deserved.

Many of such good people in the university community and beyond have been visiting me at home and in office while some even undertook immediate journeys to Ibadan to commiserate with me. Such an action cannot come at the instance of the Head of my own department, wherein I am not just a pioneer member but have sunk some 13 years of active professional life of mine to help build and which I was also once the HOD. Rather, I could only get a half-hearted condolence letter accompanied by a memo of calumny characterized by mindless faultfinding against me and aimed to discredit me in the eyes of well-meaning people.

I am to observe that the same approach to find unwarranted faults at me was used the last time when the sponsored seven gunmen came to my residence but failed to find me as well as my wife. While you sent a letter of sympathy to me on the matter, you also attached to it a query as to where I was (that made them not to find me!) and advised me to always stay in my house (for such operations to be successful!). Honestly, I cannot understand the sense in persistent double-speak and therefore reject your condolences, which I don't appreciate. So the first memo is hereby returned to you as is.

I hereby respond to the second memo that reflects the real intention you have to write to me. This memo you have copied to several functionaries in the university including the out-going Vice Chancellor, the Chairman of Governing Council, Registrar, ASUU Chairman, university lawyer, and so-called committee on investigation of allegation of serious misconduct of Dr Ayoola, among others. Just as done before without success, you have tried to use my recent travel when my father died to find new faults at me, so I can be suspended or sacked from my job again when the last attempt failed to produce desired results. And if not for the reason that I got to know how widely you have circulated the memo in question, my initial attitude during this active mourning period of mine is simply to ignore it. But the opinions of well-meaning people in the society would not permit me to do that. They advise that I should quickly clarify some cloudy aspects of the matter without necessarily taking you on measure for measure for now. I appreciate the wisdom in this advice and hereby proceed as follows to react on a point-by-point basis to the memo.

1. **That you do not have the slightest idea of the specific reason for my trip:** What is important is the fact that I filled a travel authorisation and the reason that I gave for the journey which was "to attend to urgent family matter". I think that is sufficient for official purposes and owe nobody the specific facts of my family matters. If we had a normal situation prevailing in the department, the specifics should have been discussed with HOD but this is presently not the case in the department.

2. **That you quickly embarked on the process of authorising my travel:** Having being a HOD myself before in that same department, I don't know that it takes any ceremony to give approval for journey other than selecting the appropriate option on the travel authorisation form and appending signature. I noticed that you have used the word process here as if it entails more than an instant action for a request for two days so as to mislead the readers of your memo. In any event, short of any intent to do another mischief, you should have put it clearly that you indeed authorize the journey. You did not put it like that because it would prevent you from the exercise of fault finding as the real motive. The mere fact that you did not mention at all in your widely circulated memo that you gave approval for the journey which I have in my hands till now, shows that you have something sinister or phony as the motive of your memo. In this regard, your memo betrays a desperate venture to find a fault at all cost, in the balance of the time, and no matter how flimsy, because time is fast running out on the assignment. I must sympathize. ...

3. **That senate had planned to commence deliberations on result today (i.e. 20 July 2001) and you had called for raw results whose deadline expired Tuesday 10 July, and as the date of my submission of your travel authorisation (i.e. 13 July 2001),**

I had not submitted my raw results. It is amazing to notice how you struggle with dates here and there and other aspects in the effort to paint a picture of wrong doing on my part in respect of examination results. The fact is as follows: that UNIAGRIC resumed activities on Monday 9 July 2001 after about 5 months of strike actions in series embarked upon by ASUU at local and national levels: that I was around throughout the week of that Monday 9 – Friday 13 July and involved in the arrangement to commence academic activities in the college: that you set the overly ambitious deadline of Tuesday 10 July for examination results to be submitted and that you were the only one among the many HODs to set such a tight deadline which none of us in the department could meet: that on Wednesday 11 July 2001, a meeting of the college board was held at which I was present and at which meeting more realistic deadline was set for the submission of examination results on following week Wednesday 18 July 2001: that I travelled out on Sunday 15 July 2001 after receiving my copy of your approval on the travel authorisation form on the Saturday 14 July 2001, which was passed under my office door: that my plan as stated on the form was for me to return on Tuesday 17 July 2001 and be in office on Wednesday 18 July 2001. Your own sequence of dates and associated events conceal several aspects so I can be seen as an irresponsible officer who undertakes unofficial travels without authorisation. Most interestingly it conceals, among other facts, the fact that you gave approval to the journey as shown on the copy of the travel authorisation form returned to me. And also that you even attached a piece of paper to the form in your handwriting, name and signature with date, and on which you inscribed a note to urge me to remember "to kindly submit results before leaving". For the same person to turn around and publish memo indicating that I have travelled out unofficially without authorisation is, to say the least wicked and mischievous.

4. **That I sent unknown person to you on Monday 16 July 2001 to bring results to you, without a note from me, and that I trusted students results to him etc. That IT WAS ON Wednesday 18 July that Dr Femi Agbede who was known to you came in with the results and information with my bereavement (which made you to collect the items from him).** Again you hid many facts of the mater in this respect. One important fact you concealed at your convenience is that local ASUU had proceeded on another strike action during the week in question over the issue of non-payment of June salaries. And though I had that information with me at Ibadan, I chose the matter of examinations in my department as being more important. Otherwise the strike action was a suitable cover for me not to worry a hoot about examination matters under the emergency situation prevailing around me in Ibadan at that time. That I struggled by telephone to describe where the materials were and informed you through people of great value about what happened and that I made special arrangements for you to have the results before the expiration of the deadline was just being my natural self as a loyal and dedicated officer with a full sense of responsibility. But that is exactly the feature of me that you are capitalising on to find new faults at me now: what an Irony! There is no need to exploit the sentiments of the people by insinuating that I had handled examination matters in a wrong way. I am sure that if there were any elements of that in my action, you would have explored that avenue to nail me down as usual rather than publishing an image-destroying memo only. And if and when you do that, I will defend myself as usual. My motive is clear and that is to get the materials across so the processing of the results of the college would not be held up in case the senate meeting scheduled for 20 July would hold. In any case, the senate meeting did fail to hold for no other reason than that the local strike action remained in force till Thursday 26 July 2001. So where is the crime I have committed here?

5. **That I should note that I have not done well: but for my bereavement I ought to be cautioned.** Please leave my bereavement alone and answer the question posed as to the crime I have committed. Two issues are at stake in all and it is your word against mine on both issues. One, you approved the travel authorisation and you have acted in falsehood to say you did not do so. Two, I acted in the interest of the department and college to send items to you when it was not possible for me to return from my journey as planned: you called it an offence worth cautioning me for. What you have done is tantamount to cautioning me already, which I reject totally. Given that I am still in the period and mood of mourning, I am constrained to overlook the pain inflicted on me by the high degree insensitivity to my situation as implicit in this statement of yours, for the time being.

6. **That I should recall that it was this kind of attitude and behavior that attracted a suspension to me, which I contested and lost.** You must be making reference to the suspension letter issued to me by the Vice Chancellor in January 2001, which I challenged in court and succeeded to obtain a court order to the effect that the suspension should not be given effect pending determination of substantive suit. Therefore the letter did not have effect on me as nobody touched my salary or prevented me from carrying out my job. Subsequently, the matter was heard and overruled whereby the court overruled me and the order was no longer in force. I filed a notice of appeal immediately together with a motion of injunction that prevents anybody from touching my salary or preventing me from carrying out my job. This is the situation till date, which you are very much aware of. At least it is to your knowledge that I undertake my teaching and research works including student supervision in the department up till now. I also receive my pay slip monthly in full value. In fact the need for you to put up the memo that I am responding to at present would not have arisen if I am on any suspension whatsoever: you wrote the memo

in full knowledge and recognition of the fact that I am fully on duty.

So where lies the reason to say I have lost (the case)? I know what would have happened to me under the atmosphere of desperate executive witch hunting that I have lived for a number of years now. Indeed the intention was for neither of the sponsors of the suspension letter to leave me to receive my salary (and in full for that matter); nor for me to even remain on my job. So where some people celebrate an illusory victory by thinking that I have lost, they know better in their minds that the present situation with me is drastically different from their original intentions. So there is no basis for such celebrations. Rather I am in the best position to celebrate on account of having survived systematic official tyranny and despotism orchestrated against me for no just course. In this regard, let me refer you to what a judge of High Court of Benue State had to say to castigate the university administration and its hatched men while ruling in my favour in a case of fundamental human rights violation instituted by me: "Even though we have many despots here and there in the country it is the collective will of Nigerians that they be governed by rule of law and not that of despots ... Where a people who are supposed to be civilized behave as if they are not, they have to be shown the correct thing to do and they should not be encouraged in their misconduct". That is by the way.

Your reference to the court case of suspension conceals as usual some important elements of the issues involved. Let me say that there is no committee investigating any act of misconduct against me at present. I noticed that you copied your memo to a committee about such a thing and will like to advise you not to dive into murky waters that can expose you to a contempt charge and make you step on the ground of prison once again. I wouldn't say more than that concerning that aspect for now. First, you conceal your role in the suspension saga for people to see and judge.

Specifically you failed to mention that you acted as the person (or HOD) who issued three queries in a single day (!) based on fictitious allegations and even before delivering them to me, you have found me guilty at my back and reported back on the assignment to the Vice Chancellor (!). Second, you cleverly concealed the facts that the events leading to the suspension letter indeed played the role to you as the source of a surreptitious memo in falsehood against me from where the three queries were subsequently concocted. Third, you concealed the fact that apart from the civil case you mentioned, the undeserved suspension of me by the Vice Chancellor actually earned you a criminal trial for varied charges bordering on behavior unbecoming of someone trusted with a position of responsibility like managing people as HOD. Indeed this case led to your being bundled in a vehicle and taken to the prison where you spent some time before your bail was satisfactorily secured (!). It was in sympathy of that event that I released pressure on you by instructing my lawyer to hold the case in abeyance, coupled with the fact that you approached a number of good people to rescue you out of the bad situation. Moreover, subsequently the university governing council has embarked on an intervention exercise with a view to settling this and other cases out of court, which I have obliged in the interest of peace. I thought you were sober and indeed you expressed sobriety to the people who talked to me at that time. However, the content of your memo to me shows clearly that I have misread (you). When I resuscitate this and other cases involving you as defendant or accused, I will report back to the Pro-Chancellor to inform him that your actions are at cross purpose with the good intention of governing council.

Meanwhile I cannot resist the urge to remind you of certain aspects of the High Court ruling on the civil suit on the suspension saga indicating some negative findings of the Honourable court about your role in the sequence of events that culminated in the suspension letter and generally your official conduct. This will help the university authorities that you copied your memo to not only to understand your real motive behind the memo but also to estimate your chances in the criminal prosecution. The following findings pertaining to you were made by the court of law (see his ruling in motion No. MHC/25M/2001 delivered by his Lordship, Honourable Justice I. Hwande, dated 12/4/2001).

> "On the queries issued to the applicant (i.e. Dr Ayoola) I need to emphasise that they were effective against the applicant on the date served on him. To merely post the queries on the dispatch book of the university will not bring the facts of those queries to the attention of the person queried. To refuse to consider the response of the applicant on the ground that he did not respond when the query was not yet brought to his attention is mischievous and oppressive ... He (i.e. the applicant Dr Ayoola) is not to be punished by churning out queries to him in his absence and closing the door against him to reply.
>
> The 4th Respondent (Dr Umeh) is certainly hasty in the manner he queried the applicant and proceeded to refer the matter to the Vice Chancellor ... The motive of the 4th Respondent (i.e. Dr Umeh) is of no much value provided they do what is correct and fair in respect of the applicant (i.e. Dr Ayoola)."

Those are the facts of the case you described to have been lost by me and probably won by you! What remains to be lost in character by somebody trusted with an administrative responsibility as important as the HOD of an academic department in a university, but who is found by a court of law is administratively mischievous and oppressive; and who involves himself in "churning" out queries, hasty to inflict injury to other people, unfair among other unworthy attributes. Such a person(s) can only be found to remain in office at UNIAGRIC where he/they can continue in his/

> their criminal activities unchecked namely criminal defamation, framing incorrect evidence, injurious falsehood, and most terrible of all, alteration of documents or forgery as correctly alleged against him/them in the magistrate courts.
>
> In the final analysis, however, the quality of job of such people reflects in the poor state of the institution that they govern, which is there for everybody to see and everybody has, indeed seen at UNIAGRIC.
>
> Dr G. B. Ayoola

Furthermore, in terms of taking concrete action, I had followed up with the police regarding the earlier report of the matter by my lawyer. Also, I deposed an affidavit under a judicial oath to the effect that Gyang was after my life, which I caused to be broadcast on radio and television far and wide. My letter to the commissioner of police was titled "Report of an Attack of My Residence by Unknown Gunmen".

The main elements of the report that I received are as follows:

1. One of the gunmen headed straight to the male children's room and appeared to my son through the window. My son by name Iyinoluwa was at his study desk, which faced one of the windows. Gun was pointed at Iyinoluwa through the window, and the gunman ordered him to open the entrance door without raising any alarm. The gunman observed that somebody was sleeping on a bed in the room and he asked Iyinoluwa if that person was his father. The person sleeping was my cousin by name Adefisoye. The gunman threatened Iyinoluwa that if he raised any alarm on his way to open door, he would shoot at Adefisoye in his sleep. Iyinoluwa obeyed and moved out of the room to open the entrance door for the gunman.

2. Iyinoluwa was ordered at gunpoint to take the gunmen to his father's room. The gunmen entered the female children's room where they kicked my niece, by name Tunrayo awake but left my little daughter,

Similolu who was asleep undisturbed. They entered all the rooms and conducted an extensive search. The gunmen asked for my cellular telephone, which was not available. They also asked for the key of my wife's car parked outside behind the house at that time. The children were held captive and bitten up as the search continued. One of the gunmen picked a new wristwatch in the male children's room, and another one picked the pocketsize tape recorder on the reading table in my study.

3. Afterwards, the gunmen held Tunrayo hostage and took her outside with them. They ordered her to take them to the next house where there was light. After a few meters towards the house one of the gunmen sighted a policeman and confirmed from Tunrayo that policemen were on guard there. They asked for the name of the occupant of the house and Tunrayo answered "DVC". They asked for the meaning of DVC and Tunrayo answered "Deputy Vice Chancellor". They asked for the actual name of the DVC and Tunrayo answered Professor Ikurior. Then the gunmen ordered her to turn back from the direction of the residence backwards. They asked further the name of the occupant of the house on the other side of my house and Tunrayo answered Architect Daudu. The gunmen pushed her to lead them there.

4. Tunrayo was used to gain entrance into Arc. Daudu's residence where the family members were also harassed and dispossessed of valuable items and money. I understand that one of the gunmen suggested that Arc. Daudu should be shot in the chest. But another gunman disagreed on the ground that it was not Arc Daudu that "gives us trouble" but the other man at the back who was not found at home" (i.e. myself).

Preliminary Remarks

I have searched my soul and could not see where I had given anybody troubles. I don't have any disagreement with anyone in particular, save some fundamental issues that I am presently seeking judicial decisions in relation to my 'duties. And I don't see how these could constitute troubles for anybody except those averse to the tenets-of civil society and believe in or want to perpetrate the use of brute power of oppression and repression against fellow citizens.

Action Sought

Although the event appears as a robbery incident from the face of it, the elements of the report received indicate that it is not. Rather it is an attempt to assassinate me at my residence in the late hours of that day.

Therefore I nurse the fear that my life is presently in danger in the University, and would like to seek the quick action of the Police to assure me of my security and to ensure adequate security for me. Meanwhile, I take liberty to also report the matter to the police.

This time, police command in Makurdi was sufficiently sensitised to quickly take action in terms of protection for me: two uniformed men to guide my residence, and one undercover policeman carrying a gun under his clothes to serve as my bodyguard for the next six months. I became what Oyindo termed *omo government* (i.e., government child), a euphemism for someone untouchable without incurring the wrath of law enforcement agents.

Going by the tone of this letter, Gyang was noticeably embarrassed and was summoned to both the police station and the court to quickly depose a counter-affidavit, given the damning content of my letter, wherein he trivialised the attack and manufactured a cover-up as story. He said that what happened in my house on 25 October 2000 was not an assassination attempt but part of a generalised state of insecurity on campus involving people other than me. He attempted to achieve this by staging a fake visit of a similar gang of gunmen at Ikurior's house. In the night when the script was acted, I heard a noise and peeped through the window into Ikurior's compound. From my vantage point, I could watch the drama being acted out. I saw how his night guards fired a shot into the air to create a sense of panic, and how Ikurior himself arrived in his car at his gate during the fake operation, blast the horn, and drove in the direction of Gyang's residence. In reality, no incident happened and it was all theatre.

Year 3—2001

Twelfth Onslaught

On the first working day of the year, I resumed work at the department office on the ground floor, where I collected my mail from the pigeonhole and then climbed the staircase up to the college office to exchange some New Year's pleasantries on the way to my office. As I walked through the long corridor on the first floor of the college building, my mail still in my hand, I saw a lady from afar leaning against the rail in front of my office door. I recognised her as a messenger in Kureve's office. It looked like an ambush, and so it immediately struck me that a new trouble might be waiting for me over there. As I moved closer, even without the courtesy of saying good morning, she handed over a stapled letter to me together with the dispatch book for me to sign.

I entered my office and prayed for a peaceable New Year, and then I opened the mail one by one. Amongst them were three queries Umeh had churned out since December, as well as a reminder containing a twenty-four-hour deadline that had fallen due many times over. The last one that I received at the door was a suspension letter. I sat back on my chair and heaved a heavy sigh not of relief but of trepidation: It appeared the world around me had ended, and I had been finished professionally. Speechless for a moment, Gyang's words resonated in my mind a few times: "I have got what it takes to nail you down, and I will do so at all costs."

I read the letters one by one again. The senseless queries were based on allegations of travelling without permission and other fictitious offences, and the three of them were staggered in dates over three days—11 December 2000, 13 December 2000, and 14 December 2000—as Christmas break was approaching. He had delayed their delivery to me until he was sure I had travelled home, thereby denying me an opportunity to respond to them on time. On 20 December 2000, when the university had closed for Christmas and I had travelled home with my family, he wrote a reminder saying, "I had written you three queries on very serious offences you committed … As at today you have not responded to any. You should send me your response within the next twenty four hours please."

I had a premonition of Umeh's capacity for mischief making. I stood up and walked briskly to the department office, where I asked the messenger for his dispatch book. I was stunned to see that all four letters were posted at the same time and on the same day after I had travelled home! Subsequently, I felt the need to report this development to the pro-chancellor regarding how my prediction had come true. My letter was dated 25 January 2001 and entitled "Re-Overview of Situation at UNIAGRIC with Particular Reference to Me".

> I am to notify the Pro-chancellor now that as I predicted to him … the characters of the game plan have all played out. Dr Umeh helped VC to raise three fictitious queries within three days together with a spontaneous reminder; all in one day but with staggered dates (all) within the last working week of December 2000 prior to Christmas break declared by the university. And immediately the university resumed work on 3rd January 2001, my suspension letter had been written and signed (and also delivered to me).

The letter of suspension under reference, dated January 03, 2001, contained a most offensive aspect - that "During the period of your suspension, you should not leave Makurdi town without the expressed permission in writing by the Vice-Chancellor", which struck me immediately that a cause of action was imminent.

As usual, there was no response from the pro-chancellor, and so I went to court again with a case of criminal mischief against Umeh and with a civil litigation to enforce my fundamental right to free movement and fair hearing. On the one hand, the alleged infringement of my right to free movement was anchored on the statement in the suspension letter, that I should not travel out of Makurdi; while, on the other hand, the alleged infringement of my right to fair hearing was premised on the hurried issuance of the same letter by Gyang without first giving me an opportunity to defend myself against the allegations levelled by Umeh in his sporadic memos. The haste was understandable against the need for them to prevent me from stopping them by an order of court before the deed was done.

This haste notwithstanding, my lawyer quickly entered court before Gyang could direct my salary to be stopped, as he had done to other people on suspension. In this way, my counsel displayed the utmost dexterity as a human rights lawyer, coupled with commendable industry to get me off the hook of Gyang. With deft legal courage, he filed a motion in the High Court of Benue State before the Honourable Justice Ejembi Eko (High Court 2) for the suspension of the letter issued to me by Gyang, preventing it from taking effect immediately. He premised it on the wickedness of Gyang to insert a clause in the letter that restricted me from "traveling out of Makurdi" till the disciplinary process would end. Assuming without conceding that Gyang had the power to suspend a senior staff from his job the way he did, Okutepa found this clause most objectionable as a breach of my fundamental human right to freedom of movement and fair hearing—both guaranteed to a Nigerian citizen in the constitution.

However, following a technical argument between Justice Eko and Okutepa, though the honourable justice anticipatorily agreed about the merit of our case in fundamental human rights enforcement, he denied us the leave we sought to enter court the way Okutepa had, based on technical grounds against our course of action. Eventually the judge ruled,

> In spite of the tenacity Mr Okutepa has argued the application I am not persuaded in any way that the course he has adopted in pursuing the redress of the applicant accords with the due process of the law. Accordingly, I refuse to grant the leave sought. The application is therefore refused.

On that day, Okutepa, who was so passionate about my situation in the university, became so emotional that he cried in court. I spontaneously joined him, and both of us sobbed like children. Then we, including my wife and friends who'd accompanied me to court, sheepishly moved out of the courtroom. Outside the courtroom, Okutepa quickly firmed up; his will was so strong that the same day, he amended the application and refiled it for reassignment, this time to Honourable Justice I. Hwande (High Court 3), who took a painstaking look at our application to suspend the suspension letter before proceeding to the substantive matter. Happily for us, he granted me the leave and issued the order as follows.

> For the avoidance of doubt ... an interim order prohibiting the Respondents (i.e. Gyang & Co), their officers, servants agents or their privies from giving effect to or acting on the letter of suspension with reference ... dated 3rd January 2001 pending the hearing of motion on notice is hereby made.
>
> Respondents are also restrained from harassing, preventing in any way interfering with the rights of the applicant to his employment, full salary, allowances and other benefits pending the hearing of the motion on notice.

This was the breather I needed, both to be able to remain afloat financially and also remain on duty to the shame of Gyang in the academic community. The ruling of the court jolted Gyang beyond measure, which made him whine openly about the role of Benue State judiciary in providing refuge for me and shielding me from the poisonous penetration of his arsenal. Therefore, going further in the same letter, I briefed the pro-chancellor thus.

> In any event, Sir, I had headed for the courts again and succeeded to obtain an order to suspend the suspension letter from taking effect ... And, as expected the university (still) wished my dismissal to be a quick disposal action, and so a panel of investigation was quickly set up under the chairmanship of Professor B. A. Kalu (my submission to this panel upon invitation also attached herewith). So I hope to update you from time to time about subsequent developments, Sir.

What's more, when the substantive matter was decided, the pronouncements of Honourable Justice Hwande was most devastating in the way it dealt a terrible blow on Umeh. To say the least, the damning judgment constituted a judicial indictment of Umeh for the irresponsible role he played in the suspension saga. Here are some excerpts (emphasis mine).

> To merely post the queries in the department book of the university will not bring the fact of the queries to the attention of the person queried. To refuse to consider the response of the applicant on the ground that he did not respond when the query was not yet brought to his attention is *mischievous and oppressive* ... He is not to be punished by *churning* out queries to him in his absence and *closing the door against him to reply.*

As these pronouncements of the judge constituted both moral and professional baggage on Umeh, having impugned his suitability as a Head of my Department so badly, he became frightened and restless in his behaviour towards me, but not sober nonetheless.

Meanwhile, the criminal case on the same matter against Umeh had also been opened, which I filed at the Upper Area Court in Makurdi, for mischief, falsehood and other criminal acts against me on his part, which produced consequential injuries to me. It is in this case that Umeh suffered humiliation the most, when in the process to perfect the bail granted him something went wrong, and so he was taken to prison custody. Although his friend, Odoemenem, who'd accompanied him to court on that day, ran like a madman out of the building to seek help, it was late in coming; at least not before Umeh was hurled into a bus waiting outside the courtroom to take some hardened criminals back to prison yard after the day's session. It is only he who could tell the story about the humiliation he suffered at the hand of his co-travellers on the way and afterwards, before Gyang's help came for his release. Consequently pressure was mounted on the court in securing Umeh's release as obvious during court proceedings on the adjourned date, when the magistrate abruptly withdrew from adjudicating in the matter any further. And soon afterwards, apparently in fear of his possible conviction in the case eventually, Umeh had soberly requested a friend of mine - Mr S. S. Haruna - to intercede on his behalf and to save him from such a disaster befalling him – ever having to serve a prison sentence in his lifetime.

* * *

Perhaps the mother of my cases was the one couched in legal terms as originating summons. A lull ensued immediately after the suspension cases had progressed in my favour; which contrary to Gyang's calculation was supposed to be his last onslaught to destabilise me. He had thought that putting me on suspension would not only kill my personal ego but also deny me of my much-needed salary to prosecute the cases in court. Whatever the outcome of the Kalu Committee, positive or negative, he would have used the report as a basis to dismiss me from the university. But all that was not going to be, because surprisingly for him, my lawyer was competent enough to secure an interlocutory injunction to prevent the suspension letter from taking effect until the substantive motion on notice was determined. Gyang knew that my lawyer was too smart to bring the case to an end quickly and while Gyang was still in post as VC. As the lull lengthened, it appeared that Gyang had resigned to fate and resolved to leave me alone.

In packaging the case of originating summons, some fourteen staff members were identified as plaintiffs, including myself, who had suffered one way or another from Gyang's policies or actions, thereby providing evidence upon which to anchor such policies or actions as being aberrant in the absence of a governing council, as prescribed by the enabling law of the university. Then the question was put to the court, whether these and similar policies or actions were or were not ultra vires the power of VC; if they were, they should be declared null and void and of no effect whatsoever. The import of the case was to nullify policies and actions such as appointments and promotion exercises carried out by Gyang since inception, which were obviously beyond the powers of VC; contracts awarded by Gyang beyond the stipulated spending limits of the VC; termination and dismissal of staff, which passed the powers of VC; and more. In this case of originating summons, if judgment was entered in our favour, we intended to overturn all conceivable legacies attributable to Gyang at

UNIAGRIC after vacating office soon. Gyang was practically jolted by this case, and he mounted a stronger team of lawyers than in the previous cases to fight it out with all the university money he could deploy to prevent it from being opened in court.

By the end of 2000, it had probably dawned on Gyang that he might not win the fight against me after all. It appeared that his spirit had dropped and his eagerness to nail me down had waned, just as the whole campus had turned their backs against him and judged him a non-performer. He was at loggerheads with virtually all elements of the university community, particularly all the unions on campus that had gone on strike for one form of his maladministration or another. Not even members of his kitchen cabinet spared him, except his principal hatchet men, who had been ostracised in the university community for their ignoble roles as the symbols of Gyang's wickedness to many people. In particular, it dawned on Gyang that he had a couple of months to go, and he had been so embattled that he had not been able to organise a single convocation for the cumulative sets of graduating students year after year. He rushed up a proposal to hold a joint convocation for the large number of final year students who had finished during his time. The governing council, looking at the short time left and having been totally disenchanted about Gyang's performance, turned it down. That meant that no single student under his administration would ever carry his signature on his or her certificate. What a shame.

As soon as we entered the last calendar year of Gyang's tenure as VC, 2001, the governing council was somewhat dejected by the appalling state of the university under Gyang, and it embarked on a general peace and reconciliation move for the aggrieved staff to take their cases out of court. This was with a view to putting the university's house in order before the appointment of Gyang's successor, which going by the university statutes should commence at latest six months from the end of his tenure. First, an interactive meeting of aggrieved staff with council chairman Dr Phillip Atamuo was held in January 2001. Subsequently, acting outside Gyang's pleasure, a committee of council was formed to explore the possibility of resolving the staff cases out of court. The committee convened a damage control meeting with aggrieved staff on 29 January 2001, for the purpose of "exchanging ideas with former/serving staff of the university who for one reason or the other had grievances with the university and had consequently instituted court cases against the institution". As listed in the minutes of the meeting, the aggrieved staff who attended the meeting were nine in number: Arch. V. S. Daudu, Dr G. B. Ayoola, Mr P. O. Odiansiye, Mr J. E. Alabi, Dr O. O. Agbede, Mr L. T. Oparaugo, Prof. I. Onyido, and Dr I. A. Shoremi.

As soon as the purpose of the meeting was introduced by the chairman of the governing council, Gyang stormed out of the room in palpable displeasure, and like a dog with its tail tucked in between its hind legs, he recused himself, citing the need "to create a free atmosphere for the discussion". The administrative officer, Miss M. I. Agogo, who served as the legal officer of the university in all the litigations, was also asked to leave the meeting.

The minutes of the meeting stated as follows.

> With the assurances of the Chairman, the aggrieved staff, who spoke forcefully and frankly stated their grievances as follows:
>
> i. Official high-handedness on the part of the university administration.
> ii. Open discrimination against Southerners in the University.
> iii. Absence of due process in handling staff matters
> iv. Executive witch-hunting
> v. Determination to eliminate "Idachaba Boys"
> vi. Injustices in appointments and promotions leading to elevation of undeserving staff over more productive ones, e.g. Dr Shoremi who claimed to have been suppressed as Lecturer I since November 1989
> vii. Over-emphasis on personalities rather than principles
> viii. Lack of academic freedom to apply professional capacity to attract external funding for research projects.

> In addition they highlighted their personal grievances, which included denial of rights and privileges as well as undeserved persecution. In particular, Dr G. B. Ayoola reported that the Vice Chancellor had sent hired assassins after him. He appealed to Council to guarantee his security.

Arising from the meeting, a number of decisions and immediate actions were agreed, specifically with respect to me: "The matter would be taken up in writing with the Vice Chancellor immediately to provide adequate security for the staff", and also with respect to all aggrieved staff. "The affected staffs are also expected to discuss with their Counsels with a view to exploring the option of out-of-court settlement".

But like someone destined for perdition at all costs, all that scolding of Gyang was thrown away, which infuriated the governing council against him. Indeed, nothing concrete came out of these last-minute efforts of the governing council to resolve the many cases out of court and spare Gyang from his impending departure from the university with ignominy. Nonetheless, in the spirit behind this meeting, I truthfully embarked on taking long adjournments in the cases I had filed in court. After a long, deafening silence on the part of the university administration, I wrote a letter to update the pro-chancellor and chairman of council about the status of the court cases about six months after the meeting (dated 9 July 2001).

At the tail end, Gyang, now totally spent and confused as his final days in office loomed so large, issued a memo of lamentation about how things had turned so badly for him, stating he regretted his poor administration of the university, and blaming members of his ruling cabinet one after the other in the Mzough U'Tiv caucus—Kucha, Uza, Ikurior, and Kureve, to mention a few—for misleading him all along. He was asking for forgiveness from everybody except me, whom he'd battered so much that personal pride would not let him. Embarrassed, he particularly expressed sadness that the unions would desert him "at this eleventh hour", and he begged them to call off their strike actions to pave way for a happier exit for him. The union leaders discountenanced all his pleas.

Nonetheless, as the end of Gyang's tenure approached, I noticed that he had become somewhat sober in his recent actions towards me. At first it appeared as if he was rethinking his vow to nail me down at all costs. It was an unexpected gesture when he extended an invitation to me for celebration with him at the VC's lodge when two children of his became university graduates. Having arrived too late on the same day of the event, I was not favourably disposed to honouring the invitation, and I did not honour it anyway. Instead, I wrote, "On behalf of my wife, Bose, and children, I wish them a successful career practice devoid of environmental hostility and unwarranted executive witch-hunt later in life (like the one I suffered under their father at Makurdi)."

One day, as I recall, we met at a public event in town, the inaugural meeting of the Benue State Council on Agriculture, at which I was the keynote speaker at the instance of the state government. Gyang was seated at the high table with two chairs between him and me. After the presentation of my well-received paper, it was time for a short break. Gyang sent his aid to me. As I looked in his direction, he stepped aside a few steps from the crowd and beckoned to me. I instinctively moved close, my right hand in my pocket to avoid having a handshake with him.

Gyang quietly said to me, "Let us put an end to all this madness. I am ready to take you back as director of CEFAS."

I managed to say, "VC, you've got it all wrong. That is not in my least contemplation, and I take exception to a diminishment of the issue to such a low level as a desire to be a director." I waved with my left hand and reminded him, "You will recall that you begged me to be director of CEFAS and HOD at the same time, and it took us two meetings to negotiate it before I agreed to take up the two posts."

Further, as I became more confident in his presence, I said in a pedagogic tone, "At issue for me is the penchant I have for responsible governance of the university by our leaders, for responsibility and probity of our leaders in public office, and for merit and excellence in public service generally—all of which you naturally abhor from outset. It is not about post holding, and it's definitely not about directorship of CEFAS or even VC-ship of the university."

As I continued to pump words into his head, the bell rang for the commencement of the first technical session of the workshop. He cut in apologetically and in a low tone said he would like me to have a meeting with him in his office next Monday "so we can talk things over". I immediately felt that Gyang was brought to his knees right before my eyes, and he played straight into my hands that afternoon.

Back home that day, I reflected on my encounter with Gyang. He was in such a helpless situation, which put him at the receiving end of my own punches for a change. My mind flashed back to his manifest capacity for theatre and mischief, and I cancelled the possibility of seeing him at his office on Monday as he had requested with a humble disposition, which might not have been genuine. Truly, as brethren feared when I shared my encounter with Gyang at fellowship that weekend, he was such a character that he could possibly have planted a camera somewhere in his office so he could tender mischievous photographs as evidence against me in court. Later, I learned that my decision to skip the appointment outright irked him and probably worsened his mood at the eleventh hour of his tenure of office as VC. In any event, there was little or no time left for him to plan and launch another onslaught against me, and so as I supposed, he had probably given up on the mission to nail me down at all costs.

Then came a moment of lamentation for Gyang as he began to wind down. As required by law, he delivered an address to the governing council of the institution to give notice of the impending expiration of his five-year non-renewable tenure of office in early September 2001, as well as to flag off the race for his own successor. The address was published in *The Voice* newspaper of Wednesday, 11 April 2001, as an extended statement in self-evaluation of his administration since his fortuitous appointment in September 1996 to succeed Idachaba. In the publication, Professor Gyang blamed the sorry state of UNIAGRIC largely on an initial absence of governing council to superintend over him, as well as the role of "a group of staff opposed to my administration and who has resented my coming from outside"—that is, because he was appointed from Ahmadu Bello University (ABU), Zaria, where he'd been a professor of Veterinary Medicine. According to him, "this group of staff formed cleavages to harass me out of office within six (6) months of my tenure". Furthermore, he said, "When this strategy failed the same group resorted to advising me wrongly to mess me up, and discredit my administration." What a lame excuse for his woeful performance in office as VC, one which offends the intellect of academics and indeed abuses it as an explanation of the weird situation at UNIAGRIC Makurdi during his tenure.

No one was impressed by this lamentation of Gyang. Rather, to spite him further, the university went into sporadic closures towards the end of Gyang's tenure, arising from multiple developments. All the academic staff unions on campus—ASUU, SANU, WASU, and ASUTON—had embarked on a prolonged strike action for non-payment of salaries for four months. Although Gyang hurriedly paid two months arrears, his appeals for the staff to resume work fell on deaf ears of union members, who were bent on disgracing him out of office. In parallel to this development was an ongoing students' rampage following the death of their union officials on mission from the national headquarters to Makurdi, at which time the action group sacked Gyang and took over control of the university. Somewhere in between these sporadic events, rumours filled the air that the embattled Gyang was arrested at Abuja Airport for being in possession of a huge sum of money (allegedly university money to be ferried abroad), so frantic calls were made to his kinsmen and other prominent Benue people to rescue him including General Malu, a Tiv man and who was in government as chief of army staff at a point in time.

By that time, all members of Gyang's cabinet had deserted him. In particular, the likes of Kucha and Uza became outspoken against him and stated openly at the ASUU meeting of 13 September 2000 that the university administration under Gyang had totally collapsed. Adding to his woes in his last days, Gyang's official car was involved in a ghastly accident on the road between Makurdi and Abuja. Not a few students and staff of the university jubilated openly about the unfortunate event. The car was a total wreck, and he sustained a broken right hand, following which he wore a cast for a protracted time before the end of his term as VC and his eventual exit from the university. He went back to Zaria.

In the end, Gyang left UNIAGRIC much unlike the way he'd come five years earlier. This time there was no drumming or dancing, or any organised send-off party from any section of the university community, not even from the members of Mzough U'Tiv, who'd orchestrated his appointment as VC, or members of his cabinet, who'd benefitted from him in various ways. Indeed, all the unions on campus rejected the spirited appeal by Gyang for them to call off their multiple strikes in order to pave the way for his peaceable exit. Thus much unlike the glorious exit of Idachaba in 1995, Gyang left the office of vice chancellor in September 2001 practically unsung.

In the Aftermath

Professor James Ayatse, also a Tiv man and previously a lecturer at the Benue State University, was on sabbatical leave at UNIAGRIC at the material time, and he was the successor to Gyang as VC of the university. His appointment happened as if he was deliberately planted and strategically positioned for that purpose. Following another intensively contested race to the post that, again, had Professor Ikenna Onyido as a contestant (and he, Onyido, was tactfully edged out a second time), Ayatse eventually emerged as VC consistent with the wish and desire of the Tiv elite. My wife and I paid him a congratulatory visit at his home within a couple of days after the announcement and before he assumed office.

The day he assumed office at the north core coincided with the meeting of the UNIAGRIC branch of Academic Staff Union of Universities (ASUU) at the south core, at which I was present. He addressed the members present in a mien of humility and friendship, which struck me in certain aspects and copiously featured in my first official communication to him.

26 September 2001

The New Vice Chancellor
Professor J. O. I. Ayatse
University of Agriculture Makurdi.
P M B 2373, Benue State, NIGERIA

Dear Professor Ayatse,

Memorandum of Congratulations

The news of your recent appointment as the Vice Chancellor of the University of Agriculture Makurdi have been received by us with considerable delight, and I would like to congratulate your good self on this important achievement. My wife and I have paid you a visit at your residence in Makurdi town on Saturday 5 September 2001 in the cherished company of Professor Ikenna Onyido and his wife. Now that you have assumed duty fully, it is considered necessary to express my friendly disposition and favorable mindset more formally. In doing so, 1 would like to seize the opportunity to offer a few words and make some clarifications as well, if you don't mind.

To start with, by virtue of this appointment, you have succeeded Professor E. O. Gyang-Gyang who was the Vice Chancellor of this University for five years, between September 1996 up and September 2001. Unfortunately, as you have noticed and expressed at the ASUU meeting that you quickly appeared and addressed, the university being inherited by you is in a sorry state in every conceivable aspect - financial, infrastructural, and academic, etc. Although your predecessor entered and was received with fanfare five years ago (with a grand reception for him at the tollgate where people danced *Konkomo, Kpalongo* and *Kwaghir* before television cameras), his departure could not have been more inglorious: The dominant union ASUU declared a strike action two days to the end of his term; there was no official send-off party for him; the wholesale convocation ceremony conceived in a hurry was put off; the sitting of a ad hoc committee of governing council to implement the unedifying report of the presidential visitation panel that indicted his administration severally had begun in earnest; there is pronounced negative publicity arising from media calls including paid adverts in print media for probes and investigations by all and sundry (see past issues of News Watch magazine, The Punch newspaper, etc.). This kind of exit only reminds one of the biblical king in Israel who for being utterly wicked to his subjects and so despotic during his reign, that when he died no one desired him; and though "he was buried in the City of David, but not in the tombs of the kings" (2 Chronicles 24: 25).

The major problem with the administration of Professor Gyang was that it was premised on the use of brute force to crush any dissenting voice at all costs. Some of us, including my humble self, were targets of sporadic attacks and persistent executive witch-hunting for no reason other than maintaining principled stand about issues that affect the institution. We had no option other than to seek refuge in the temple of justice. As you may have learnt sir, in my own circumstance, several cases were filed in courts against the university administration to avoid being unjustly sacked from my job and to ward off the unpleasant effects of the desperate mission of the administration to destroy me personally and professionally. I was also compelled in the circumstance of intense official hostility to institute civil and criminal proceedings against certain staff members who lent themselves as instruments of oppression and repression, to help nail me down at all costs. The administration of Professor Gyang, instead of interdicting the staff members in question as stipulated by civil service regulations, used public money to hire lawyers defense of them, thereby elevating criminality to the level of official policy. It is within this context of primordial tyrannical governance that his Lordship, Honourable Justice I. Hwande employed the harshest words to describe Professor Gyang's administration thus; his words:

"Even though we have many despots here and there in this country it is the collective will of Nigerians that they be governed by rule of law and not that of despots ... Where a people who are supposed to be civilized behave as if they are not, they have to be shown the correct thing to do and they should not be encouraged in their misconduct."

Let no one hear someone idly saying again, like Professor Gyang did, that we have offered him a bad advice. I do not wish your tenure to end up in the same way as your predecessor's. The major recipes for success include the following: One we must shun despotism as a style of administration; one must beware of professional sycophants in our midst and people with sharp criminal instincts; one must uphold and appreciate the truth, as well as adopt fairness, justice and restitution, transparency and other elements of good governance, as a matter of deliberate policy.

I would like to identify with the parable of the farmer which you gave at your unscheduled appearance at the ASUU meeting, albeit rather cautiously. Concerning the question posed about the outstanding salary for the month of August, you shared with us how your father had instructed you that it was better to begin to make your own heaps anew, on arrival to the farm, than to repair the bad heaps previously made by other people. There is tremendous wisdom in that and my sense is that you are talking of the types of extra-big yam heaps characteristics of Benue farmers and you imply that the heaps of your predecessor as a farmer are bad enough. Agreed. But my immediate concern, which I chose not to express at that occasion, is that the overall output of the whole farm will be determined by the combined yield of your own heaps and those of others before you. I would like to infer that succession in a government office is intricately continuous; it is like one locomotive train following another so that if the one in the front crashes (remember the old Langa Langa crash), there is no way for the one following to pass until the mess is cleared. Sometime ago, close to a year now, someone in our midst described Professor Gyang s administration as a knocked engine that must be completely dismantled and dismembered and reassembled. Thus it will be a miracle that the speed at which you desire to move this institution forward will not be affected or retarded by the completely knocked down (CKD) state of its growth engine passed down by your predecessor. My advice in this regard is that you be swift, resolute and decisive in attending to the issues of the past so that the future can be explored more successfully and faster. Unless we follow up our findings about the sharp and bad practices or the past administration with necessary actions to thoroughly investigate the circumstances and bring perpetrators to book our quick expressions or disgust about the terrible state of things will soon be misconceived as mere platitudes.

Lastly, as a pioneer staff of the university and as a holder of responsibility positions in the past (Director of CEFAS, 1995–1998; HOD of Agricultural Economics Department, 1996–1998), I am also capable of describing for you the academic development pathway of the institution reasonably well enough. An initial takeoff stage that was full of intellectual enthusiasm and challenge derived from purposeful, visionary and mission- oriented leadership was succeeded by an era of intellectual sterility, frivolities, incompetence, and inordinate ambition of people in leadership. Suffice it to stay that the expectation of this community is very high pertaining to the way forward toward revamping and rejuvenating the system. A critical aspect is the need for conscious effort for redesigning and reformulation in order to rediscover the institution with respect to key elements (e.g. the Land Grant concept; the Collegiate system; the Policy context; the special farmer focus; the practical farming approach etc.).

To conclude, it is saying the obvious that there is much to be done to bring UNIAGRIC back to normal life alter the five years of drifting and wasting. Therefore I would like to wish you God's guidance while pledging my unflinching loyalty to serve in my little way. Please accept the hearty congratulations of my humble self, my wife Bose and our children (Taiwo 16; Kehinde 16; lyinoluwa 14: Similoluwa 7).

Kindest personal regards and respects.

Sincerely,

Dr G. B. Ayoola.

Ayatse came with a heart of reconciliation, and on 5 November 2001 he convened a meeting with the so-called Idachaba boys in his office, including Dr I. A. Oluremi (formerly Shoremi), pleading with us to take our cases out of court and asking us to propose what should be done for us to achieve that as quickly as possible. We discussed it freely and openly with the new VC, who lamented about the empty treasury he had inherited from Gyang and the problem he faced to settle the bill of lawyers defending the university in many cases, particularly in my own cases, which numbered ten at the last count! One of the demands I placed before him was the withdrawal of the suspension letter his predecessor had unjustly served me while in office, so that I would not withdraw the case to walk blindly into suspension. To this Ayatse categorically agreed, and he immediately gave a verbal directive to the registrar to withdraw the letter. Others made similar demands, including Daudu, Onyido, and Agbede in turn. Another demand I made to Ayatse was the release of my promotion letter. Though successfully concluded before the fight with Gyang broke out in 1997, it had suffered undue delay in being released. The meeting ended on a friendly note, and Ayatse agreed to our conditions, which immediately led me into taking long adjournments and putting the prosecution of all cases in abeyance while the peace process progressed. In any case, I put up a letter to the new VC that properly documented the critical conclusions of the meeting, which was signed by all of us except Professor Onyido, who had earlier taken his cases out of court to pave the way for his participation in the recent appointment exercise. The letter dated 17 November 2001 read in part:

> Re: Resolution of Court Cases
>
> We the undersigned would like to thank the Vice Chancellor for the recent meeting with him and the Registrar on the above subject matter. The conclusion reached was to the effect that details of the terms of settlement should be worked out to facilitate the action of university administration in resolving the various cases.
>
> Attached herewith, find the table of terms on a case-by-case basis as produced collectively by us. The missing aspects relate to actual financial implications in terms of the legal or travel expenses ... Meanwhile the attached material contains the main issues and will help the Registrar to commence action as agreed.
>
> Thank you, sir,

Signed:
Arc V. S. Daudu
Dr O. O. Agbede
Dr G. B. Ayoola
Dr A. O. Oluremi

However, no sooner had we concluded this pact than some hiccups ensued and Ayatse began to backpedal. Ayatse succumbed to pressure from those within and without who taunted us with the notion that the institution was greater than us, and so we should be unconditionally compelled to come out of court. One such person was Njike, who was very bitter about the bruises he had suffered in court at different stages. He would not live to see us walk free on campus again, let alone be reintegrated into the university community so effortlessly. At that time, he was still an internal member of the governing council Gyang had left behind.

Meanwhile, I had sent a passionate appeal to the chairman of the council to update him about ongoing action to implement the decisions reached at the meeting in good faith.

> 9 July 2001
>
> The Pro-chancellor, and Chairman Governing Council,
> University of Agriculture, Makurdi
> Attention: Chairman, Ad Hoc Committee on Peace and Reconciliation
>
> Dear Sir,
>
> Cases in courts against the university administration
>
> The letter dated 19 January 2001 (R/E/UAM/PE/605) signed by Mr M. T. Atsaka refers. I attended the meeting conveyed to discuss the circumstances surrounding the various suits pending in courts against the university administration. It was decided that the governing council would examine the various issues raised and soon contact the affected staff for further discussion with a view to reconciling the parties involved and resolving the situation.

As a result, I have secured long adjournments to facilitate council's effort toward re-establishing peace on the campus.

However, I have not heard from the governing council till date but recently learnt that a committee has been set up for the purpose that has commenced work. In this regard, I am to register my willingness to co-operate fully with governing council in respect of those cases involving me as a plaintiff.

This is to remind the Pro-Chancellor about the state of affairs and urge that 1 should be contacted as previously agreed. The status of cases involving me against the university administration (less those involving criminal prosecution of certain staff) are listed as follows:

1. In the High Court of Nigeria at Jos (Case No. Il 1C/5L 80 1 7199, filed on 24/5/99) between Professor 1. Onyido; Arc. V. S. Daudu; Dr G. B. Ayoola; Dr O. O. Agbede: AND UAM: VC of UAM: Permanent Secretary of Federal Ministry of Agriculture and Natural Resources Abuja. The motion on preliminary objection raised by defendants has been moved and argued, awaiting ruling. Professor | Onyido has subsequently withdrawn from the case as a plaintiff.

2. In the High Court of Benue State at Makurdi (Case No. MCI305/99: filed on 26 July 1999) between Dr G. B. Ayoola AND UAM; Professor E. O. Gyang; Administrative Committee on CEFAS. The case has been concluded and judgement delivered in my favour to quash an undeserved letter of warning issued to me. The trial judge castigated the university administration in strong terms.

3. In the High Court of Benue State at Makurdi (Case No. MI1C/225M/2000; filed on 7 April 2000), between Dr G. B. Ayoola; V. Ehigiator AND UAM: Senate of UAM; Governing Council of UAM; VC of UAM. Judgment was delivered in our disflavour and a notice of appeal was given.

4. In the High Court of Nigeria at Abuja (Suit No. FITC/ABI/CS/222/2000, filed on 17 July 2000); between Arc. V. S. Daudu; Dr O. A. Shoremi; Dr G. B. Ayoola; Dr O. O. Agbede; Mr P. Ododo; Mr S. Agha; Mr M. Idachaba; Mrs. M. M. Alagheny: Mrs. M. N. Yaor; Mr S. Ozioko; Mr T. K. Yesufu; Dr 15 O. Omoregbe; Dr S. Ochai; Mr A. I. Omoike; AND UAM; Senate of UAM; Governing Council of UAM; Minister of Agriculture and Rural Development. The case was dismissed upon the ruling on the preliminary objection of the defendants. We have gone on appeal and we are already in Federal Appeal Court Abuja, while a motion subsists in the Federal High Court to seek injunction pending appeal.

5. In the High Court of Benue at Makurdi (Case No MIC/16M/2001; filed on 12 January 2001) between Dr G. B. Ayoola ANDUAM; VC of UAM; Governing Council of UAM; Dr J. C. Umeh. Court ruled on an ex-parte motion in my favour to give an order prohibiting the respondents from giving effect to a letter of suspension issued to me. Subsequently court ruled on a motion on notice to vacate the order. I have given a notice of appeal and filed a motion in court to seek an injunction to maintain the status quo pending appeal.

Thank you sir.
Dr G. B. Ayoola

Subsequently, the news that the Benue elite, who would never leave things for the VC to decide on his own, had mounted their own pressure on Ayatse in the same direction. Such pressure had dragged the peace process into muddy waters, and it began to look like another round of trouble was brewing for me. Meanwhile, the series of adjournments I sought in court had started to expire without headway in the settlement programme to report back to court. In particular, within a week or so, the criminal matter against Njike regarding the forgery of Magit's thesis was reopened, and I had quickly concluded my evidence in chief to close my case. Another matter in the criminal prosecution of Njike and Umeh was also reopened, and my evidence in chief was at an advanced stage. During the session, Njike fainted in the courtroom, thereby compelling the magistrate to forcibly adjourn the case for two hours. When Njike was unable to return, then it was rescheduled for a later date. Amidst these events, information came that the chancellor of the university at the time, a traditional monarch from Ibo land where Njike hailed from, was quickly reached to intervene in the situation at UNIAGRIC before his subject could be sentenced to jail. As the information had it, the chancellor hurriedly summoned the pro-chancellor/chairman of the governing council, Dr Atamuo. Arising from these frantic efforts was the decision to convene an emergency meeting of the governing council, at which point a rescue scheme was put in place for Njike. He was thoroughly castigated and tongue-lashed for his ignoble role in the hullabaloo that had enveloped the university for years and which had retarded the growth of the institution.

Suddenly, a letter of subtle threat dated 3 June 2002 came from the registrar that was intimidating and cited an unknown "Public Service Code of Conduct". It read:

Resolution of All Court Cases Out of Court against the University

In its quest for peace and stability on Campus, administration held several meetings with all those aggrieved staff who took the University to Court towards amicable resolution of the issues that necessitated court actions. This was done either jointly or on individual levels. In addition, several appeals were made to them to withdraw such cases from the courts as the threats to loss of job and individual liberty were no longer tenable.

Consequently, some of the aggrieved staffers who took the University to Court withdrew such cases unconditionally following the appeals; and informed University administration accordingly. However, few who are still on the payroll of the University have refused to do so. This clearly is in violation of Public Service Code of ethics that an employee cannot take his employer to court while still remaining on such employer's payroll. Some of the aggrieved staffers had written to administration giving preconditions for the withdrawal of their cases from Courts.

The University Administration presented the conditions for the withdrawal of these cases given by you to Council for consideration and further directive. Council at its 42" Statutory meeting held on the 30th and 31st May, 2002 discussed our submissions for conditional out of Court Settlement and resolved as follows:

[a] The University is not a competent authority to administratively vary or review the findings or conclusions of a Court of Law. It is noted that the Courts at the first instance have concluded seven (7) of the Lawsuits with two (2) of them on further appeal to Higher Courts, and two at preliminary stages.

[b] Findings and recommendations of panels set up with the backing of the University statutes when accepted by the appropriate authority are binding and cannot be set aside or overturned, except in compliance with due process.

[c] The University has on its part incurred huge legal expenses in the bid to defend herself in the cases instituted against her and her functionaries and cannot therefore accede to the request for monetary compensation for lost cases.

Council frowned at the fact that you are yet to withdraw the cases and appeals you instituted against the University and its principal organs and functionaries from the various Courts in spite of Council and the University Administration's intervention based on its mandate to maintain peace and engender a conducive academic and working environment and directed that you do so without any preconditions.

Based on Council directive:

{i} You are hereby given one month from the date of this letter to unconditionally withdraw all cases you have against the University.

{ii} While these 'cases remain in Court, within the time period given in (i), you will not be eligible to hold any position of responsibility in the University

{iii} Council will review the situation after the specified time frame above and take appropriate action.

Thank you

Dr S. A. Ede
Registrar and Secretary to Council

Distribution:

1. Arch. V. S. Daudu
2. Dr G. B. Ayoola
3. Dr A. O. Oluremi

The true message of this letter was not lost to me, which was to harass and force me to take the cases out of court without reference to the terms agreed to with Ayatse. I noticed how Ayatse had been clever by half; he had tactfully escalated the battle to the level of governing council, which carried the weight of my employer, thereby weakening my strength relative to his as the head of administration. Now face-to-face with governing council and standing by myself with rage, I began to backpedal in trepidation of the full weight of the governing council unleashed on me. My initial response was on the side of caution, trying to avoid a new round of hostilities with the governing council as my employer by statute.

At first I flexed some muscle by agreeing to take the civil cases against the university administration out of court, but the personal cases, civil or criminal, against Njike, Umeh, and Odoemenem were not considered. The real target of the administration were those personal cases that I'd left out, and they wanted to rescue my three stalkers from going to jail upon conviction. Therefore my action in this regard angered the university the more. The battle between me and the governing council at this stage was fought through punches thrown at each other in terms of letters and other unrecorded exchanges with the registrar, in the latter's capacity as secretary to the council, wherein I succumbed to the pressure of governing council at last.

24 July 2002

The Chairman
Governing Council
University of Agriculture Makurdi

Dear Sir

Compliance with Council Directive

I am writing in respect of the recent developments about the court cases that I have instituted against the university authorities and certain individuals over time since 1999, when the governing council had not been constituted for six years. The governing council has recently issued a directive that these cases be withdrawn from the courts with a view to looking into the issues that necessitated the court actions. ...

Compliance

I would like to draw attention of council to the following correspondences and actions that clearly indicate that l have since complied with the directive of council in totality.

On cases with university (5 cases, all civil):

1. My anticipatory letter to Vice Chancellor dated June 10, 2002, based on informal knowledge of the impending action of governing council. This indicates my initial willingness to pull out of courts in three out of the five cases while stating my constraints in two cases.
2. Memo by Registrar and Secretary to Council dated 3rd June (ref. R/UAM/LIT/30; received 11 June

2002). This memo formally communicates the Council directive to me, with explicit reference to cases with university.
3. My reply memo to Registrar and Secretary to Council dated 12 June 2002, which communicates my compliance to withdraw from three cases and my constraints in two cases as presented in my previous letter to VC.
4. My letter to Pro-Chancellor and Chairman of Council dated June 15. 2002 reporting my disposition to comply and the constraints and seeking his action to assist in removing the constraints so the balance of two cases could be taken out of court
5. My letter to Registrar and Secretary to Council dated June 16. 2002 indicating my decision to take the balance of two cases against the university out of court. Based on some assurances given.

On cases with individual persons (4 cases, 3 criminal and 1 civil)

1. Memo from Registrar dated 17 June 2002 (ref R/UAM/LIT 1'30) advising me to take the cases that I instituted against individuals in their personal capacities out of court, as well.
2. My letter to Registrar and Secretary to council dated June 23 2002 indicating my decision to withdraw the four cases against individuals from the courts

Instruction to Lawyer

My successive decisions to come out of court in each case as indicated above was accompanied by concurrent instructions to my solicitors, which was promptly acted upon. I have provided a copy of the action of my lawyer in this regard to the Registrar including the notices of discontinuance addressed to the courts in respect of active cases. And I would like to assure the Chairman that the cases have been withdrawn from court as directed.

Action Sought

The attached summary of cases shows that I have embarked on sporadic court action to save my job, to save my career and my integrity at a time when council was not constituted and when the normal university process to seek redress was not available to me anymore. These cases have emanated from the intense official hostility against me, which was sponsored by the former Vice Chancellor, Professor E. O. Gyang. The origin of this hostility could be traced to my honest contribution at an official meeting at Abuja in May 1998, after which the former VC openly swore to nail me down at all costs, notwithstanding my profound apologies.

The victimization process involved incessant fault-finding against me in which certain staff members played unedifying roles to commit crimes as variously alleged in the courts, including deliberate falsehood, forgery, deceit of senate and other bodies, mischievous queries, to mention a few. These actions were carried out unregulated and unchecked with a view to nailing me down at all costs, as mandated by the former VC. As the highlights of cases show, the principal arrowheads for the purpose are Professor M. C. Njike, Dr J. C. Umeh and Mr I. U. Udoemenem. Although the cases against them were inconclusive at the time of pulling them out of court, it is on record that these people were all judicially indicted during the proceedings, criminally or otherwise. Therefore I humbly seek the action of Governing Council to critically look into these issues as assured, since I have now taken the first step of faith to fully comply with council directive and take all the cases out of court.

I remain loyal and dutiful, as well as pledge my disciplined hard work as usual, and promise to faithfully monitor events in the courts at Makurdi, Abuja and Jos to ensure effective withdrawal of the nine cases. Meanwhile, I await the reciprocal actions of the Governing Council to remedy the situation and prevent further injuries to me, as assured.

Thank you, Sir.

Yours truly

Dr G. B. Ayoola

Afterwards, my lawyer, with his letter of 27 June 2002, began the process by filing a series of notices of withdrawal of cases from all the courts in which I had sought refuge and got it. Looking back, from the date that the first case was filed (24 May 1999) and to this date of my lawyer's letter of withdrawals was written, I had spent no fewer than 1000 days in court!

* * *

Ayatse began to untie the knots with a view for him to making good on his own side of the bargain. A "Senate Committee on the Operational Modalities of Postgraduate Programmes in the Department of Agricultural Economics" was set up towards redressing some of my grievances and re-establishing sanity in the postgraduate programme in the department. As correctly discerned by him, the postgraduate programme in my department was the fertile ground for witch-hunting me by the university administration under Gyang and with the instrumentality of my three stalkers, Njike, Umeh, and Odoemenem.

The membership of the committee comprised Professor M. A. Akpapunam (Chairman) and five other members (Dr D. V. Uza, Director, Linkages; Dr Mrs. H. J. Kaka, Ag. Head, Department of Home Economics, Dr M. O. Adeyemo, Ag. Head, Department of Crop Production; Dr A. A. Agbendeh, Ag. Head, Department of Physics; and Mr P. T. Amando, Secretary, Postgraduate School, Secretary). Although the committee failed to properly castigate Umeh for the role he played initially in his personal and later his official capacity as HOD, its report contained explicit indictments of Njike in its findings and attributed the bad state of affairs to him in strong enough words to pass a verdict of guilty on him in the saga. Specifically, the report blamed Njike for the "Overbearing attitude and intrusion into the affairs of the Department of Agricultural Economics by the Dean of Postgraduate School (i.e. Njike)" and the "Deliberate delay in the processing of requests (such as in the appointment of

External Examiners) from the Department by Postgraduate School", which eventually led to frustration of many postgraduate students in my department, not the least Patrick Magit and Victor Ehigiator, who were used as fodder in their desperate bid to nail me down at all costs. And what's more, the committee's report recommended Njike for removal as the dean of postgraduate school. In a courageous move by Ayatse as VC, Njike was so removed—vintage Ayoola!

I saw this action of the university administration under Ayatse more as in the pursuit of truth and justice than as an effort in restitution, as I'd demanded and desired. Nonetheless, it marked the beginning of the end of an era of academic tyranny, administrative impunity, and executive recklessness at Makurdi, to say the least. Subsequently, the governing council was reconstituted, and Njike lost his seat on council because no one would cast a vote for wickedness in that body anymore. Soon, Njike's ego sagged, and he buried his head in shame on campus, gradually receding into academic oblivion.

* * *

Next, Ayatse granted me a breather in terms of sabbatical leave from the university, effective September 2013. My sabbatical leave placement with the famous International Fertilizer Development Centre (IFDC), which also came with a rising profile for me professionally and materially, was simply for the asking. My request coincided with the time the organisation had just won a seven-million-euro project code-named MIR (Mache d'Itrant Regionale, or Marketing Input Regionally) from the Dutch government (DGIS), covering the whole of the West Africa subregion. I had been associated with IFDC since late the 1980s as a consultant, along with its staff from its headquarters in Muscle Shoals, Alabama, to conduct the nationwide fertiliser liberalisation study for Nigeria. It was most gratifying for me to be appointed as the Policy Economist and technically positioned as Head of Nigerian Office for MIR. By virtue of this position, I also served as the Policy Economist to the DAIMIA project (Developing Agri-Input Market in Nigeria), a USAID-supported project but also implemented by IFDC. Both positions combined, exalted as they were, far more than CEFAS or HOD positions at UNIAGRIC, was not just a proof-of-concept opportunity for me but also uncommon practical exposure to serious policy implementation work to liberalize the farm input sector across many borders in the ECOWAS region.

Fortuitously, no sooner had I settled down at my office of the MIR project in the ECOWAS building in Abuja than another presidential visitation panel was constituted for the university. Its period of investigation covered Gyang's time in all ramifications, and its terms of reference was damning. Professor Olorunimbe Adedipe, who was the pioneer VC of the Federal University of Agriculture Abeokuta at the same time Idachaba had been the pioneer VC at Makurdi, chaired this the panel. He was someone I knew back in Ibadan as a no-nonsense and disciplined academic who, like Idachaba, had been fired by the philosophy behind an agricultural university. He was instrumental to building the triple-helix model of this philosophy for Nigeria from the outset, anchored on teaching, research, and agricultural extension operating under the same administrative umbrella.

With enthusiasm, nay excitement, I submitted a memorandum about my situation to Adedipe's panel and tabled the core issues in the settlement process on which Ayatse had been dragging his feet for so long. In my memorandum, I wrote,

> I would like to humbly invite the visitation panel to discern and act upon the numerous issues embedded in the events and cases presented, and to specifically request as follows:
>
> - That the various letters and charges against me be invalidated in quick time.
> - That the issue of culpability and criminality inherent in the court cases be determined consistent with the social responsibility of university as a government institution that should not encourage crimes or harbor criminals in any guise;
> - That the issue of innocent students that became victims of the situation be considered and resolved so they can receive their hard earned degrees;
> - That the circumstances under which the former council directed staff to get out of court be examined

with a view to ensuring justice and restitution for the people concerned.
- That the collateral damages and injuries suffered in the process be alleviated in terms of speedy completion of promotion and other incentives.

In conclusion one has had a harrowing experience as a staff of the university, associated with considerable collateral damages and injuries personally and officially. However, the university needs to undertake a conscious effort towards reformulation and redesign of its programmes in consonance with the original mission and mandate.

It was after the panel's work, and at a most unexpected time, that Ayatse quietly released my promotion letter to the rank of professor, which obviously reflected the favourable recommendations of the Adedipe-led panel to government. Even though the positive assessment had come in since 1997, Gyang permanently sat on it in the wake of hostilities till this time. However, possibly in an attempt to not offend the sensibilities of godfathers and other Benue elites who'd backed Gyang all along, the letter of promotion was wrongly dated to take effect in 2003 instead of 1997, when I'd actually been assessed for the purpose. Nonetheless, the promotion came at the right time to further boost my profile at IFDC, where I spent a three yearlong leave – one-year sabbatical leave back-to-back with a two-year leave of absence.

Later, I gathered that the panel not only vindicated me on all counts but also recommended that the tenure of Gyang be completely audited, having found concrete evidence of financial corruption against him. They scrupulously investigated my petition. When I laid my hand on the white paper, it was observed that the government had approved the recommendations of the panel in my favour, which included the finding of the panel that indeed Gyang and his hatchet men—Njike and Umeh, to be specific—had acted without conscience by victimising my postgraduate students Patrick Magit and Victor Ehigiator for the sins purportedly committed by me as their major supervisor. Following this finding and the recommendation of the panel, it was explicitly stated in the white paper that university authorities should revisit the matters of my students. Unfortunately, Ayatse and his successors have not complied with that to this date.

The recommendations of the visitation panel, together with the decisions of federal government, include the following on term basis.

> Term of Reference 3
>
> "Look into the financial management of the institution over the recommended period and determine whether it was In compliance with appropriate regulation."
>
> **Recommendations:**
>
> (a) The **former Vice-Chancellor Professor, Erastus O. Gyang should be held responsible for the enormous losses encountered by the University amounting to N20,392.430.00** as a result of decongestion of Stores exercise which became necessary on those Store items he (the former Vice Chancellor) purchased to overstock the Stores as well as the indebtedness of the University, variously put at between N176 and N500 million, during his tenure as Vice Chancellor. This is despite cautionary notes by the internal auditor.

Comment: The Visitor accepts the recommendation and directs the Federal Ministry of Education to investigate the matter.

> (b) In order to determine the extent of Prof. E. O. Gyang's personal involvement in the heavy financial mismanagement during his tenure as Vice-Chancellor, there is an urgent need to set up a financial investigating Panel.

Comment: The Visitor accepts this recommendation and directs the Ministry to set up an Administrative Panel of Inquiry on the matter.

> (c) Consequent on Recommendation 6 above, all outstanding personal entitlements due to Professor Festus O. Gyang should be suspended forth with,

pending the outcome of the recommended Financial Investigating Panel.

Comment: The Visitor accepts this recommendation and directs the University to comply.

Term of Reference 9

Advise on any or all other aspects of the Institution that you consider should be of interest to both the Visitor and the public, and to the attainment of the objectives for which the institution was set up.

Findings/Observation/Recommendations

The Case of Dr G. B. Ayoola

a. It has adequately been shown that the period, January 1, 1999 to September 6, 2001 under Prof. Gyang was a period characterized by unrests. It has been alleged that Prof. Gyang from onset had fixed his mind on punishing those he had assumed to be his predecessor's loyalists. The campus was divided into two camps thus escalating incidents of tribalism, favoritism, frivolities and incompetence. During the period, several people of the University community, especially the non-indigenes were harassed, molested and humiliated. Many members of staff who could not stand the rigours resorted to the law courts for succor and one of such persons was Dr G. B. Ayoola who instituted 9 (nine) cases in the law courts (i.e. not including the one I instituted in the name of my student's name, Patrick Magit).

b. With the inauguration of the Governing Council on July 1, 2000 and the appointment of Prof. Ayatse as the new Vice-Chancellor on September 6, 2001, the new Vice-Chancellor and Council made spirited efforts to get all the cases withdrawn from courts.

c. Series of negotiation culminated in the withdrawal of the myriad of cases. There is however, the case of Dr G.

B. Ayoola in which the University has not yet honoured the terms as follows:

> Invalidating the various offensive letters and charges against him.
>
> The issue of the innocent Students who became victims of the situation has to be considered and resolved so they can receive their degrees.
>
> The withheld promotion of Dr Ayoola and other related matters.

11.0.1 Recommendation

The University Governing Council should take necessary action on the unresolved issues of Dr Ayoola and others soonest in order to lay the matter to rest.

Comment: Visitor accepts this recommendation and directs Council to revisit the Issue of Dr Ayoola and all concerned with a view to finally resting the case.

I resumed at UNIAGRIC in late 2006, by which time Ayatse's tenure had expired and Professor D. V. Uza had succeeded him in office as the next Tiv man in line. Uza was well known to me since I'd joined the university in 1988. He was a sympathiser, if not accomplice, to the course of Mzough U'Tiv against Idachaba, and he was also a strong influencer in Gyang's cabinet from the outset. To be honest, I couldn't vouch for what might or might not happen to me during Uza's time—hence the fear I nursed that made my return less enthusiastic than it should have been in a post-Gyang era. Specifically, he probably would have forgotten a harsh statement he made to me sometime in the past at the North Bank mechanic village. At that time, he was still basking in the arrogance of power he'd wielded during the reign of Gyang. He cast a dry joke with me, saying, "If I were Gyang, it wouldn't have taken me such a long time [since Abuja meeting] to get you sacked from the university."

Besides my fears about what Uza's regime portended for me when my leave expired, it also appeared to me that the scars of the protracted war I had fought and won at the institution could not have healed completely. With the likes of Njike, Umeh, and Odoemenem still around, no one needed to tell me that cultivating new friendships at the institution would be an arduous if not impossible task for me. Thus, obeying the message in my spirit, the thought of an exit strategy grew stronger by the day. And afterwards the thought crystalized in my mind, as was readily agreed with Bose for implementation of the strategy without qualms; what a painless decision for me to step down from UNIAGRIC as an academic staff – take an initial terminal exit with the accumulated annual leave, followed by withdrawal of my service from the institution, which dovetailed into an early (voluntary) retirement at 55, when under the new regulations governing academic service in the country's university system I still had a decade and a half years in sight to do so.

Surprisingly, in the twilight of my final exit from UNIAGRIC, it gladdened me that my adversaries had begun to soften their hearts. One day while I was on terminal leave already, Pastor Femi Agbede came to pray with my family at morning devotion, as he occasionally used to do since the outbreak of hostility against me. He read Psalm 124:7 in part, wherefrom he anchored the message he had for us, that "the sneer is broken, and we are escaped"; which message implying that the battle was over and I have been vindicated. Afterwards, in a most gratifying spirit I saw him off to his car outside the building. As if to stamp that message as true and devine, another car drove into my compound. Alas, the person driving was Professor Ikurior – my next door neighbor and the person for so long in self-imposed hostility against me at the instance of Gyang! As Deputy Vice Chancellor and chairman of the Students Rampage Investigation Panel, Ikurior he was who did Gyang's bid to invite me to appear before the panel, as what he termed "aggrieved person against Gyang's administration". In the process he succeeded in roping me in, thereby laying a good foundation for Gyang to sack me from the university. Standing beside myself in surprise, I wondered what he could be looking for at my residence for the first time ever and so early in the day! My wife and I gazed at him curiously and in awe of God's works as he quietly followed me into my sitting room. He hurriedly sank in a chair opposite mine, and began to deploy words of apology and regrets in my ears, blaming Gyang for the ignoble role he played during my travails in the university.

A couple of days later, Umeh also flip-flopped, with an unexpected courage though, when he came up to me at a workshop in Abuja to tender apology for his own role in my travails, as well. During the tea break that immediately followed the presentation of my paper at that workshop, he personally delivered to me a short note he had written in his unmistakable long hand. As he tucked it into my left hand, both he and I avoided an eye contact. I opened the small piece of paper, still wondering what on earth it could possibly contain. On it was written a familiar Bible passage usually cited by Christians for seeking forgiveness. When our eyes eventually met, I was a little lost about the look of self-pity he wore, and was speechless for a moment in sympathy. I couldn't explain how my spirit so quickly acceded his remorseful disposition in my presence. Following that encounter, I paid Umeh a friendly visit at his residence the next weekend in the company of my wife, and he returned my visit the next day. Now I heaved a heavy sigh of relief, fully convinced in my spirit that truly "the sneer is broken …"!

In any case, my sympathy for Umeh subsisted forever. So much for the irony of the faith compelling a Christian to seek forgiveness at all times, just as he did from me. Such an act of repentance, if genuine, was good for his soul but equally bad for his reputation. Umeh had lost his reputation, according to not only me but also to the university community and society at large, when he surreptitiously lent himself as an evil instrument for Gyang and Njike to use innocent students (Patrick Magit and Victor Ehigiator) as fodder in fighting a senseless war against me at Makurdi. What a shame.

UNIVERSITY OF AGRICULTURE, MAKURDI

Head

DEPARTMENT OF AGRICULTURAL MANAGEMENT

From: Prof. Umeh   To: Prof Ayoola
Ref: Date: 25/02/09

Kindly read this passage: Matthew 18: 21-35. I read it this morning and God laid it on my heart to give it to you to read.

Prof. Umeh

Part Three
Legal Tussle

♪
When burdens press, and seem beyond endurance,
bowed down with grief, to Him I lift my face;
And then in love He brings me sweet assurance:
'My child! For thee, sufficient is my grace

Res ipsa loquitur – that is, the facts speak for themselves

My struggle in the fight for truth against lies and right against wrong is hereunder X-rayed in sync with the sequence of the respective onslaughts that gave rise to them in the previous chapter. In each case, and at the minimum risk of unavoidable repetitions, the synopsis of what happened in a particular court starts with a brief recap of the individual contexts followed by an extract from the minutes or record of selected proceedings and, where strictly warranted, by rulings or judgments and critical pronouncements of the court.

Case 1

Direct Criminal Prosecution of Professor M. C. Njike for Forgery in the Matter of My Postgraduate Student Patrick Magit

In the Chief Magistrate Court of Benue State of Nigeria
In the Makurdi Magisterial District
Holden in Makurdi

CASE NO/DCR/60C5/99

Before His Lordship: Bakare C. I., Esq (Chief Magistrate II); Dan Ogo, Esq (Chief Magistrate II)

Between: Dr. G. B. Ayoola (Complainant) and Prof. M. C. Njike (Defendant)

Case sequel to Seventh Onslaught: This case was filed on 18 June 1999 against Professor M. C. Njike, who had maliciously altered the oral examination results of my postgraduate student, Mr Patrick Magit, which I had forwarded to the senate of the university through him as dean of postgraduate school for final approval for the award of the MSc degree. The actual results form was altered by changing the decision or recommendation of the oral examination panel, from option B, meaning pass, to option C, meaning fail. As stated on the standard form "Examiners' Report on Master's/Doctoral Thesis", the original interpretation of option B is "That the thesis be accepted and degree be awarded subject to correction to be certified as may be determined by the panel", but the original interpretation of option C on the same form is "That the thesis is referred for amendments to be certified by the External Examiner". Njike also made an insertion in front of option C as follows: "(Major Supervisor and External Examiner)". As a result of these fraudulent alterations and insertions, the thesis was rejected and the student dismissed by the senate. Furthermore, I was disparaged and ridiculed on the floor of senate and subsequently subjected to disciplinary process for professional negligence, punishable by dismissal.

The defense entered a preliminary objection on the basis that the case was statute barred, that the case was groundless and frivolous, and that I did not seek the sanction of the attorney general before commencing with the case. For these reasons, he sought that the accused person be discharged and acquitted. The defense also posited that Professor Njike had committed the alteration on 29 August 1998, and the case was statute barred because I'd lodged my complaints on 18 June 1999, more than three months after the actual act. The defence also reiterated, in a counter-affidavit, that Njike was discharging his duties when he made the alterations, and if the complainant felt an injurious act had been committed against him, he should have commenced his proceedings within three months of the alteration. The "groundless and frivolous" argument was hinged on my not being specific on the nature of injuries I'd suffered when the senate decision was reached; if I suffered any injury at all, it was so slight I had no basis to complain. On the third issue of my not seeking the sanction of the attorney general, the defence cited a non-compliance with the provision of a section of the Criminal Procedure Code, which barred any law court from taking cognisance of a case involving forgery until the consent of the attorney general was sought.

My lawyer, S. O. Okpale, Esq., from Eche Ada Chambers, vehemently opposed the defence application, urging the court to dismiss it as unmeritorious, vexatious, and an attempt to thwart the course of justice. In our better and further affidavit, we submitted that the sections of the law relied on by the defence didn't apply to our case, and that they were distinguishable from ours. On this basis, my lawyer urged the court to dismiss the defence's objection.

On 29 July 1999, the court gave its ruling in my favour, which implied that Njike had a criminal case to answer. He was visibly jolted, and his spirit was broken.

> Ruling:
>
> In this application, the applicant seeks for the following order: An order dismissing or striking out the complaint on the ground that the initiation of the proceeding is time barred.
>
> 1. An order striking out the proceeding on the ground that the necessary sanctions of the Hon. Attorney General have not been obtained.
> 2. An order striking out the proceeding on the ground that it is groundless and frivolous.
> 3. Any other order as the court may deem fit.
>
> The application is supported by a seven (7) paragraph affidavit and a further and better affidavit (4 paragraphs). The applicant relied on all paragraphs of their affidavits.
>
> The gist of the applicant's application considering their affidavit evidence is that the applicant who is arraigned on a direct criminal proceeding for the offences under section 364, 392 and 393 of the penal code is a public officer by virtue of his being a staff of the University of Agriculture. The applicant counsel submitted that the action complained against in the proceeding took place on the 28/9/98 and that the direct criminal complaint was instituted against the applicant on 18/6/99 a period of more than three months. The counsel to the applicant further argued that this being so, the action was statute barred. The learned counsel submitted that since the action complained of was done in the course of official duty the action ought to have commenced before the period of three months from the date of the alleged action being complained against by the respondent by virtue of

the provision of section 2(a) of public officers protection Act Cap. 379 Laws of the Federation of Nigeria 1990. The applicant referred to the decided cases of Cluaka vs. Local Government Civil Service Commission and Anor. 1989 BNLR page 126 at 128. Fred Egbe v. Hon. J. A. Adefarasin 1987 vol. 1. SCNJ page 1 at 2. The learned applicant counsel submitted that the ratio dicendi of these cases are applicable to this case.

The learned applicant counsel further submits on the 2nd arm of their objection that the complainant respondent has not complied with the provision of sections 140 and 141 of the CPC. He submits that the court is authorized by virtue of the provisions of section 141 of the CPC to take cognizance of the offence of forgery under section 393 of the penal code without the sanction of the Attorney General. The applicant counsel submitted further that in the absence of the sanction of the Attorney General, the court ought to decline taking cognizance.

The learned applicant counsel submitted that the allegation complained of against the applicant is groundless and frivolous. The learned counsel submitted that some particulars of injury allegedly suffered by the respondent ought to have been indicated. The counsel submitted that if the respondent suffered any injury at all, it was so minor or slight that it should not be complained against. He referred the court to section 58 of the penal code. He finally urged the court to dismiss the whole action.

The respondent objected to the application and filed a counter affidavit of 6 paragraphs. They relied on all paragraphs of their counter affidavit.

The respondent counsel in summary submitted that all the sections of the law relied upon by the applicant counsel are inapplicable to this case. The respondent counsel submitted that the acts complained of by the respondent were not done by the applicant in the confines of his duty. The learned counsel submitted further that the public officer protection law is only meant to safeguard officers from civil actions and that it does not apply to bar criminal actions. He referred to the case of Yabugbe vs. COP. 1992 NWLR at 234 page 153 at 155. He submitted that they do not need the sanction of the A.G. to make this complaint. He submitted that the issue of slight injury raised by the applicant under section 58 of the penal code is premature. The respondent finally urged the court to dismiss the application.

I have considered the entire application before me, all the affidavit evidence, the submissions by brother counsels that where any action prosecution and all the decided cases cited herein and I intend to take the issues raised in order in which they were raised.

The first issue raised in this application is that of the provisions of the public officers protection law which provides in section 2(a) that where any action, prosecution or other proceeding is commenced against any person for any act done in pursuance or execution or intended execution of any law or of any public duty or authority or in respect of any alleged neglect or default in the execution of any such law, duty, or authority, the following provisions shall have effect.

> (a) The action, prosecution, or proceeding shall not be or be instituted unless it is commenced within three months next after the action, neglect or default complained of ... A close look at all the decided cases cited apart from the case of Yabugbe vs. COP supra shows they all related to civil proceedings. Also a close look at section 2(b) (c) and (d) of the public officers protection law, the mention of plaintiffs and defendants is clearly seen. It is trite law that there is no bar to criminal prosecution except where time is limited by statute. The pertinent question for consideration in this application is whether looking at the provision of section 2 (a) (b) (c) (d) of the public officers protection law and the decided cases before me, can it be rightly said that the public officers protection law avails a public officer standing trial for criminal allegation.

To answer this question, the intention of the legislators have to be made out and this can be deduced from the provision of the law itself. It is obvious that the legislator by their use of the words plaintiffs and defendants in the same section 2 intended that the provisions of section 2(a) of the same law should be applied to civil proceedings and not criminal prosecution. This interpretation was clearly adopted by the Supreme Court in the case of Paul Yabugbe vs. COP 1992 4, NWLR page 152 at 155. The fire supreme court Judges anonymously held that the word "prosecution" "within the context of section 2 of the public officers protection law means the constitution and carrying on of civil legal proceedings. This is made apparent by subsequent use of the words plaintiffs and defendants in the explanatory sub-sections (b), (c) and (d) and the complete absence of the words prosecution and accused in these subsection". They held further "It could not have been the intention of the state to shield or protect public officers from criminal prosecution for criminal offences committed by them in the guise of performing their official duties by limiting the time to initiate prosecution to only three months. "Per Uwais J.S.C. held in this same case. "Is it the intention of the legislature in enacting the public officers protection law, to protect public officers from prosecution in respect of any crime committed in the course of their duty? I do not think so. It does not stand to common sense and reason that a public officer is free to commit any offence in the course of his duty so long as criminal prosecution is not brought against him within 3 months. It will be absurd and ridiculous."

From the foregoing, I hold that section 2 (a) of the public officers protection law is not applicable to this case being a criminal prosecution and therefore does not avail this applicant.

On the second arm of the application as regards the sanction by Attorney General, the relevant section for consideration is 41 of the CPC with specific reference to the section 393 which is the one of the sections under which applicant is arraigned. Section 141 states, No court shall take cognizance of any offence falling under chapter xxi or xxii of the penal code or under sections 383, 386 of the same code except upon complaint made by some persons aggrieved by the such offence but where the person so aggrieved is a woman who according to the customs and manners of the country ought not to be compelled to appear in public or where such person is under the age of eighteen or is an idiot or lunatic or is from sickness infirmity unable to a complaint some other person may with the leave of the court make a complaint on his or her behalf and in this case of an offence under section 393 of the penal code where the party aggrieved is the Government or Local Government Authority, Attorney-General may make a complaint on behalf of such Local Government Authority and in the case of an offence under section 393 of penal code where the so aggrieved is other than the Government or Local Government Authority, a police officer may in public interest and with the sanction of the Attorney General make a complaint on behalf of such party. "Upon a close look at the relevant provision of the section 141 of the CPC touching on section 393, I am of the view that the word 'may' used there is generally a permissive or an enabling expression prima facie. See the authority of Alhaji Chief A.B. Bakare vs. The Attorney-General of the Federation 1990 9 SSCNJ 43. The provision therefore not being a mandatory provision cannot debar an individual from instituting an action under that section. My understanding of that provision is that where the individual chooses to use police to prosecute, he needs the sanction of the Attorney General since the police shares function with the ministry of justice. They are partners in progress.

I hold that the respondent does not need sanction of the A.G. since he has come by way of direct criminal prosecution.

On the third arm the facts giving rise to this prosecution has been clearly stated in the complaint and even the applicant in his affidavit has admitted in his paragraph 3(b)(c) that the act which the complainant respondent has complained of though the applicant contends that he did the said Act in course of his duty. The case therefore cannot be said to be groundless or frivolous in the circumstance.

On the whole, the objection to this application is sustained and the application is hereby dismissed.

(Sgd): Bakare C. I., Esq.

Chief Mag. II.

29/7/99

Afterwards, Njike's plea was taken and he was admitted on bail. However, in the stupor that he found himself, Njike resorted to delay tactics, ostensibly to evade justice, by absenting himself from court sessions on the matter. After a number of adjournments, on 20 January 2000, when the matter was fixed for definite hearing and Njike was still absent in court, my lawyer, Okutepa, applied for a warrant of arrest for having jumped bail, which was granted immediately by the chief magistrate. Then the defence lawyer, Ejale who was also initially absent hurriedly surfaced in court with the accused person. He requested to recall the case, pleading spiritedly for his client to be spared this time. He complained of an information gap that made Njike be absent that day. Eventually the chief magistrate graciously revoked the bench warrant and extended the bail.

Hearing of the case resumed on 3 March 2000, by which time the Coram had changed, as another chief magistrate had taken over the case in person of Dan Ogo. As soon as this was noticed, the defence team contemplated exploring the change to introduce further delay of trial. They filed an appeal against the previous ruling of the court that overruled their initial objection, implying that the court should not take cognisance of the offence alleged against Njike, as "necessary sanctions from the Attorney General were not obtained before the proceedings were initiated". He went on to make submission that the plea of the accused should not be taken until the motion was heard. My lawyer objected on the grounds that there was no law saying that a plea of an accused should not be taken before the new magistrate when there were changes in Coram, and that an appeal did not operate as a stay of execution. That, "the issues of whether or not the sanction of the Attorney General was required to prosecute the issues already decided by the court would operate as an estoppel, and that the court should take the plea of the accused, after which the motion could be looked at." The ruling was fixed for 24 March 2000, but this was extended to 5th April after the defence filed a notice of withdrawal of objection—an action described as an afterthought by the chief magistrate. The chief magistrate ruled in favour of the defense; and the plea of the accused would be taken.

A melodrama ensued on 5 April 2000 when the case came up for hearing, and again Njike was absent in court. As in the previous instance, my lawyer applied for a bench warrant to be issued on him, which was granted. His lawyer rushed out to inform him about this, and he hurled himself into the court to recall the case as he had done before. Unfortunately, before they'd arrived, the court had risen for the day's sitting, and so Njike was arrested and bundled into a waiting patrol wagon containing some criminals heading to prison custody. A heavy pressure was exerted by the university on the police authorities, who graciously decided to keep him in police custody overnight, instead. As I later learnt, he was offered a narrow bench on which to pass the night. The next day, the defence lawyer recalled the case, citing an information gap as the reason for Njike's failure to come to court. The chief magistrate grudgingly discharged Njike of the arrest warrant, thereby extending his bail, leading to continuation of the case.

After a series of adjournments, hearing in the substantive matter eventually commenced on 2 April 2001, with me as the first prosecution witness (PW1), as led in evidence by my lawyer, J. S. Okutepa, Esq., and subsequently cross-examined by defence counsel, S. P. Ejale, Esq., before the case was eventually closed.

17/7/2002

Coram: -   Dan Ogo, Esq. Ag. Chief Magistrate II.

Accused: -   Present, speaks English.

Mrs. M. Nwadioke (standing in for Okutepa) for complainant and Pros.

Mr S. P. Ejale for accused.

Mrs. Nwadioke: Case for continuation of hearing. The complainant, Dr G.B. Ayoola has instructed us to withdraw this matter because of some fundamental development. This instruction is based on the directive of the governing council of the University of Agriculture Makurdi. We therefore apply for the matter to be withdrawn at the instance of the complainant.

Mr S. P. Ejale: We have no objections to the application for the withdrawal of the case per se. However, I am not aware of any directive against the complainant to withdraw this matter from the Governing Council of the University.

Court: It is good to make peace for indeed nothing is superior to peace making especially when two parties disagree. In the application before me, since both parties have consented to the withdrawal of peace, I have no reasons to stand in their way or against their wishes. Accordingly the application by Mrs. M. Nwadioka on behalf of the complainant, Dr G.B. Ayoola for the withdrawal of this case is hereby granted. The complaint is therefore terminated and the accused discharged forthwith.

(Sgd): Dan Ogo, Esq.

Ag. C/Mag. II.

17/7/2002

Case 2

Libel Suit against Professor M. C. Njike, Mr I. U. Odoemenem and Dr J. C. Umeh

In the High Court of Justice of Benue State of Nigeria
In the Benue State Judicial Division
Holden in Makurdi

MHC/70/99

Before: His Lordship Justice I. Hwande (Judge)

Between
Dr. G. B. Ayoola (Plaintiff)
And
Prof. M. C. Njike, Dr. J. C. Umeh, Mr. I. U. Odoemenem
(Defendants)

Case sequel to Fourth Onslaught: I instituted this case against the defendants on 29 July 1999 for libel and defamation of character. The first defendant, Professor M. C. Njike, was the dean of postgraduate school at the University of Agriculture Makurdi. The second Defendant, Dr J. C. Umeh, was a senior lecturer in the Department of Agricultural Economics at the same time as me. The third defendant was a research fellow at the Centre for Food and Agricultural Strategic of the university at the time. I was also a senior lecturer in the same department as Umeh.

The defendants have jointly or severally acted to forge, falsify, and alter supervision sheets I had forwarded to the senate of the university for the assessment and approval of the thesis of one Patrick Magit, a postgraduate student under my supervision in my department. The trio conspired and collaborated with one another to defame my image in some papers sent to the senate of the University of Agriculture, Makurdi. Gyang, who chaired the senate meeting in question, called me a liar and other bad names on the floor of the senate.

Specifically, Umeh caused the dismissal of my student and the rejection of his thesis by the university senate, which he did in wickedness against me. Subsequently, the senate recommended a disciplinary action against me. As a result of this, various university organs, including the senate, castigated me and raised questions about my personal integrity, professional standing, and reputation. Professor Gyang, who was the VC at that time and also one of the people who had a grudge against me, was the person who sponsored the trio of Njike, Odoemenem, and Umeh on a witch-hunt against me, based on the knowledge that the trio had scores to settle with me severally and collectively. The third defendant, Mr Odoemenem, had gone to town to slander me on the issue of a computer under repair, which he alleged I had stolen. He accused me of conniving with the repairer to steal the computer. Furthermore, at the instance of Gyang, Njike headed a one-man panel that investigated me on the query I served Umeh when I was his HOD. It became clear the instruments professor Gyang was using in the plot to destroy me comprised these three people, on which basis I sued the trio at the High Court of Benue State, Markurdi.

Proceedings commenced on 29 of July 1999. I affirmed faith in getting justice without being deterred by the deteriorating condition of my health. The main suit was anchored on a claim magnified on acts of libel and defamation of character of my humble self, through the combined efforts of Njike, Umeh, and Odoemenem. The act complained of was allegedly done at various times between 1998 and 1999. However, preceding the substantive matter, my lawyer, Okutepa, brought a motion pursuant to S. 105(1) and (2) of the High Court Laws of Northern Nigeria and Section 6(b), Constitution of the Federal Republic of Nigeria 1999, seeking an order restraining the law firm of Messrs. Adejo Ogiri, Chief (Senator) Adejo Ogiri, S. P. Ejale, A. G. Abah, or any other lawyer from the law office of Adejo Ogiri and Associates from representing the respondents. Also, we sought an order restraining the University of Agriculture, Makurdi, as well as its agents or servants, from funding the defence of the defendants or engaging the defendants for the purpose of their defence. The motion was supported by a ten-paragraph affidavit.

My lawyer contended that I was a staff of the university, and it was against public policy for the university to be seen as supporting one of its employees against another. That it was against the goal of the university of ensuring peace within its environment and staff. In this regard, the court should order the university to stop funding the defence. He further contended that the only condition when the University of Agriculture could engage the services of a solicitor was when its revenue is involved. None of the defendants was sued in his official capacity. No one was allowed to make a trade out of felony, and if the allegations against the defendants were approved, they could not affect the revenue of the University of Agriculture, Makurdi. Our reasoning, amongst others, was that it would be against public policy for the university to be seen as expending its resources to defend people alleged to have committed certain offences and being prosecuted principally for criminal defamation of character.

As expected, the threesome through their Counsel Ejale vehemently opposed the motion. He argued that the defendants were servants of the university and were carrying out their duties when sued and acted in their official capacity. If a servant was performing the duty of his master, and he was sued in the course of that duty, he contended, the master was under obligation to ensure his defence. The defendants had been carrying out their official duties when they were sued. The lawyer further stated that the application was frivolous. He urged the court to dismiss the application and go into the substantive matter. My lawyer argued against this, saying that Benue State laws must govern anyone who submitted himself or herself to the jurisdiction of this court. He argued that a person guilty of committing a crime couldn't be acting in their official capacity. The prima facie nature of the case should take precedence at this stage, and the court should stop the university from funding the defence of the defendants.

On 26 July 2000, the judge gave a ruling.

> Ruling:
>
> In the main suit the plaintiff who is also the applicant in this motion is claiming various sums of money from the defendants/ Respondents for acts of libel and defamation of character. The Respondents as well as the plaintiff are staff of university of Agriculture Makurdi that is a Federal Institution. When the Respondents were served with the claim of the plaintiff/applicant, they got in touch with the university authority and the chambers of Adejo Ogiri & Co. was briefed to handle the defence of Respondents. Exhibit 'A' attached to the supporting affidavit speaks to this fact. The chambers of Adejo Ogiriaccordingly filed a memorandum of appearance, dated 17.6.99 on behalf of the defendants Respondents. This motion is a reaction to exhibit 'A' signed by Miss M. Agogo for the Ag Registrar of the university.
>
> On the motion filed for the applicant by his learned counsel J. S. Okutepa Esq the applicant is seeking: (i) An order restraining the firm of Miss Adejo & Co, Chief Senator Adejo Ogiri, S. P. Ejale A. G. Abah or any other lawyer from the law firm of Miss Adejo Ogiri or its Associates thereof from appearing and defending the defendant/Respondents in this Case. (ii) An order restraining the University of Agriculture Makurdi, its agents/servants from funding the defence of the defendants or engaging the defendants for the purpose of their defence in this Case any internal or external solicitors of the university and any order that the court may deem fit to make. Relying on the 10 paragraphs supporting affidavit the counsel to the applicant submitted that the application is made pursuant to S. 105(1) & (2) of the High Court Law of NN (Northern Nigeria) applicable to Benue State and S. 6(6) of the 1999 constitution.

It is the further contention of Okutepa for the applicant that the only condition when the university of Agriculture can engage the services of a solicitor is when its revenue is involved.

That none of the defendants is sued in his official capacity. That if the allegations against the defendant are proved that cannot affect the revenue of the University of Agriculture, Makurdi.

He cited in support of the case of Kondoun Anor v. Abari (1979–80) 1 BSLR 165. He also referred to S. 15 & 16 of Decree 46 of 1992 on Universities of Agriculture, and submitted that what was inserted falls within conduct that can be described as scandalous. That this falls within S. 15(3)(d) of Decree 48 of 1992. He urged on the court to grant prayer (1) on the motion paper.

On prayer 11 it is the submission of applicants' counsel that it will be against public policy for the university to be defending people alleged to have committed certain offences. He relied on S. 74 of the Evidence Act and contended that 1st defendant/Respondent is being prosecuted for criminal defamation. That some of the allegations involve forgery. That no one is allowed to make a trade out of a felony. That as both parties are staff of the university, it is against public policy for the university to support some staff against another. He urged the court to grant the 2nd prayer also.

Learned counsel for the Respondents S. P. Ejale Esq opposed the application. It is his submission that the Respondents are servants of the university. That where they are sued for acts done in performance of their duties the master is under obligation to ensure their defence. He relied on the counter affidavit and submitted that the Respondents were carrying out their duties when they were sued. He referred to S. 6(6)(6) of the 1999 Constitution. He also placed reliance on the already cited case of Kondoun Anor v. Abari.

It is also the submission of Respondents counsel that under the S. 105(1) & (2) of the High Court Law, it is the

Attorney General who should complain and not someone else. It is his further contention that, S. 105 of the High Court Law of Benue State does not affect the University of Agriculture Makurdi being a Federal University. He urged the court to dismiss the motion. S. 105(1) of the High Court Law of Northern Nigeria states that: -

"In the case of a prosecution by or on behalf of the state or by any public officer in his official capacity, the state or that public officer may be represented by a law officer, Director of public prosecution, state counsel administrative officer, Police Officer or any legal practitioner or other person duly authorised in that behalf by or on behalf of the, Attorney-General or in revenue cases authorized by the head of the department concerned".

That above section was interpreted by Idoko J, in the Case of Kondoun Anor v. Anthony Abara and another (1979-80) BSLR 165 more particularly at p. 168 where he stated that: -

"Bearing in mind the advice of the Federal Supreme Court in the above case that it is left to each court to decide on question of legal representation to be provided by the Attorney-General in a case such as this, it appears to me that where a public officer in the execution of his official function or under the colour of his Official function is alleged to have committed a tortious wrong, the state has sufficient interest to enable legal representation to provide for the public officer in court even though sued in his personal capacity because it could appear at the end of the day that the public officer had apparent or ostensible or implied authority of the state to do what he had done.

I think Ahura J, was right when he held in the case of Prince C. A. Obaje v. Fit Lt MM Kunlere & 1 Or, unreported decision of Benue State High Court in suit No. MHC/3/98 that the disagreement arose in a joint venture business between the parties and as there was nothing official about it, it was wrong for the Attorney-General to send a counsel to defend the defendant even though a public officer.

In the suit before the court for consideration the defendants are not represented by the office of the Attorney-General of the state, The chambers of Adejo Ogiri is a private chambers consisting of private legal practitioners. It is not an appendage of the Attorney General's Office. The university of Agriculture is not a state Ministry and is usually not assisted in its legal matters by the state Attorney General. Interpreting S. 105(7) of the High Court Law to stop the University from acting in a situation like the one under consideration will be overstretching the S. 105(2) of the High Court Law beyond its elastic point. Whereas S. 105 (2) of the High Court Law of the state can be a guide to the court I do not think it can be used to restrict the hands of people not affected by it to a position of helplessness.

The position of the case as I see it is it as held by Idoko J, in Anor v. Abdri Supra: -

"Where a public officer in the execution of his official function or under the colour of his official function is alleged to have committed a tortious wrong, the state has legal representation".

It is my view that the above principle applies to the state as well as the university as it is the common law position on the issue.

Where the university authority are of the view that the defendants acted in their official capacity or at least under the colour of their office in the facts that have led the plaintiff to court, the university will be in order to arrange representation to the defendant.

It is for the plaintiff to show that the defendants did not act in their official capacity or even under the colour of their office, Under the circumstances of the case before me, I am yet to be presented with facts to convince me that the defendants were on a voyage of their own when they were acting as alleged by the plaintiff in his statement of claim. I will not therefore restrain the chambers of Adejo Ogiri from representing the defendants as prayed by plaintiff.

It is also my view that it is not against the public policy for the university to choose to assist in the defence of the people it believes was functioning for it. It is not possible to be a striker and at the same time a goalkeeper for the same side. The university cannot be expected to fund plaintiff to prosecute the case and turn round to arrange defence for the defendants as suggested by Okutepa J. S., Learned counsel for the plaintiff. For the reasons given above, I declare to grant the orders sought.

SGD.

(Justice I. Hwande) J

26.7.2000

The motion of the defendants was fixed for 9 October 2000. On the said date, the defence asked for an adjournment because he had attended a meeting of the governing council, and there was a recent development. The council had expressed desire to resolve all the legal matters against the university. As a first step, all the plaintiffs should withdraw their cases from the court. But this decision had not yet been communicated to me, and I requested an adjournment so that the decision would be properly committed to me, upon which channels of communication could be opened on the matter. Mr Okutepa, my lawyer, opined that such an application ordinarily ought not be objected to because as a minister in the Temple of Justice, it was the duty of both counsels to see that parties settle out of court. However, my counsel had heard in court that morning that the matter, still in court, was a subject of disciplinary committee, and I was expected to appear before the committee the next day. The first defendant, Professor Njike, was a member of that committee. My counsel submitted that the application for adjournment was intended to ensure I did not get justice on the matter. Because the issue was already before the court, it was Mr Okutepa's view that the council was not sincere in their approach that they wanted to settle the matter of court. The defence replied that he'd go to the university to warn them about the presence of the case in court and to urge them to withdraw their letter of invitation to me. In response to this, Mr Okutepa added that he'd also write and draw the attention of the disciplinary committee on the matter, which was being addressed in court.

The judge held that it was rather sad and curious that the university had been impatient in knowing the decision of the court on the matter by going ahead to serve me with a letter of invitation to appear before a disciplinary committee. Because both parties had promised to remind the governing council that the matter was still in court, the court hoped that the university authority would see reasons to suspend the action, pending the outcome of the case.

Meanwhile, in September 2001, a new vice chancellor was appointed, and there were renewed efforts from the administration to take all my cases out of court. But while this was going on, Njike and Umeh showed no inclination towards helping out with the peace process. My lawyer made this known in court, and the defence told the court that there was a reconciliatory committee set up by the council to look into the various disputes the university administration was involved in. The council was asking for more time to enable them settle the parties involved, and he'd want an adjournment to report on the settlement efforts.

On 6 May 2002, my lawyer complained to the court that the university was paying lip service to settling out of court. It seemed as if the settlement was being attempted only in theory and the proposal we had written to the university thus far on the matter had not yet been responded to positively. He further stated that though we were desirous of giving the new administration room to ensure peace on the university campus, we'd appreciate they took a more serious step. The defence responded, saying that most of the conditions given by the plaintiff for settling out of court were unacceptable. But the counsel was playing its part by encouraging the university to settle out of court. The court decided to adjourn the case for the final time so that both parties could reach a settlement out of court.

Thereafter, the defendants' counsel raised a preliminary objection pursuant to section S.2 (2) of the Public Officers Protection Act, which interestingly provides a cover for public officers. The section provides that no action shall lie against a public official unless such action is commenced within three months of the action complained of. It was argued that, the section under reference had caught up with the plaintiff (i.e. myself) in this instance, as three months had elapsed before the action was filed. In responding, my counsel submitted that the objection was misconceived and premature owing to the reasoning that when an objection is raised that an action is statute barred, the court looks at the statement of claim to determine when the cause of action arose, and because it was not possible to determine when the cause of action arose, the argument would not stand in law. Furthermore, it was submitted that for the Public Officers Protection Act to avail any person, evidence must exist that the act complained of was done within the limits of the powers of such public officers. When a public officer embarks on the trip of complete illegality, he loses the protection of the law. The dean of postgraduate studies, Professor M. Njike, acted outside the scope of processing results to the senate. Ultimately, the defendants were not doing what they were paid to do.

Ruling

The defendants through their learned counsel S. P. Ejale Esq moved this court on 2.2.200; to strike out this suit as being statute barred. That the defendants are all public officers in the employment of university of Agriculture, Makurdi and that the acts complained of were performed in the course of their employment. That by S. 2 (a) of the Public Officers Protection Act, no action shall be against a public officer unless such action is commenced within 3 months next after the action complained of. That University of Agriculture is statutory institution established under the Act No. 48 of 1992. It is a Federal Institution. That from the pleadings filed and exchanged, the defendants are staff of the university. That whereas the Act complained of took place in 1998 this suit was filed on 10th May 1999; that, the defendants are alleged to have sent some papers to the senate of the university in 1998. That this was in the normal course of their duties. That the defendants are alleged to have conspired and collaborated with each other in order to defame the image of the plaintiff who was a major supervisor of Post Graduate

Students. That for defamation the effective date is that of publication. That as three months had elapsed before the plaintiff filed this suit he is caught up by S. 2(a) of the Public Officers Protection Act and the case should be struck out. Reliance is placed on the case of Odiasinye v. University of Agriculture Makurdi and Others, case No. FHC/J/CA/81/99 discussed on 6.4.2000 in Jos.

In his response learned counsel for the plaintiff J. S. Okutepa Esq contented that the objection is misconceived. That it is not clear on the statement of claim to determine when the cause of action arose and as such it will not be proper to throw out the suit. That it is not possible to decide if the action against 2nd and 3rd defendants is statute barred from the claim. It is also the submission of defendants counsel that for the Act to cover a public officer, he must be performing the duties within the purview of his employment. That, when a public officer goes all out, to embark on an action that is illegal he loses the protection of the Act. He cited in support Ibrahim vs. Judicial Service Committee (1998) 14 NWLR (pt. 584) P1 at p32. Mr Okutepa conceded that 1st and 2nd defendants are lecturers and are therefore public officers but that their work is to research and lecture. He referred to the University Regulations and submitted that to alter and call a person a thief is not part of the work of a lecturer.

It has been conceded that the defendants as employees of University of Agriculture, Makurdi are public officers within the meaning of the public officers Protection Act. The area of disagreement as to the applicability of the Act is whether the events complained of in the claim have been properly stated within the time of occurrence as to enable the court calculate and arrive at the arithmetic of three months envisaged in S. 2(a) of the Act or not and whether the defendants did not go outside their public duties when they did what is complained of by the plaintiff. Paragraph 11 of the statement of claim indicates that when the result of Patrick Magit was presented to the senate on 27.8.98, 1st defendant inserted the words complained in this suit.

Paragraph 15 of same claim states that when the Senate again reconvened the result was again presented. That 1st defendant with active connivance and instigation of 2nd defendant presented a memo objecting to the thesis of Patrick Magit. That date of this second meeting of the senate is not disclosed. Paragraph 18 refers to what 3rd defendant wrote to the Vice Chancellor when he took over from plaintiff as Director of Centre for Food and Strategic Studies. Again no date is given in the pleadings.

From the pleadings before the court, it is not possible to pin down all these happenings to the date of 27.8.98 as erroneously assumed by counsel to the defendants. As time is of essence in considering the objection and as no enough evidence has been disclosed from the pleadings relied upon to support the defendants objection, the objection cannot stand. I do not consider it necessary under the circumstances to consider the 2nd issue, which relates to whether the defendants acted within their duties or not as that will be touching on the merit of the case. I dismiss the objection of defendants for inadequate date on the event from the pleadings.

SGD.

(Justice I. Hwande) J

50.6.2001.

3.10.2001.

Plaintiff in court.

Defendant absent.

Mr J. S. Okutepa with him Mohammed Adeniyi Esq for the plaintiff, Mr S. P. Ejale for the defendants.

Mr Okutepa. This matter is for hearing. I had been working under assumption that there was a move for settlement initiated by the university council. I hoped that we would be "able to settle the matter out of court. I did not take steps to subpoena the university for vital documents that I needed to tender in the matter today. Just Yesterday I got to hear that the conduct of 1st and 2nd defendants towards plaintiff appears to show that they are not serious with the efforts at settlement. It was too late to apply for a subpoena to serve on the university to tender the documents today. It is in light of the above that I apply for a date to enable us prove our case.

Mr Ejale. On the contrary my instructions are that the university Governing Council has set up a reconciliation Committee to look into the various disputes. I got this information from the legal officer of the university. The university council has asked for more time to enable them settle the parties out of court. On that instruction I ask for adjournment to report on the settlement efforts. We are however not forcing the hand of anybody.

Mr Okutepa. I will ask that matters should remain as they are for settlement to take place.

Court. The court is of the view that following the appointment of a new Vice Chancellor for the university and the interest of the Governing Council to settle this matter out of court, another opportunity should be given for parties to attempt settlement out of court as prayed by defence counsel. The suit is adjourned to 22.11.2001 for patties to settle out of court if they can end report back on that date.

SGD.

(Justice I. Hwande) J. 3.10.2001.

23.1 •. 2002.

Parties absent.

Mr T. A Ihua holding the brief of J. A, Okutepa for plaintiff.

Mr S. P. Ejale for the defendants.

Mr Ihua. I have instructions that parties are making moves to settle out of court. That the process of settlement is almost completed. We ask for another date to enable the parties complete their settlement efforts.

Mr Ejale. I have similar instructions. We have almost reached a settlement.

Court. The suit is further adjourned to 15.3.2002 for parties to complete their settlement efforts.

Sgd: (Justice I. Hwande) J. 23.1.2002.

6.5.2002. Plaintiff in court.

Mr J. S. Okutepa with him is Mrs Okwo Nwadieke for the plaintiff.

Mr S. P. Ejale for the defendants.

Mr Okutepa. The matter is for report of settlement. It will appear as if this settlement is attempted only in theory. We made proposal to the administration of the university in writing. There has been no reply and there has been no positive response. While we are desirous of giving the new administration room to ensure peace on the campus we will appreciate if they take a more serious step than the lip service they are paying to the issue of settlement out of court. We are not encouraged by failure of defendants to respond even to basic issues we raised.

Mr Ejale. I understand that the plaintiff is demanding some condition to be fulfilled before he will accept a settlement. Most of these conditions are such that they cannot be accepted. We have encouraged the university to settle out of court.

Court. The parties are given one more adjournment to see if they can settle out of court. The suit is adjourned to 1.7.2002 for parties to reach a settlement out of court.

Signed

(Justice I. Hwande) J.

7.5.2002

1.7.2002.

Parties absent.

Mr J. S. Okutepa with him Mrs. Nwadieke, Nomji, and Pepe for the plaintiff.

Mr Okutepa. The matter is for report of settlement. I have instructions from my client to withdraw this case also. The plaintiff is directed by the Governing Council of the University to withdraw this suit and all the suits my client has against the university. I therefore apply to withdraw the suit.

Court: Upon the application of learned counsel for the plaintiff to withdraw this suit for amicable settlement out of court, this suit is hereby struck out.

SGD.

(Justice **I.** Hwande) J.

1.7.2002.

Case 3

Fundamental Human Rights Enforcement in the Matter of Centre for Food and Agricultural Strategy (CEFAS)

In the High Court of Justice of Benue State
In the Benue Judicial Division
Holden at Makurdi

MHC/305m/99

Before His Lordship: Hon. Justice D. T. Ahura (Judge); Hon. Justice I. Hwande (Judge)

Between
Dr G. B. Ayoola (Applicant)
And
University of Agriculture Makurdi, Prof. Erastus Gyang (VC), University of Agriculture Makurdi, Administrative Committee on CEFAS (Respondents)

Case sequel to Sixth Onslaught: I instituted the case against the respondents in 1999 for the enforcement of my fundamental human rights. My lawyer filed a motion ex parte seeking an order of the court to grant me leave to enforce my fundamental rights to fair hearing, as guaranteed by the constitution. He also asked for an order restraining the respondents from further interfering with my fundamental rights to fair hearing and an order staying all actions relating to the application. The motion was brought pursuant to Fundamental Human Rights Enforcement 1979 for an order to issue to stop the respondents in their desperate bid to punish me at all costs. It was granted by court, to the effect that they be restrained from any further disciplinary steps to be taken against me, pending determination of matters in court.

The court, after reading my counsel's application, granted me leave to apply for the enforcement of my fundamental human rights within seven days of granting the application. With the leave, the respondents were restrained from entertaining matters relating to me in respect of the application until the substantive case was determined.

In the substantive matters, I claimed that the allegation made against me by the second respondent was a result of the fact that the relationship between us had deteriorated, and the second respondent threatened to deal with me because of that. Consequently in order for the second respondent to carry out his threat to deal with me, he set up an improperly constituted committee to investigate my tenure of office as director of CEFAS at the material time. As argued by my lawyer in the application, the acts of the respondents were ultra vires and a clear violation of my fundamental human rights. A series of interlocutory applications ensued, filed by both parties. After a series of adjournments were granted at the instance of both parties, the court proceeded to trial.

Meanwhile, in spite of this order, the committee had continued to hold its sittings and submitted its report, based on which a letter of warning was issued to me. My lawyer contested the decision of administration to issue me a warning in court, thereby applying for the VC and the registrar to be summoned to appear before the court to explain why they acted in contempt of the order of 17/08/99. The opposition lawyer responded by saying that the cause of the warning was because the applicant had refused to hand over the office since 1998 and that these facts were not stated in the affidavit for which the leave was granted.

Advancing his arguments, my lawyer posited that the CEFAS committee was set up as a result of Professor Gyang's disappointment on the refusal of the minister of agriculture to implement the recommendations of his UNIAGRIC administration and the VC to get me and some other lecturers dismissed because of our alleged roles in the students' rampage. As a result, the fairness of the CEFAS committee could not be guaranteed because I had not been accused but was invited to the committee as a witness. The committee had gone ahead to serve me a warning letter without a chance to defend myself.

Warning, according to the university constitution, is a form of punishment. Because the allegation of theft levelled against me was a criminal offence, the committee had no competence to investigate the matter. No administrative body had the competence to investigate crime; therefore, the warning letter served me was a product of ultra vires. Not only did the letter have no basis to stand, but also it was issued after the court had issued an injunction restraining the respondents from acting on the act complained of, pending the determination of the substantive suit.

My lawyer posited that the registrar had been hasty in issuing the warning: he had contravened a section of the senior staff regulations that held that he must obtain evidence of three warnings served me by my HOD before going ahead with serving me his own letter.

The opposition counsel opposed the application. He contended that the terms of the committee were not spelt out and its members were not named. He further argued that the ex parte motion was granted on 17/08/99, whereas the warning letter was served on 01/11/99, about three months after the stay order. He urged the court to discountenance the application because it could not know whether the senate or the vice chancellor set up the committee without the terms of reference.

On 5 April 2001, judgment was delivered in the matter.

> Ruling
>
> The applicant in this matter is seeking for the following reliefs:

(1) A Declaration that 3rd Respondent as set up by 1st and 2nd Respondents is unconstitutional, null and void of no effect whatsoever being a breach of applicant fundamental right to fair hearing.

(2) A declaration that the setting up of 3rd Respondent and its composition is null and void and of no effect whatsoever as there is no provision for such a committee in the law establishing 1st Respondent.

(3) An order directing that the Respondent stop any further sitting or investigation or doing whatsoever anything whatsoever related to any such sitting or investigation or acting in consequence thereof.

(4) An order of perpetual injunction restraining the Respondents by themselves, their representatives, agents or privies from interfering with applicant's right to fair hearing or doing anything whatsoever arising from such breach.

The motion is brought pursuant to the Fundamental Rights enforcement Procedure Rules) 1979. It has been deposed in the affidavit in support of the application that the applicant is the past director for Centre for Food and Strategic Studies (CEFAS) of 1st Respondent. That 3rd Respondent was set up by 2nd Respondent who is the Vice Chancellor and Chief executive of 1st Respondent to investigate the applicant. That before 3rd Respondent was set up the relationship between 2nd Respondent and the applicant was far from cordial. That the relationship deteriorated when in 1998 the applicant aired his view concerning the incessant problems in the University to Minister of Agriculture. That when Mr I. U. Udoemenem became head of CEFAS, he made false allegations against the applicant. That relying on those false allegations the 2nd Respondent set up two committees to investigate the applicant. That the two committees found nothing against the applicant.

That when the Minister of Agriculture refused to implement the recommendations of a panel set up by 1st and 2nd Respondents after student's rampage as relates to the applicant the 2nd Respondent felt disappointed and set up 3rd Respondent.

That the membership of 3rd Respondent is such that its fairness cannot be guaranteed. Moving the application J. S. Okutepa Esq. learned counsel submitted that a person who is not accused and has no opportunity of defense of himself cannot be punished. That applicant was invited before the committee only as a witness.

He referred to Exhibit 'B' and contended that by the University Regulations at page 55 warning is punishment. That S.36 of the 1999 Constitution guarantees the applicant's Right of fair hearing. That the applicant was investigated regarding theft of books and theft of his personal file. That the investigation also covered matters involving criminal breach of trust. Okutepa submitted that 3rd Respondent was not competent to investigate criminal offence, as no administrative body is competent to do so. He relied on Garba V. University of Maiduguri (1986) 1 NWLR (pt. 18) 550 at 576–578. It is the submission of Okutepa also that Exhibit 'B' is a product of an ultra vires and it has no foundation on which to stand. That the University had no authority to set up 3rd Respondent.

It is also the submission of Okutepa that Exhibit 'B' was issued after the High Court has issued an injunction restraining the Respondent from acting on the facts complained of pending the determination of the substantive action. That this order was served on 1st Respondent and yet it was ignored by the Respondents. That this undermined the dignity of the court. He referred to Military Governor of Lagos State **V.** Chief Odumegwu Ojukwu (1986) 1 All NIR 194 at 201–203. He urges the Court to issue an order of mandatory injunction to quash Exhibit 'A'. That no evidence was taken before Exhibit 'B' was issued. It has to be quashed for lack of fair hearing also. He referred to p.56 of Senior Staff Regulations and argued that before the Registrar will issue a warning there must be evidence that there were three warnings from Head of Department on the person involved. That there is no such evidence in the case of the applicant. The rules have actually indicated that after three warnings from the Head of Department any further offence shall attract a more severe disciplinary action as may be recommended by the Head of Department concerned to the Registrar for further necessary action.

It has not been made clear by the Respondents whether the applicant was warned up to three times before this conduct was referred to the Ag. Registrar of the University. Mr Okutepa submitted that the Registrar was hasty in issuing the warning in Exhibit 'B'. Okutepa also submitted that the Vice Chancellor or University can only set up panels that are backed by the University law. That the 1st and 2nd Respondents cannot set up 3rd Respondent. It is only the council that can do it.

S.P. Ejale learned counsel to the Respondents has opposed the application. The Respondents filed two counter affidavits. He contended that the terms of the committee are not spelt out and members of the committee are not named. That exhibit 'C' cannot be the term of the committee.

Mr Ejale submitted that Ex parte Motion was granted on 17-8-99. Whereas exhibit 'B' was authorized on 1-11-99 after the stay order. He contends that the warning relates to an event that happened in 1998.

It is also the submission of Ejale Esq. that Exhibit 'B' relates to handing over of office and it does not involve criminal investigation as contended by applicant counsel.

It is the contention of Respondent's counsel also that bias has not been established by the applicant in this application. That he who asserts must prove. He urged the court to discountenance the application submitting that whether it was set up by Senate or Vice Chancellor without the terms of reference the court is not in a position to know.

On the 1st relief I am inclined to agree with Respondent's learned counsel that it has not been established before this court who set up 3rd Respondent. In that document is not before the court. In the absence of actual proof I will not act on speculation and as such I see no basis for granting 1st relief. It is refused on the ground that it has not been established before the court.

2nd relief is that the court should declare the setting up of 3rd Respondent null and void. Mr Okutepa argued that 3rd Respondent was set up to investigate criminal allegations against the applicant and that it lacks the power. S. 16 of Decree 48 of 1992 empowers the Vice Chancellor or Senate to set up an investigative panel to determine whether a prima facie case has been established against any member of staff.

From the tenor of the contents in Exhibit 'B' it does appear that the Administrative Committee on the Centre for Food and Agriculture Strategy (CEFAS) was set up to consider the issue of failure of applicant to hand over to his successor as the new Acting Director of CEFAS. The complaints that applicant refused to hand over certain number of books and computer to his successor to my mind did not relate to any criminal investigation. Nowhere in the letter is it alleged or concluded that applicant converted those items to his own use and did not handover with intent to cause wrongful loss to the University and unduly enrich himself. Garba V. University of Maiduguri is not to the effect that if the matter investigated is looked into by an administrative body is capable of criminal interpretation, the panel should hands off the issue. The substance of what was set out to be investigated is what should matter and not what such investigation is capable of confirming in the minds of the person investigated or some other people.

As the main complaint in this application was our lack of handover to a new Director and not to investigate any Criminal complaints against applicant, I am of the view that the ease of Garba V. University of Maiduguri is no assistance to the facts under consideration. I am also unable to hold that the 1st and 2nd Respondents lacked the power to set up the committee. That was administrative in nature. I hold that 3rd Respondent was not set up to investigate crime and its setting up cannot be declared void ab initio. I refuse to uphold.

3rd relief appears as belated in most of it as by exhibit 'B' the Report has been submitted and the result is what is confirmed in Exhibit 'B'. The relevant aspect of the relief is that the court should direct the Respondents to stop any action based on the investigation. This order the court will make if there are good grounds for doing so. The next relief has its basis on fair hearing.

Applicant submitted that there is no indication anywhere that applicant was confronted with any allegation accusing him to enable him respond before he was served Exhibit 'B'.

Mr Ejale for the Respondents did not contest the fact that warning is a form of discipline under the University Regulations.

The applicant was not queried to enable him face the allegations made against him from such report granted that the Respondents were right to consider it at that time. In University of Agriculture **V.** Grace Jack (2000) FWLR (pt. 20) p720 at 742 Mangaji JCA stated in his lead Judgment:

"I think only one issue will settle this question one way or the other and that is whether the Respondent_was confronted during the sitting of the investigating panel as a person accused of a crime that she was simply invited as a witness. If indeed she was only invited as a witness, then she could not at the end of the day be found guilty without changing her with specific misdeeds for which notice should be given her."

The University has repeated the same error in this case where by issuing a warning letter exhibit 'B' to applicant after he appeared before 3rd Respondent only as a witness. Such a letter cannot be allowed to stand.

Apart from the above fact it has been conceded by counsel to Respondents that exhibit 'B' was authored at the time the High Court made an order suspending any further action on the facts in this application pending the hearing and determination of the matter. This order embodied in Exhibit 'A' was served on the Respondents. Exhibit A is dated 17-8-99. Not moved by the existence of exhibit 'A' the Respondents went ahead and issued exhibit 'B' warning the applicant on the outcome of the work of 3rd Respondent on 1-11-99.

Mr Ejale, hard put by the Respondents' conduct, gave a lame excuse that the facts in Exhibit 'B' occurred in 1998. Where the facts occurred in 1998, the investigation was carried out in 1999 and the court made an order restraining any action against the applicant based on the report.

Even though we have many despots here and there in the country it is the collective will of Nigerians that they be governed by Rule of Law and not that of the despots. It is in this wise that S. 36 of the 1999 Constitution has the provision of fair hearing on any citizen accused of wrong doing embodied in court. Where a people who are supposed to be civilized behave as if they are not, they have to be shown the correct thing to do and they should not be encouraged in their misconduct.

By issuing exhibit 'B' after the court made an order in Exhibit 'A' the Respondents took a step in futility and for this reason to exhibit 'B' cannot be allowed to stand. In Governor of Lagos State V. Ojukwu (1986) 1 NWLR (pt.18) 621 Obaseki JSC stated at p. 638 that.

"The Nigerian Constitution is founded on the rule of law the primary meaning of which is that everything must be done according to Law, It means also that Government should be conducted within the framework of recognized rules and principles which restrict disciplinary power."

Because exhibit 'B' was issued without respecting the Constitution requirements for fair hearing and because it was issued at the time the respondents were restrained by an order of Court from dealing with the subject matter pending the determination of this application and it was issued in violation of the procedure laid down in the regulations regarding discipline of the staff of applicant caliber I hereby declare exhibit 'B' which is the warning issued to applicant as null and void of no effect whatsoever.

Respondents are hereby restrained from interfering with the right of applicant to fair hearing or doing anything whatsoever to him arising from such breach.

(Justice I. Hwande) J

5-4-2001

Plaintiff in court

Defendants represented by Mary Agogo

Mr J. O. Okutepa for the applicant with him is S. Nomji

Mr Ejale: For the respondents.

Mr Okutepa I will not ask for cost.

Court: No cost is awarded.

> (SGD)
>
> I. Hwande, Judge,
>
> 5-4-2001

Okutepa: We will urge that motion number MHC/149M/2000 be withdrawn for the sake of peace.

Mr Ejale: No objection

Court: The court commends the attitude of applicant seeking to withdraw the motion citing the VC and Ag. Registrar for contempt.

The motion stands withdrawn and it is struck out.

> (SGD)
>
> I. Hwande. Judge,
>
> 5-4-2001

Case 4

Direct Criminal Prosecution of Dr J. C. Umeh for Mischief and Related Offences in the Matter of My Wrongful Suspension

In The Magistrate Court of the Makurdi Magisterial District Holden in Makurdi

Case No/DCR/47c1/2001
Before His Lordships: T. M. Wergba (Senior Magistrate II/ PACJ); E. A. Arii, Esq., Chief Magistrate I

Between
    Dr. G. B. Ayoola (Complainant)
And
    Dr. J. C. Umeh (Defendant)

Case sequel to Twelfth Onslaught: This case pertained to the role Umeh played in his capacity as the head of my department, at which time he wrote three queries in one day to be issued to me. He mischievously inserted staggered dates, and without waiting for my response, he also wrote a report to the VC in which I was alleged of several fictitious offences in order to help the VC nail me down at all costs. In particular, he said that I was absent from duties without authorisation, amongst other spurious allegations. Unfortunately for him, the innocent departmental messenger entered all the letters and the report in the departmental register at once and in a single sequence, thereby providing me with proof of criminal mischief on the part of Umeh as contained on the charge sheet.

i. Criminal defamation pursuant to section 39, and 372 of Penal Code;
ii. Injurious incorrect document with intent to commit injury (section 124 Penal Code) and
iii. Giving false evidence, S. 158 Penal Code.

The trial of Dr J. C. Umeh as charged commenced on 30 of January 2001. He pleaded not guilty on all charges. The court declined to take the plea of the accused person for the offence of giving false evidence under S. 158 Penal Code, for want of jurisdiction. The counsel to the accused person applied for the bail, building his argument on the factors and conditions for the grant of bail. My counsel took objection to bail, and the argument ensued as follows.

> Mr Ejale: I ask for bail of accused under section 341 (2) Criminal Procedure Code (CPC). All the offences are bailable and subject to your discretion. I have the instructions of the accused person to say that he will comply with all bail conditions if granted it. He will provide a fit surety, he will not interfere with investigation and he will not jump bail. I also apply that bail be on self cognissance. The purpose of bail is to secure the accused attendance at his trial. The accused person is an associate Prof. with the Federal University of Agriculture Makurdi. He is on permanent and on pensionable appointment.

> J. S. Okutepa: Appearing for complainant along with two counsels. We take objection to bail being granted the accused. If bail is granted, he will commit other offences of similar nature brought to this court. Indeed after filing this document, he committed another offence. We have documents to prove this. The offences for which accused is arraigned are not ordinarily bailable. The status of an accused person is no determinate factor of bail operating otherwise Mohammed Abacha, Mustapha and Co. will not be in Prison today. The accused person is the head of Department of the complainant if released on bail

will continue to use his biro in framing complaints as already done.

The accused person's plea for the offence under section 158 (2) P.C. is not taken. Views show that the court views very seriously the nature of the offence in question. I submit that before an accused can be entitled to bail under section 341 (2) Criminal Procedure Code, he should demonstrate with concrete evidence with determination not to further commit other offences. The Professorship of this accused is also questionable. In one breath, accused person is addressed as a Doctor and in another as a Prof. without any back up proof.

The Justice of this matter demands that this accused person be kept in prison to learn his lessons. On the issue of safe bail, I submit that there is no law that says that a Prof. who is arraigned before a court should be granted safe bail. There are known cases of Professors running away from this country. Prof. Wole Soyinka is one such example. I urge you to refuse bail for this accused person. We are ready now to proceed with hearing in this case.

Mr Ejale: It is trite law that the issue of bail should not be lumped together with the issue of punishment. The issue of bail should not also be mixed up with complainants desire to humiliate. This court should distance itself from such sentiments. Justice must be manifestly seen to be done. If the accused is remanded in prison for frivolous direct criminal case, what will the public feel? This court has declined jurisdiction for the offence under section 158 (2) Criminal procedure case not for the seriousness of the offence alleged but for lack of jurisdiction.

Court: The offences alleged against this person under sections 391, 393 and 124 penal code are offences that attract a jail term of 2–3 years. The offence alleged under section 158 penal code attracts jail term of 7–14 years. This shows that these offences are ordinarily not bailable particularly that under section 158 penal code. The refusal of bail to an accused person is never for the purpose of punishing or humiliating him or her.

The court refuses bail to an accused if the bail conditions contained in section 341 (2) criminal procedure code in addition to those to be imposed by the court are not met. The accused person in this case is a well-known person from what is before me. It is therefore not likely that he will breach the bail conditions if granted. Moreover, he has orally undertaken through his counsel to abide by all bail conditions as contained in section 341 (2) criminal procedure code. In the absence of any evidence to the contrary, I shall exercise my discretion under section 341 (2) criminal procedure code in accused's favour to enable him prepare for defence. Self-bail shall however not be granted this accused as prayed by her counsel. The accused is hereby granted bail in the sum of #5,000.00 with one fit surety in the same amount. Surety's passport photograph only is to be deposited with this court.

(Sgd)

T. K. Wergba

We were prepared to delve into the hearing straightaway, but counsel to the accused person came up with the usual gimmicks of raising a preliminary objection on grounds of abuse of court process, which were hinged on the absence of the fiat of the attorney general in respect of charges of criminal defamation of character and injurious falsehood alleged. Therefore at the accused counsel's instance, the case was adjourned to 26 of February 2001.

On the next adjourned date, 26 February 2001, which was for hearing, the following exchanges took place.

26/2/2001

Coram: T. M. Wergba, Senior Magistrate II/PACJI

J. S. Okutepa, Esq., appearing with S. Nomji, Esq. for complainant

S.P. Ejale, Esq., for accused

Complainant: Present

Accused: Present

Mr Ejale: This matter was adjourned to this day to enable defence counsel file preliminary objection. Due to a variety of reasons, the objection is not ready and therefore not placed before the court. We have taken some of our actions however, but which is not for the consumption of this court. We therefore ask for date, the preliminary objections are not in place, and then we will go on with hearing.

Mr Okutekpa: We take objection to the application for an adjournment. We came this morning ready to argue the objection my learned friend orally applied and the matter was accordingly adjourned to today. We are therefore taken by surprise that their objections are not ready. We cannot continue to take adjournments at the wishes of the defence. I urge the court to order that the defence should go on with the objections today or make a clear cut statement that they are not ready to go on with the preliminary objection so that we can take an adjournment and proceed with hearing at the next adjourned date. If the other actions taken by my learned friend are not for this court consumption, then, he should not have ever mentioned them in the first place.

Court: I hereby decline to proceed with the trial of this case. I cannot work under pressure as to do so will not to be in the interest of justice. I shall therefore transfer this matter to another court of competent jurisdiction.

Mr Okutepa: We have no choice of court. It can be transferred to any competent court

Mr Ejale: I suggest that the matter be transferred to Chief Magistrate Court Makurdi for reassigning maybe to another court.

Court: Case hereby transferred under Section 147 criminal procedure code to Chief Magistrate Court I Makurdl. Case to be mentioned in that court on 8/3/2001.

(Sgd)

T. M. Wergbaa, Senior Magistrate II/PACJI

26/2/2001

The case resumed on 28 September 2001, and Umeh's bail was extended by the new magistrate, Mr E. A. Arii, Esq. Further adjustments were granted, but eventually the case progressed to hearing on 14 May 2002. My counsel contemplated merging the case with another case involving Professor Njike, which he quickly withdrew after putting an oral application forward as follows.

> We apply that this case be merged with that (another) case to enable us prosecute the two accused together because the allegations against the accused there and the allegations against this accused were committed in the course of the same transaction. We also intend to adduce evidence to show that Dr Umeh and the accused in Suit NO. DCR/12c1/2000 ordered and abetted themselves in the commission of the offences. By Section 221 (a) (b) (c) (d) Criminal procedure Code both cases can be tried together. We submit that it is not the sameness of the transaction that matters here, but the continuity of purpose. We refer to the case of Maruna V. state (1972) 8/9 S.C. 174 at 205. The purpose is to portray the complainant as an irresponsible academician. I withdraw my application. We are to go on separately.

> Then the proceedings continued with my evidence as the complainant.

> I know the accused. He is Dr J. C. Umeh, a colleague in the department where I work. I knew him in the postgraduate school of the University of Ibadan, first. I joined the University of Agriculture in 1988. Dr Umeh joined us about 1990 or 1991 in the Department of Agricultural Economics. I was first Director of the Centre for Food and Agricultural Strategy and also the Head of Department (HOD) of Agricultural Economics, from 1996–1998. By December, 7, 2000, the accused had become the Head of Department of Agricultural Economics for six months. The first HOD was Prof.

Patrick Erhabor. Dr J. C. Umeh succeeded him as HOD. I took over from Dr J. C. Umeh. And after two years Prof. Erhabor took over from me. Next Mr N. I. Achamber took over from Prof. Erhabor. Dr J. C. Umeh took over from Mr N. I. Achamber. Of all these HODs, I have had problem with Dr J. C. Umeh only. The accused became bitter when I took over from him as HOD in November 1996 when I was still the Director of the centre. A new Vice Chancellor has just been appointed in the previous September by name, Prof. E. O. Gyang, who met my department in a "bad situation", with Dr J. C. Umeh as HOD of my Department and Prof. Erhabor as the Dean of the College. The "bad situation" had many parts, but one was very outstanding, and that one was that since 1991 up to 1997 when the Department and the College had started postgraduate Programmes and have been admitting students into these programmes year after year no single student had graduated as at 1997 - under the leadership of the accused as HOD. The Vice Chancellor invited me to two meetings as Director of the Centre where he expressed all his feelings to me about the situation in my department. He said he had been inundated with petitions about my department from inside and outside the university. Therefore, he urged me to take over the running of the department from the accused. My initial reaction was to decline politely, because the reason why he wanted me to go and administer the Department was the same reason why he did not want me to leave my Post as Director of the centre. And that reason was for me to go and rebuild the Department as I built the Centre before he came. After much persuasion, I took up the challenge and took over from the accused. The accused was practically unfriendly throughout my tenure of two years. He expressed that he felt humiliated out of the post. He did not co-operate to run the Department with me. He gave me pressure from behind constantly. I can remember the case of one Victor Ehigiator who was his student before I took over the headship position. Victor had problem with the accused as his supervisor before I became HOD. His case was one of the Postgraduate studies students the Vice Chancellor wanted me to address. The Senate of the University gave me only one Semester to clear all the backlog of M.Sc. cases. I organised seminars and examinations for the students but the accused refused to release Victor to join the others in this exercise, by totally refusing to read his draft thesis since the student came back from the field. I intervened and begged the accused and sent the University Community to the accused to no avail. He insisted that he would take his pound of flesh from that student because he offended him privately. Eventually, after six months of my intervention, I went to the senate to change the accused as the Supervisor of this student to myself. The accused petitioned the senate against me through the Dean of the post-Graduate school who supported him. The Dean of postgraduate school is one Prof. Njike. The senate changed him from supervising the student and I was formally assigned to supervise the student. We applied for external examiner for the student. The accused person and the same Prof. Njike opposed it. Again the matter went to senate. The senate overruled their joint objection and an external examiner was appointed for the student. Thirdly, the accused and Professor Njike delayed the invitation of the External Examiner for one and half years. I generated several memos to senate before the examination panel was constituted. On the day of the examination, the accused was made to be one of the examiners of the same student by the same Prof. Njike not minding the previous problems and his bad relationship with the student. The accused delayed in coming for the oral examination for 30 minutes in order to frustrate the holding of the examination. We had already started the examination for about 10 minutes before the accused showed up. He interrupted the examination and insisted that he wanted to raise an issue. He made his point and wanted the panel not to go ahead with the examination. Before the end of the examination, the accused again brought out a list of farmers the student interviewed when accused was the supervisor. He claimed that list contained 194 names of farmers. But that when he read the draft thesis, he saw a list of 528 names. He then concluded that the student had told a lie in the draft thesis which he supervised. The student denied the allegation. Rather, the student raised counter allegation of falsehood and witch hunting against the accused. The student alleged that the list he gave to the accused then was longer than what the accused was presenting to the panel. The student asked for ten minutes to allow him to bring the full list he gave to the accused. This request was not granted. Instead the Panel asked the student to show his list to the HOD and the accused for verification later. The panel has resolved that the student passed the examination. Accused was a member of the panel who endorsed the form 16 stating that the student passed the examination. After that examination, the student immediately provided to me the list which I asked him to submit formally. When he did, I invited the accused to a meeting for verification of the list together with me, but he refused to attend. What we saw next was a publication by Prof. Njike intending to repeat the examination this student passed, which intention failed to materialise. In February 2002, the accused produced what he called "attestation" of this same examination I have been talking about. I have read the further and better counter-affidavit filed by Professor Njike. This is the affidavit. The so-called "attestation" of the accused is exhibit 2 in the said further and better counter-affidavit.

Okutepa: We wish to tender the said further and better counter-affidavit in evidence.

Ejale: I object to its admissibility. One, the affidavit sought to be tendered is not the original—nor is it an office copy. I rely on Section 79 Evidence Act. We submit that the affidavit was not filed in this court and it is only such affidavit that this court can recognize. The case in which this affidavit came from was a civil matter in the high court. And the person standing trial here is not the person who deposed to the affidavit. That the deponent is not deposing to any fact that is before this court. An affidavit should be headed in the court in which the affidavit should be used. For the reason I object to the admissibility of this document. We refer to Section 78 Evidence Act.

Okutepa: We submit that this objection is misconceived and should be overruled. The affidavit sought to be tendered is a private document of the complainant. The complainant has laid foundation that he read the affidavit and that he has seen the document made by the accused attached to the Affidavit. It was not a Photostat copy of the document. The stamp of the Commissioner of Oaths is thereon. Therefore it qualifies as the official copy as defined in Section 79 of the Evidence Act. The Section empowers this court to recognize this affidavit for all purposes. It is wrong to say that the words "court's use" meant to be the court where the affidavit was filed. This court is also a court. We submit that Section 78 of Evidence Act is not relevant here. The court is not directing that the facts be proved; rather we are tendering it in evidence. Sections 6 and 7 of the Evidence Act makes this Document very relevant in this case. The affidavit is no longer a public document since we have been served with it. It has become our private document. Section 109 Evidence Act refers. The complainant can therefore tender it.

Ejale: We refer to Section 90 Evidence Act.

Court: Case further adjourned to 1/1/2002 for ruling and continuation of hearing. Bail extended.

>(Signed)
>
>E. A. Arii, Esq.
>
>Chief Magistrate I
>
>14/6/2002

1/7/2002

Corams: E. A. Arii, I. Chief Magistrate I.

Accused present

Counsel absent—bereaved

Complainant absent

Counsel absent

Court: Case further adjourned to 9/8/2002 for ruling and continuation of hearing

(Sgd)

E. A. Arii, Esq.

Chief Magistrate I

1/7/2002

9/8/2002

Coram: E. A. Arii, Chief Magistrate I

Accused present.

S. P. Ejale, Esq, for accused Complainant absent

Counsel absent

Ejale: Neither the complainant nor the accused is present. I am, however aware that the complainant has filed a letter of discontinuance (at the instance of the new VC who has sued for peace and is seeking out-of-court settlement). His lawyer also talked to me that they intend to withdraw the complaint. I therefore apply that the complaint be struck out and accused discharged under Section 165 Criminal Procedure Code.

Court: The complaint is hereby struck out for want of appearance of complainant.

The accused is discharged under Section 165 Criminal Procedure Coode.

(Sgd)

E. A. Arii, Esq.

Chief Magistrate I

9/8/2002

Case 5

Fair Hearing in the Matter of Student Rampage

In The Federal High Court of Nigeria
in the Jos Judicial Division
Holden at Jos

FHC/J/CS/77/99

Between
Professor Ikenna Onyido, Arch. Victor Salau Daudu, Dr G. B. Ayoola, Dr. O. O. Agbede (Applicants)

And
University of Agriculture Makurdi, the Vice Chancellor, University Of Agriculture Makurdi, the Permanent Secretary, Federal Ministry of Agriculture and Natural Resources (Respondents)

Case sequel to First Onslaught and Second Onslaught: Following the student rampage in the university on 24–26 January 1999, which resulted in the destruction of some private and public property, a panel of investigation was set up to investigate the rampage. Without any allegations leveled against us, but by invitation as witnesses only, I and three others (Prof. Ikenna Onyido, Arch. Victor Salau Daudu and Dr O. O. Agbede) were indicted by the panel of investigation. The recommendation of the panel was approved for implementation, which clearly was to further the pursuit of the ethnic cleansing agenda of the vice chancellor and the executive witch-hunting of me in particular. Our only hope, as per the justice of the report of the panel of investigation, was to approach the court by taking a writ challenging the report and subsequent approval by the senate before its implementation commenced.

During the pendency of the suit, by means of a motion on notice, we asked the court (Federal High Court, Jos Division) for an order of interlocutory injunction restraining the defendants/respondents, who were the University of Agriculture Makurdi; the Vice-Chancellor, University of Agriculture Makurdi; the Permanent Secretary, Federal Ministry of Agriculture and Natural Resources; their servants, agents, or privies; and anyone acting on their instruction in implementing the report and recommendations of the senate panel of investigation vis-a-vis the student rampage of 24–26 January 1999. This was pending the determination of the substantive suit, and for such further order or orders that the honourable court may deem fit to make in the circumstance. The order was expressly granted, and the case eventually proceeded to hearing.

However, owing to the incessant and long adjournment of the hearing from one date to another, the hearing never took place until the settlement out of court took effect, and the case was literally abandoned. Hereunder, the main gist of the case can be gleaned from the affidavit of the applicants.

> Affidavit in Support of Motion
>
> I, Arc. Victor Salau Daudu, Male, Christian. Director, Physical Facility, Nigerian Citizen of House No. 28, Senior Staff Quarters, University of Agriculture, Makurdi, Benue state do make oath and say as follows:
>
> 1. That I am the 2nd Plaintiff/Applicant herein as well as the Director, Physical Facility with the 1st Defendant/Respondent and by virtue of my position I am conversant with the facts deposed to hereunder

2. That I have the consent and authority of the other Plaintiffs/Applicants who are Lecturers with the 1st Respondent as well as our Solicitors, AKUBO & CO., to depose to this Affidavit.

3. That I know as a fact that there was a Student rampage on 24th and 26th January, 1999 at the University of Agriculture, Makurdi, Benue State in the course of which some Public and Private Property were damaged.

4. That I know as a fact that following the said Students Rampage on 24th and 26th January 1999, a Panel of Investigation was set up to Investigate the matter.

5. That I am informed by the 4th Plaintiff/Applicant and I verily believe him to be true that the students of the 1st Defendant/Respondent visited his house at No. 43, Senior Staff Quarters, University of Agriculture Makurdi on 26th January, 1999 and thereupon caused series of damage consequent upon which he wrote a memorandum to the Senate Panel of Investigation. The copy of his Memorandum is attached and marked as Exhibit 'A'.

6. That I know as a fact that the 2nd Defendant/Respondent who was himself a victim of the said Rampage especially as the Vice-chancellor's lodge/Residence was set ablaze leading to personal losses of Property, presided over the meeting at the Senate that constituted the Panel in question.

7. That I know as a fact that the 2nd defendant/Respondent manipulated the composition of the Senate Panel of Investigation to suit his Personal purpose.

8. That specifically, I know as a fact that the Committee of Deans and Directors which modified and/or interfered with the composition of the Senate Panel of Investigation on 27th January1999 Presided over by the 2nd Respondent was unknown to the University set-up.

9. That I know as a fact that the senate of the 1st Respondent on 29th January, 1999 under the chairmanship of the 2nd Respondent merely rubber stamped or ratified the change in the 'composition of the Senate Panel of Investigation as effected by the committee of Deans and Directors held on 27th January, 1999.

10. That I know as a fact that the Senate Panel of Investigation variously invited I and the other Plaintiffs/Applicants to testify before it. The letters of invitation are attached and marked as Exhibits 'B' 'C' 'D' and 'E' respectively.

11. That I know as a fact that none of us was put on trial or invited as a suspect or accused person before the said Senate Panel of investigation.

12. That I know as a fact that the said Senate Panel of Investigation submitted its Report in four various volume the 1st and 2nd Respondents on 6th May, 1999.

13. That I know as a fact that the 2nd Respondent in his address on the receipt of the said Report on 6th May, 1999 and which was widely Published on both print and Electronic Media made statements that were highly Prejudicial of the final outcome even before the Senate met to consider same. The copy of 2nd Respondent address is attached and marked as Exhibit 'F'.

14. That I know as a fact that the senate met on 10th May 1999 to consider the Report of the Senate Panel of Investigation and thereupon approved the recommendations of the Panel against us for implementation.

15. That I know as a fact that the said Senate Panel indicted I and the other Plaintiffs/Applicants and made recommendations that the Authority takes appropriate action against us.

16. That I know as a fact that the Chairman of the said Senate Panel, to wit: Professor S. A. Ikurior is a friend, confidant and a former classmate of the 2nd Respondent.

17. That I also know as a fact that the 2nd Respondent initiated and effected the promotion of the said Professor S. A. Ikurior to professional status with the 1st Respondent at a time when there was no Governing Counsel, Appointments and Promotions Committee or any known Ad-Hoc Committee vested with powers of appointing or promoting staff of the 1st Respondent.

18. That I know as a fact that five members of the Senate Panel of Investigation namely Dr C. C. Ariahu, Dr (Mrs.) H. J. Kaka, Dr I. N. Itodo, Dr A. Onoja and Mr D. A. Orkar are all members of the Senate (themselves) who later sat on 10th May, 1999 to consider the said Report.

19. That I know as a fact that presently, the Report of the Senate Panel of Investigation is with the 3rd Respondent for final approval, which could be any moment from now.

20. That I know as a fact that the 2nd Respondent has already started his ethnic cleansing agenda by terminating the employment of various staff of the 1st Defendant/Respondent who are not from the same ethnic group with him.

21. That I am further informed by the 4th Plaintiff/Applicant and I verily believe him to be true that his appointment with the 1st Defendant/Respondent was terminated on 18th November 1998 at the instance of the 2nd Respondent and that same is being presently challenged before this Honourable Court.

22. That I know as a fact that I and the other Plaintiffs/Applicants are challenging the composition, Proceedings and recommendations of the Senate

Panel of Investigation and the Report already submitted inter alia on grounds of bias and breach of the Principles of Natural Justice.

23. That I know as a fact that our case before this Honourable Court raises substantial issues to be determined.

24. That I know as a fact that unless this Honourable Court intervenes, an irreparable damage will be done to I and the other Plaintiffs/Applicants should the Defendants/Respondents proceed to implement the Report and the Recommendations of the Senate Panel of Investigation on the Students Rampage of 24th and 26th January 1999 during the Currency of this Suit.

25. That I know as a fact that I and the other Plaintiffs/Applicants are committed to the expeditious Prosecution of the substantive Suit.

26. That I know as a fact that damages will not adequately compensate us for the injury and irreparable damage that will be done to us should the Respondents go ahead to implement the said Report and Recommendations of the Senate Panel of Investigation of the Students Rampage of 24th and 26th Jan. 1999.

27. That I and the Other Plaintiffs/Applicants undertake to pay damages to the Respondents if our case turns out to be useless at the end of the day

28. That it will be in the interest of Justice to grant this application.

29. That I depose to this Affidavit in good faith.

Case 6

Fair Hearing in the Matter of My Postgraduate student Mr Patrick D. Magit

1. In The High Court of Justice Benue State of Nigeria the Makurdi Judicial Division Holden at Makurdi MHC/186m/2000

    Before His Lordship: Hon. Justice D. T. Ahura

2. In The Court of Appeal Ca/J/220/2000

    Before His Lordships:

    > Aloma Mariam Murktar JCA, Ibrahim Tanko Muhammad JCA, Isah Abubakar Magaji JCA

3. In the Supreme Court of Nigeria Sc 416/2001

    Before His Lordships:

    > Salihu Modibbo Belgore JSC (Presided), Akintola Olufemi Ejiwumi JSC, Ignatius Pats Acholonu JSC, Ikechi Francis Ogbuagu JSC (Read the Lead Judgment)

Between
Patrick Magit (Applicant)
And

University of Agriculture Makurdi, the Senate of the University of Agriculture Makurdi, the Governing Council University of Agriculture Makurdi, the Vice Chancellor University of Agriculture Makurdi (Respondents)

Case sequel to Seventh Onslaught: The case progressed far, from the trial stage at the High Court of Benue State to the appeal stage at the Federal Court of Appeal, before it was finally disposed of at the Supreme Court of Nigeria. The thesis of Mr. Patrick Magit, a postgraduate student under my supervision, was wrongfully rejected and he was wrongfully dismissed from the university based on a paper secretly produced by Dr J.C. Umeh and presented to senate by Professor M. C. Njike. I filed on behalf of the student a fundamental human rights proceeding through my lawyer, J. S. Okutepa, Esq. The res of the case was formulated, as highlighted below; that:

1. Mr Magit did his project defence before an oral Examination Panel; which verdict was: "thesis be accepted and degree be awarded subject to correction to be certified as may be determined by the panel". In addition, the panel produced a report indicating that: "Thesis is concise and appropriate. The literature review, problem statement and justification for the study are very well written. The conceptual framework is clearly stated. The panel also made some "Suggestions for Improvement" as follows:

    a. "Each chapter should have a title. Suggestions have been made in the text."
    b. "The abstract is over three pages long. It can be reduced to the required length."
    c. "Please note the suggested phrasing of the objective on p. 5.
    d. "The bottom of p. 5 should be sub-headed "Justification for the study."
    e. "The use of only the Cobb-Douglas Production Function is too big a risky assumption. This is borne out by the negative values of MVP for seed and other capital items... We suggest the candidate runs other

functional forms or functions to see which one gives the best fit …"

f. "The reference (p. 79–83) should be examined item by item to put them in internationally acceptable forms."

2. The correction required pertained to the need for the student to try some other functional forms with a view to choosing one with positive marginal value productivity (MPV). Overall, the "Thesis is very well written in clear, simple and understandable language".

3. That these corrections were subsequently effected, which was certified by External Examiner and the Major Supervisor (myself). With respect to the issue of MPV the External Examiner, in his letter of certification expressed his satisfaction about the corrections in the following words:

    a. "With reference to P. 35 different functional forms have been tried. Even though the Cobb-Douglas function appeared to give the best fit, the MVP for potato seed is no longer negative due to better re-definition of the variables. The interpretations of the results are now adequate and acceptable".
    b. "As was discussed in March 1998 with Dr Ayoola, HOD, Agricultural Economics, I gave him the go ahead to approve the thesis based on the satisfactory completion of the thesis corrections as stated above.

4. But upon submission to Postgraduate School the Dean, Prof. M. C. Njike who is not an expert in Agricultural Economics, but an expert in Animal Science, for reasons best known to him (and in a bid to pursue his own personal vendetta against the Major Supervisor), deliberately found fault with the thesis; whereby, according to him, an unknown "Independent External Examiner" was asked "to express an opinion" on the correction carried out by the student by comparing the corrected and the original versions). Curiously however, the name and signature of the unknown "Independent External Examiner" was concealed while the date of his report was not

shown as well. In his report this unknown person (Umeh a member of the panel of examiners that passed the thesis originally) made spurious allegations about the thesis.

5. Based on these allegations and without giving Magit an opportunity to defend himself against them, let alone finding out the facts about the correction from HOD/Major Supervisor (myself) or from the External Examiner (who had certified the corrections with me) the Dean of postgraduate school (Njike) caused university senate to reject the thesis and dismiss the student.

Therefore the following reliefs were sought from court:

1. An order quashing the decision of the Respondents on the ground that the said decision was arrived at in breach of the rules of natural justice and fundamental right of the Applicant to fair hearing as guaranteed by the Constitution of the Federal Republic of Nigeria.

2. An order quashing the decision of the Respondents in the said letter on the grounds that the said letter on the said decision is ultra vires the powers of the University of Agriculture Makurdi, and or that the said decision was taken in breach of the University of Agriculture Decree No. 48 of 1992.

3. An order compelling the Respondents herein to produce before this Honourable court for the purpose of their being quashed, every decision taken, every reports of the panel that may have been set up and the results thereof, every recommendations made to the Respondents by any person or group of persons in relation to the thesis of the Applicant contrary to the report of the Examination Panel and the accepted corrections made thereto, and accepted by Applicants Major Supervisor and External Examiner.

4. An order of Mandamus against Respondents herein, compelling them to issue to the Applicant his MSc. (Agric. Econ.) Degree Certificate.

5. Any other legal or equitable remedies that may be available to the Applicant in the circumstances of this case.

In the judgement delivered, however, the court declined to grant these reliefs. The verdict, as I strongly believed, was premised on a faulty understanding of the matter:

> I agree with Professor M. C. Njike that if the opportunity to hear him (Magit) was necessary, that opportunity was given when the applicant was called upon to correct his original thesis and submit same to the Attestation Panel. When this thesis reached the Senate, it was like placing this answer papers (the corrected thesis) before his examiners and his presence was not required. I cannot see in the procedure followed by the Respondents a breach of the rules of fair hearing.

In my own opinion, from this view on which the court verdict was premised, it is obvious that a good understanding of a postgraduate system was lacking on the part of the court. In the standard practice all over the world, the decision of the oral examination panel is sacrosanct, having been given a power of attorney on all matters about the student's thesis such that once taken, it was final and binding on the university authority to abide with it. In this case, the verdict of the examination panel, as already declared to the student and celebrated in the department, was that thesis should be accepted and a degree awarded and nobody, not even senate can change that verdict unless the thesis is re-examined by another panel of competent expertise. Thus if any other technical issue arose in the cause of corrections, as Umeh and Njike had conspired to say, such should be referred to the same oral examination panel before senate could take a decision, definitely not an Umeh masquerading as "Independent External Examiner". And this was not so in the case of Magit, which offended the principle of natural justice and fair hearing. That being our case: that is, the issue of fair hearing arose not before the student carried out the corrections but afterwards, when Umeh subsequently acted behind the entire panel he was a member of, to overturn the earlier verdict reached by the whole panel, thereby single-handedly re-determining the fate of the thesis and of the student in such a callous manner.

* * *

It was during the pendency of this and other cases that the complicity of Mrs. Lawal to help Umeh pin another offence on me became self-evident. And here lies the complexity of my situation in the university, as a litigant in multiple cases in court against the institution and its functionaries, running concurrently and numbering ten at the last count.

Fearing the negative consequence of such complicity, my lawyer filed a motion to stop the oral examination of Mrs. Lawal's thesis, when Umeh, as HOD and supervisor of Mrs. Lawal, prematurely fixed the exit seminar for her in deference to me as a minor supervisor of her PhD research, who should have read her thesis—but she did not submit to me, allegedly in criminal consequence of course. Furthermore, Umeh, in concert with Njike as dean of postgraduate school, had unilaterally appointed an external examiner and fixed a date for the oral examination of Mrs. Lawal's thesis in deference to me and without the statuary approvals of the postgraduate committees of department and that of college, both of which I was a member.

Therefore we sensed a conspiracy to railroad her to undermine the normal process. But that was not the issue, really. The issue was the sinister motive behind Umeh's action in this regard, which was not in my own interest. In consultation with my lawyer, there were two risks for me in Umeh's action about the thesis of Mrs. Lawal. One, given that I did not have opportunity to read the draft thesis as expected of me, Umeh would be able to cite it in court as an instance to buttress his accusation that I failed to perform my academic duty as minor supervisor of the student, thereby weakening my case and opening me to attack from my accusers. Second, given the capacity of Umeh for mischief, he would be surreptitiously implementing the punishment unjustly meted to me by senate by suspending me from postgraduate supervision, in which matter we had a subsisting order of court for the university to not implement the senate directive pending the determination of the substantive case. Either way, both the seminar held for Mrs. Lawal and the oral examination in view for her were objectionable and offensive to me altogether; and unless we moved against the actions, my cases in court would be put at risk.

Therefore we filed a motion at the court of appeal to stop the oral examination of Mrs. Lawal from holding, pending the determination of such cases. Though it was dismissed in favor of the university, our objection enjoyed judicial notice that could be referenced if necessary.

* * *

Back to the substantive matter of Patrick Magit: At the court of appeal, there were two issues of law for determination as formulated: "Whether the rules of natural justice and the constitutional right of fair hearing guaranteed the Applicant were infringed upon by the Respondents" and "Was the learned trial judge right to have approved of the procedure adopted by the Respondents (herein leading to rejection of the thesis and dismissal of the student)?" Nonetheless, the issues failed on appeal owing to a casual concurrence of the judges with the judgement of the lower court.

Then the case progressed to the Supreme Court, where it also failed permanently. In particular, I was struck by the basis for dismissing the suit at the Supreme Court, and its decision to do so was anchored on the principle of non-interference as stated in the lead judgement read by Hon. Justice Ikechi Francis Ogbuagu (JSC) below.

> In so far as the examinations are conducted according to the university rules and regulations and duly approved and ratified by the university senate, the court has no jurisdiction in the matter. A court of law, which dabbles or flirts into the arena of university examinations, a most important and sensitive aspect of university function should remind itself that it has encroached into the bowels of university authority. Such a court should congratulate itself of being party to the destruction of the university and that will be bad not only for the university but also for the entire nation.

That's the Supreme Court of Nigeria saying its hands were tied even against the weight of the evidence, by declining jurisdiction in a matter bordering on the very process the court intended to preserve. Here the court is not saying that the student did not deserve his hard earned certificate, since the due process of postgraduate examination was satisfactorily followed, rather that the process followed at University of Agriculture Makurdi for student Magit, though manifestly flawed *ipso facto*, simply did not matter. This implies that the court was not favourably disposed to overrule the university on matters of postgraduate examination, even if it was clear that the student had been victimised on malicious grounds, as is obvious in the case of Magit. Therefore the collateral damage is done forever, given the role of Supreme Court as the final arbiter humanly available – collateral because, in fairness to the trio of Umeh, Njike and Gyang, I as the student's supervisor was the primary target intended to be nailed down by them, not student Magit.

Nonetheless, the verdict of Supreme Court in this case is worrisome regarding the plight of the Magits of this world facing oppression in malicious circumstances and at the hand of university authorities. Here I rest my case, as the farthest limit of a supervisor's ability to defend his innocent student has now been reached. The journey was truly tortuous, and also strenuous, from the High Court to the Appeal Court and finally to Supreme Court of the land. So at this stage, I am but only spirit-bound, to turn over the rest of the matter to the Supreme Being, Almighty God for Him to judge between the righteous and the wicked, in the matter of fundamental human rights enforcement at the instance of the victim, student Magit on the one hand and the villain, lecturer Umeh and his associates on the other hand.

Case 7

Fundamental Human Rights Enforcement in the Matter of another Postgraduate Student Victor Ehigiator

In the High Court of Justice Benue State of Nigeria
In the Makurdi Judicial Division
Holden at Makurdi

Motion No. MHC/187M/2000

Before His Lordship: Hon. Justice E. N. Kpojime (Judge)

Between:

    Dr. G. B. Ayoola and Victor E. Ehigiator (Applicants)

And

    University of Agriculture Makurdi; the Senate of University of Agriculture Makurdi; the Governing Council, University of Agriculture Makurdi; the Vice Chancellor, University of Agriculture Makurdi (Respondents)

Case sequel to Ninth Onslaught: Another major victim of the power play in the department was my project student at the master's level, Mr Victor Ehigiator. Like Mr Magit, Mr Ehigiator had successfully concluded his course work, successfully defended his thesis, and passed by the duly constituted panel of examiners. He had thereby earned his MSc degree to be awarded the certificate. Our case was premised on a document titled "Paper for Senate" produced by Professor M. C. Njike as the dean of postgraduate school, in which he again employed the lethal pen of Dr J. C. Umeh to attack the corrected thesis. Specifically, after a successful oral examination followed by submission of corrected thesis to postgraduate school, the duo joined forces, as they had in the case of Magit, to destroy the thesis, based on the allegations that the student used "spurious data, fabricated estimates for variables, etc.", and they recommended to the senate that it was my own "negligence as a supervisor that caused wide fraudulent manipulation of data and forgery", so I should be subjected to disciplinary action.

In this suit, a motion ex parte was brought, praying for an order granting leave to us to apply to enforce our fundamental rights, as well as to apply for compensation and for an interim order pending the hearing of the motion if leave was granted. In support of the application were the affidavit, the verifying affidavit, and exhibits in support.

Our prayer to the court was twofold. The first was a prayer asking the court to grant an injunction that the status quo ante be maintained in respect of the MSc defence of Mr Ehigiator, or an order restraining the respondents from taking further steps that are prejudicial to the rights of the applicants. Leave was granted to us to apply for the enforcement of our fundamental rights to a fair hearing. The prayers were granted, as well as further leave to apply for compensation.

The matter was slated for hearing on 19 April 2000. Specifically, we sought the following reliefs from court.

1. A declaration that the recommendation made by Prof M. C. Njike and enforcement of the same by the respondents as they affect us were null and void and of no effect whatsoever, on the ground that we were not given an opportunity to defend or refute the allegations therein.
2. A declaration that the purported attestation and the purported report of the committee led by Prof B. A. Kalu were made

contrary to and in breach of the rules of natural justice and the constitution.
3. An order quashing the so-called attestation by Dr J. C. Umeh, the report of the 3-man panel led by Prof B. A. Kalu, as well as recommendations by Prof M. C. Njike and the decision of the senate, based on grounds that these exhibits collectively were issued against us in violation of the rules of natural justice and the constitution.
4. An order directing the respondents herein, to ratify the reports by the panel of examiners (EXHIBIT 'A') as attested to by the major supervisor (i.e. myself) vide EXHIBIT 'C' and then issue the 2nd applicant his M.Sc. certificate on the ground that the 2nd applicant, has in the circumstances of this matter earned his M.Sc. certificate.
5. An order of injunction restraining the respondents, their servants, staff and or agents from further infringing the fundamental rights of the applicants.
6. An order for N1, 000,000.00 compensation against the respondents jointly and severally and in favor of the applicants jointly for the infringement of their fundamental rights.

Professor Njike, Dr J. C. Umeh, and Mr M. I. Atsaka deposed to six counter-affidavits, with each of the deponents deposing to two affidavits each. These affidavits were objected to on the grounds of not conforming to the requirements under the Evidence Act and not containing any of the averments in the affidavit. It was the contention of the respondents that no decision had been taken by the senate, as the recommendations of Professor Njike and Dr J. C. Umeh were still pending before the senate and no decision had been made by the senate on the recommendations.

In view of the lengthy arguments advanced during the hearing in respect of the enforcement proceedings, hearing in the substantive matter was adjourned to 19 May 2000 for continuation of hearing. The court proceeded straight to hear the reply of the respondents. Starting with the first ground of objection, compliance with the Evidence Act, the court was urged to admit the affidavit and waive the technicalities considering the nature of the proceeding in the interest of justice. It was also contended by the respondent's counsel that the affidavits of the applicants fell short of the requirements of the Evidence Act and rendered it woefully defective. Summarily, the court was urged to strike out the application.

On 16 June 2000, the objections on the admissibility of the evidence in the counter-affidavit were overruled, and in the light of the arguments canvassed by both sides, the court was unable to find any infringement of the applicants' fundamental rights or any violation of the rules of natural justice by the respondents. Consequently, none of the reliefs sought in the motion were granted, and interim orders previously made were vacated.

> Ruling:
>
> Arguing grounds (i) and (ii) above, Okutepa Esq for the applicants submits that by Exhibits F and H the 2nd applicant is accused of the criminal offences of forgery, criminal conspiracy, making false document, altering and presenting it as genuine, while the 1st applicant is being accused of criminal negligence and conspiracy. He contends that the Respondents have no Jurisdiction to try the applicants for these offences. He relies on the case of GARBA V. UNI. OF MAIDUGURI (1986) 1 NWLR (pt. 18) 550 DR. SOFEKUN V. AKINYEMI (1980) 5–7 SC. 1 SABA V. NIG. CIVIL AVIATION (1991) 7 SCNJ (pt. 1) at 15. He submits that since these were allegations of a criminal nature against the applicants, their fundamental rights as enshrined in the Constitution were called into question and they (applicants) ought to have been heard before Exhibits G and H were made.
>
> In reply to these submissions, Chief Ogiri submits that the process leading to the making of Exhibit G is not an investigation of the 1st applicant but rather an investigation of Dr Umeh. He further contends that the submission that the 2nd applicant ought to have been heard before the making of Exhibit F is misconceived. It is not correct as submitted by Okutepa Esq. that Dr Umeh was only to verify area 4 on Exhibit A. Apart from this not being

part of the affidavit evidence of the applicants, there is no documentary evidence to support this contention. Exhibit A did not specify which area(s) was/were to be verified by Dr Umeh, It is clear from Exhibit G that the committee of the Postgraduate School Board, before coming to its decision, had a copy of the draft thesis Exhibit and other materials. These were necessary to enable it verify whether or not the necessary corrections were not made in areas 3 and 5 as highlighted by Dr Umeh.

This certainly cannot be a re-exam of the 2nd applicant's entire thesis behind his back. Exhibit G is very clear on the task of the committee, i.e. "to verify the data contained in the attestation presented by Dr J.C. Umeh on Mr E. V. Ehigiator's thesis." I entirely agree with Chief Ogiri that it was Dr Umeh who was under investigation and not any of the applicants. And if anybody was to be given a hearing it ought to have been Dr Umeh. I also do not agree with Mr Okutepa that the 2nd applicant ought to have been heard by Dr Umeh before making Exhibit F as Dr Umeh was simply verifying the corrections purportedly made by the 2nd applicant. Both affidavits of Prof. Njike are to the effect that all that was expected of the 2nd applicant was to lay before the attestator the documents, papers or corrected thesis he wanted the attestator to work upon. I have no evidence before me that Dr Umeh did not get all the required materials before he issued Exhibit F. Prof. Njike has deposed that "it is not the practice to have a student hanging over the shoulder of a teacher correcting scripts and thesis of his students."

This has not been denied, and no explanation has been given by the applicants why this case should be treated differently. Since the 1st applicant had nothing to do with Exhibit F, the question of his having been heard before its making does not therefore arise. If Dr Umeh had gone outside mere verification of the correction made by the 2nd applicant in Exhibit B, to the re-examination of the entire draft thesis, I believe the committee would have identified this fact in Exhibit G. There is nothing in the documents before me that Dr Umeh did more than was expected of him as outlined in Exhibit A. The submission by Okutepa that Exhibit F has not examined Exhibit B but has gone ahead to re-examine the draft thesis as approved in Exhibit A is not supported by any documentary evidence before me. It appears that the setting of a committee to verify Exhibit F was to ensure that Dr Umeh did not victimize the 2nd applicant, in view of the problem between them, which the Postgraduate School Board was aware of.

In fact paragraph 25 of the better counter affidavit of Prof. Njike to the effect that the further investigation was "for the benefit of the student" has not been denied. The applicants have not alleged any bias against the committee or any of its members or any influence on the committee by Dr Umeh. I do not think the applicants have the right to question the qualifications of the committee members. That certainly is a matter within the discretion of the Postgraduate School Board.

In view of the confirmation by the Committee of the verification by Dr Umeh as contained in Exhibit 'F' the applicants have failed to establish any bias on the part of Dr Umeh. I do not share the opinion of counsel that the applicants here were accused of any criminal offence. All that is involved here from the totality of the evidence before me are all domestic academic issues within the competence of the 1st Respondent. The Respondents refer to them as "academic fraud." See the case of BAMGBOYE v. UNI. OF ILORIN (1999) 6 SCNJ 295. All that has happened thus far from the totality of the evidence before me is a process of ascertaining whether or not the 2nd applicant has made the desired corrections in his thesis. And since the evidence before me did not indicate that Dr Umeh did not have all the required materials to work with, I agree with the Respondents that the presence of the 2nd applicant was not necessary. The committee found out in Exhibit G that the corrections have not been attended to. Pursuant to this, certain recommendations were made to the Senate. Okutepa Esq. is submitting that the applicants ought to have been given a hearing before the recommendation in Exhibit H. Since the decision in Exhibit H is only recommendatory it is not incumbent on the committee to have heard the applicants before issuing the said report.

Exhibit H is a paper for the Senate. There is no evidence before me that the Senate has acted on Exhibit H. The applicant has not so stated in 'his supporting affidavit, nor has any of the counter and better and further counter-affidavits said that Senate has taken any action on Exhibit H. My attention was drawn to paragraphs 10 and 38 of the counter and better and further counter-affidavits respectively of Prof. Njike. In paragraph 10 of the Counter affidavit he deposed, "That I know as a fact that the senate the highest academic body at one of its sittings in its collective wisdom found **Mr** Eghigiator not fit and proper to be awarded a higher degree of the University." It is not clear from the above deposition when the said decision was taken. The date of the decision would have assisted the court in arriving at the decision on whether or not it was taken pursuant to Exhibit **H.**

As I said earlier, there is no evidence before the court that the Senate has acted on Exhibit H. The applicants are relying on Exhibit I as the action of the Senate pursuant to Exhibit H. Exhibit I is a letter written by the Ag. Dean to H.O.D. (Agricultural Economics). It is dated 23/2/2000. Exhibit H requesting the Senate to consider and approve the recommendations therein is also dated 23/2/2000. The Ag. Dean in Exhibit I is conveying to the H.O.D (Agric. Economics) the decision of the Senate at its "122nd (special) meeting." The question that remains to be answered **is,** when did this "122nd (special) meeting" take place. It is not stated in Exhibit I when the said meeting took place. What is clear in Exhibit I is that on 23/2/2000 the Ag. Dean conveyed the Senate decision to the HOD. Two possibilities present themselves:

(i) The 122nd (Special) meeting of the Senate could have taken place earlier than 23/2/2000, or
(ii) The said meeting could have taken place on 23/2/2000.

If (i) above is the case then, Exhibit H dated 23/2/2000 cannot be the basis of the decision in Exhibit **I**. If (ii) above is the case, then the issue of time presents itself for determination. If the meetings in Exhibit H and T took place on the same date, then which was earlier in time. In the absence of any evidence from the applicants on the above, I cannot assume that the meeting in Exhibit H was earlier in time. If the Senate has taken a decision not to award a degree to the 2nd applicant, then such a decision has not been stated in Exhibit I nor has such a decision been conveyed to the 2nd applicant, Exhibit H recommended that the 2nd applicant's thesis be rejected. It further recommended that the 1st applicant be referred to the University administration for disciplinary action. These issues have not been dealt with in Exhibit I.

I have highlighted above why am unable to hold that the action of the Senate in Exhibit is based on Exhibit H. Further to this, the counter-affidavit and the better and further counter-affidavit of Mr Atsaka in their respective paragraphs 7–8 have deposed to the fact that the 1st applicant has many cases in various courts in the state and "many of these cases have a bearing on his conduct of his post graduate supervision and his attestation of postgraduate thesis".

That I know as a fact that complaints of his postgraduate supervision has reached the attention of the Senate of the University and Dr Ayoola is aware of this, and this dates back to 1996." These averments have not been denied. Is it not therefore possible that the action in Exhibit I could have been as a result of these other complaints on the postgraduate supervision by the 1st applicant.

This possibility has not been ruled out by the last applicant. The Applicant has not shown any nexus between Exhibits H and I. And even if they have, I would have still held that the 1st applicant is not entitled to be heard before the issuance of Exhibit I for the following reason. The applicants in their statement in support of the ex-parte application described the 1st applicant thus:

"The 1st applicant is a Senior Lecturer in the Department of Agricultural Economics in the 1st Respondent. The 1st Respondent (sic) was at one time he Head of Department (HOD) of the said Department and Major Supervisor of the 2nd applicant's thesis for Master's (M.Sc.) Degree in Agricultural Economics."

There is no evidence from the 1st applicant that as a "Senior Lecturer, it was his right to do the duties which have been taken away from him by Exhibit I. When this is viewed against the uncontroverted evidence of the Respondents that

> "--- the supervision for masters/Ph.D. programs is just a schedule of duty which Senate can assign or reassign as it considers fit"

And further that

> "--- the assignment of functions and responsibilities to any lecturer is the prerogative of the vice-Chancellor of the University".

I am unable to find in favour of the 1st applicant that the duties stated in Exhibit I are as of a right to him. The evidence before me rather suggests that they are privileges accorded him by the respondents. The 1st applicant having not established such a right cannot be heard complaining of a breach of his right without having been first given a hearing.

> Since 2nd applicant has not shown that he is affected by the decision in Exhibit I, he cannot be heard complaining that he was not heard before the decision was taken.

Okutepa submits in respect of grounds (iii) and (iv) that the court is in a position, having regard to the materials placed before it to order the Respondents to issue the 2nd applicant his master's degree certificate because he has earned it. He relies on the case of R.V. Chancellor of the University of Cambridge cited in the Nigerian Law Journal. (1986) 13 NLJ 4-43.

While counsel has conceded on the authority of some decided cases that award of degrees is within the domestic affairs of the University, he submits that such cases are distinguishable from the facts of this case. He relies on Section 7(6) of Decree 48 of 1992 which provides that

> "(6) Subject to a right of appeal to the Council from a decision of the Senate under this sub-section, the Senate may deprive any person of any degree, diploma or other award of the University which has been conferred upon him if after due enquiry he is shown to have been guilty of dishonourable or scandalous conduct in gaining admission into the University or obtaining that award."

The arguments of counsel, relying on the above provision, that the Senate has no authority to deny the 2nd applicant his degree before it is awarded cannot stand in view of Section 3(1) (f) of the same decree that "3(1) For the carrying out of its objects as specified in Section 1 of this Decree, each University shall have power (F) to hold examinations and grant degrees, diplomas certificates and other distinctions to persons who have pursued a course of study approved by the University *and have satisfied such other requirements as the University may lay down* [emphasis added]. Before Section 7(6) can apply a certificate must have been conferred upon satisfaction of the laid down conditions. Once the laid down conditions have not been satisfied, the 1st Respondent has no duty of conferring a certificate. It is only after the conferment of certificates that section 7(6) can come into play, if necessary. Since no certificate has been conferred in this case, reliance on Section 7(6) is a misconception. Paragraph 33 of the further and better counter-affidavit of Prof. Njike-has averred that

> "I know as of fact by virtue of my position as Dean of Postgraduate School that Degrees are not awarded as a result of a tribunal or judicial sittings but as a result of the course work and acceptance of the thesis written by a student."

This averment has not been denied. In view of the above deposition and the evidence before the court that the corrections in the thesis were not properly attended to by the 2nd applicant and have therefore not been accepted. I am unable to hold that the 2nd applicant has satisfied all the requirements for the award of the degree sought here. It is for this reason that I am unable to make an order directing the Respondents to issue the 2nd applicant an M.Sc. certificate as there is no evidence before me that he has earned it.

I have also been requested to order the Respondents to ratify Exhibit A and its attestation in Exhibit C and then issue the M.Sc. certificate to the 2nd applicant. I would have readily done this but for the evidence before me showing that both attestations must be in favour of the 2nd applicant before he can be considered successful. That is to say that one attestation only was not sufficient. If this was the case I do not think the respondents would have bothered themselves going through the process they went through, in view of Exhibit C. On the contrary the evidence of the Respondents is that

> Both the Internal Examiner and the Major Supervisor were to do the attestation." In view of the above I am unable to make the said order on the basis of Exhibits A and C. For this same reason I cannot make an order quashing Exhibit F.

Having carefully reviewed the entire evidence before me, I am unable to find any infringement of the applicants' fundamental rights or any violation of the rules of natural justice by the Respondents. I am therefore unable to grant any of the reliefs sought on the motion. Having found no merit in this application, I hereby dismiss it in its entirety. Consequently, the interim order of this court made pursuant to motion No. MHC/187m/2000 on 7/4/2000 is hereby vacated.

Hon. Justice E. N. Kpojime

16/6/2000

Case 8

Fundamental Human Rights Enforcement in the Matter of My Wrongful Suspension

8.1 In the High Court of Justice Benue State of Nigeria Holden at Makurdi

Suit Number MHC/3m/2001

Before His Lordship: Hon. Justice E. Eko

8.2 In the High Court of Justice Benue State of Nigeria Holden at Makurdi

Suit Number MHC. 16m/2001

Before His Lordships: Hon. Justice I. Hwande

Between
    Dr G. B. Ayoola (Applicant)
And
    The University of Agriculture Makurdi; The Vice Chancellor, University of Agriculture Makurdi; the Governing Council, University of Agriculture Makurdi; Dr. J. C. Umeh (Respondents)

Case sequel to Twelfth Onslaught: This is a two-in-one case, having moved from one High Court of Benue State (Court 2, Hon. Justice E. Eko) to another High Court of Benue State (Court 3, Hon. Justice I. Hwande) on grounds of technicality. The suit challenging my wrongful suspension was first instituted at High Court 2 before Honourable Justice Ejembi Eko. An ex parte application was brought pursuant to Order 43 R 3(1) and (10), Rules of Benue High Court (Civil Procedure) Rule S. 6(a) and (b) Constitution of the Federal Republic of Nigeria, 1999 read along with section 34(1), 42 and 46(1) Constitution of the Federal Republic of Nigeria 1999, praying for an order granting leave to applicant to apply for writs of certiorari, prohibition, and mandamus, as well as an order prohibiting the respondents and their servants, officers, or privies from giving effect to or otherwise acting on the letter of suspension issued to me, pending the hearing and determination of the substantive matter.

The reliefs sought were:

a) An interim injunction be issued restraining the respondents from preventing, harassing, or in any way interfering with my employment, full salary and allowances, and other benefits associated with my office in the university, pending hearing and determination of this application.

b) An interim order issued restraining the respondents from issuing or causing to be issued further queries, advice, suspension, interdiction, or warning to me pending the hearing and determination of this suite. A 63-paragrapgh affidavit, 48 exhibits, and another 15-paragraph affidavit by Mr N. I. Achamber supported the motion in his previous capacity as former head of my department.

However, as soon as the case opened, a technical argument ensued between the sitting judge and my counsel, J. S. Okutepa, Esq., which bordered on the appropriate legal entry into court on the matter, leading to the refusal by the court to grant us the leave being sought. The argument went on as follows, with the ruling delivered afterwards.

> Court: Has the prerogative writs not been abolished in their place orders?
>
> Okutepa: Notwithstanding s. (1) High Court Law this court can grant writs of certiorari, prohibition and

mandamus. The writs are common law remedies. S.24 (1) 1999 constitution permits any citizen to come to court if he is of the view that his fundamental right has been, is being or likely to be contravened.

The Supreme Court has stated that enforcement of fundamental rights is not limited to using fundamental right (Enforcement Procedure) Rules alone. One can go to the high court using the High court Rules to seek the remedies Order 43 Rr. 1 and 3 Rules of this court give the rights of remedies of judicial review to.

The writ is the same thing as the order. See S.10 State Proceedings Law 1988. There is no difference between an order and writ.

What is a writ? Section 110 of interpretation Act. A writ is an order commending a Respondent to appear before a court and to answer a charge or claim. No court can grant an order without a request.

Abacha V Gani Fawehinmi (2000) 4 SCNJ 4000 456—a citizen can come to court by way of judicial review i.e. writs of mandamus, prohibition and prohibition.

By S.24 (2) High court law this court has power to issue this writ and to grant leave of application to apply for the writs as sought. What S.24 (1) prohibits is the high court issuing writ and not high court granting leave for an application for judicial review to be bought. No high court issues writs of certiorari etc. anymore. They only grant leave for the motion on notice to be filled.

A writ is issued upon it being signed by the judge etc.—or S R. 15 Rules of this court.

What is prohibited by S.10 State Proceedings Law, 1988 and S.24 Court Law is the issuance of the writ of prohibition. By order 43 R.3 rules of this court all we need do and which we have is to seek leave to bring the application for judicial review. Upon the grants of the leave, the applicants under order 43 R.5 (1) (is required) to bring application by originating motion.

What is before the court is an application to grant leave and not for the court to issue the writs. What is crucial is whether there is sufficient cause of action to warrant the court granting the leave.

This court is competent to grant the leave sought.

The exhibits before the court especially Exhibit 7 show good cause. Exhibit 7 infringes on the freedom of movement of the applicant. Exhibit 7 also infringes on applicant's right to fair hearing guaranteed by S.36 1999 constitution. Exhibit 7 is a product of Exhibit 6

Applicant has disclosed prima facie case for the leave sought.

The three other prayers—this court by order 43 R.3 (10) is empowered to issue an interim order. We are praying that Exhibit 7 should be suspended in its oppressive effect. The applicant is a sick person. He has always been treated at the University Teaching Hospitals, Ibadan—see Exhibits 45, 46, 47 and 48 and Exhibits 31 and 32. See also Exhibits 15 and 16, which demonstrate the level of hatred for applicant.

I urge that reliefs be granted.

Court adjourned to 12.1.2001 for ruling.

SGD

Hon. Justice E. Eko

11.1.2001

12.1.2001

Applicant Present

J. S. Okutepa for Applicant

Court: Ruling read in open court by me

SGD

Hon Justice E. Eko

12.1.2001

Ruling

The applicant has prayed, among others;

An order granting leave to the applicant to apply for the writs of certiorari, prohibition and mandamus. The ex parte application was argued under order 43 of the Rules of this Court and sections 6 (6), 34, 42 and 46(1) of the 1999 Constitution. Order 43 R.3 (1) Rules of this Court provide that "no application for judicial review shall be made unless the leave of Court has been obtained in accordance with this rule".

Under Rule 1(1) of Order 43 of the same Rules

An application for

- an order of Mandamus, prohibition or certiorari, or
- an injunction restraining a person from acting in any office in which he is not entitled to act shall be made by way of an application for judicial review in accordance with the provisions of this Order.

The proceedings originated by this applicant are no doubt civil proceedings. Order 1 Rule 1 of the Rules of this Court provides

> Subject to the provisions of any written Law, civil proceedings may be begun by writ, originating summons, originating motion, or petition, as hereinafter provided.

Among these written laws are the High Court Law and the State Proceedings Law, 1988. Section 24 (1) of the High Court Law expressly prohibits the issuance of prerogative writs by the High Court. Section 24 thereof provides 24(1). The prerogative writs of mandamus, prohibition and certiorari shall not be issued by the High Court (2). Subject to the provisions of section 15 and section 27 the Court shall have all the jurisdiction of the High Court of Justice in England to make an order of mandamus requiring any act to be done or an order of prohibition prohibiting any proceedings or matter, or an order of certiorari removing any proceedings, cause or matter into the High Court for any purpose. Section 15 of the High Court Law is not ambiguous. It states expressly that this "Court shall not have jurisdiction in any disputes or matters or in respect of any question in relation to which its jurisdiction is excluded by the constitution." The jurisdiction of this court does not exceed those conferred on it by the Constitution, the High Court Law or any other written Law—see S.13 High Court Law.

In addition to section 24(1) High Court Law; section 10 (1) of the State Proceedings Law No.21 of 1988 states that

> The prerogative writs of mandamus, prohibition and certiorari SHALL NO LONGER BE ISSUED by the High Court.

Reading section 24(1) High Court Law together with section 10(1) of State Proceedings Law, 1988 I harbour no doubt whatsoever in me that I can not grant "leave to the applicant to apply for the writs of certiorari, prohibition and mandamus" as his counsel has vehemently urged me to do. A court Can only be competent in a matter if all the conditions precedent for its having jurisdiction exist. Bairamian FJ had clearly stated in MADUKOLU v NKEMDILIM (1962) 1 ALL NLR 587 at p.594 that

1. It is properly constituted as regards numbers and qualifications of the members of the bench, and no member is disqualified for one reason or another; and

2. The subject matter of the Case is within its jurisdiction, and there is no feature in the case which prevents the Court from exercising its jurisdiction; and

3. The case comes before the Court initiated by due process of law, and upon fulfillment of any condition

precedent to the exercise of jurisdiction. Any defect in competence is fatal, for the proceedings are a nullity however well conducted and decided: the defect is extrinsic to the adjudication.

As section 24(1) High Court Law and section 10(1) State Proceedings Law, 1988 enjoin this Court not to issue writs of mandamus, prohibition and certiorari I do not see how I can exercise the powers vested in this Court by Law to accede to the prayers of the applicant in this application. If I cannot, in Law, issue writs of mandamus prohibition and certiorari it accords common sense that I can also not grant leave to the applicant to apply for the writs of mandamus, prohibition and certiorari. The issue here is not whether a prima facie case of serious infraction of the applicant's civil rights have been violated but whether the case has come before me properly initiated by due process of law and also whether by law the applicant can pursue his remedies by any procedure expressly abrogated by law.

In spite of the tenacity Mr Okutepa has argued the application I am not persuaded in any way that the course he has adopted in pursuing the redress of the applicant accords with the due process of the law. Accordingly, I refuse to grant the leave sought. The application is therefore refused.

SGD.

Hon. Justice E. Eko

12.01.2001.

We re-entered court on the same day the ruling was delivered in my disfavour, now at the High Court 3 before Hon. Justice I. Hwande, to seek the leave again, which was expressly granted. The order issued in my favour is as follows.

Ruling

I am aware that this application was argued before my brother in High Court 3 and it was refused on points of law. I have confirmed the application before me and the one that was before High Court 3 and I have noted that applicant's counsel has withdrawn the offensive words in the application that was refused

Order 48 R 8 and 9 allow similar application to be made before different judges provided that is done within 10 days.

I have noted that this application was refused in High court 3 on 12-1-2001. It was filed within the 10 days stipulated by the Rules of this court. This court is therefore at liberty to look at the application and weigh its merit.

I have considered the supporting affidavit in support of the application, the statement in support of the application and the grounds upon which the application is based as contained in the record. I have also listened to arguments of learned counsel for the applicant J. S. Okutepa Esq in support of the application. I am satisfied that the applicant has prima facie complaints that worth looking into by way of judicial review as applied by him. This court has therefore granted leave to the applicant to apply for judicial review orders of certiorari, prohibition and mandamus.

By granting the above leave any action related to the issues complained of by the applicant stand suspended pending the hearing and determination of the motion on notice.

For the avoidance of doubt however an interim order prohibiting the Respondents, their Officers, servants agents or their privies from giving effect to or acting on the letter of suspension with reference number R/UNIAGRIC/PF/441 dated 3rd January 2001 pending the hearing of motion on notice is hereby made.

Respondents are also restrained from harassing, preventing in any way interfering with the rights of the applicant to his employment, full salary, allowances and other benefits pending the hearing of the motion on notice. Prayer iv on the motion paper is refused.

(Sgd.)

I. Hwande Judge 18/1/2001

Adjournments and motions delayed the commencement of the substantive matter, following which our argument was advanced. It was hinged on the provisions of the Senior Staff Regulations Act of 1992, wherein the power to undertake any disciplinary proceedings arises only if there is a query and three warnings. This was not complied with, and the requirement is mandatory and not advisory. Pointedly, a query was issued to me without me seeing the query. It is beyond doubt that you cannot answer a query you have not seen. Following the totalitarian and despotic approach to leadership, the vice chancellor further directed that I should not move out of Makurdi without his permission. In addition to my own affidavit in support (sixty-three paragraphs), it became necessary for someone who had been my HOD before Umeh to depose to another affidavit in support of my case, wherein to debunk the lies Umeh had told against me that led to my suspension. Mr Achamber willingly offered to do so, and he did it in fifteen paragraphs.

Affidavit in Support

I, N. Achamber, adult, Nigerian, Christian, male, of the University of Agriculture, Makurdi, do hereby make oath and state as follows:

1. That I am a lecturer in the University of Agriculture Makurdi, Department of Agricultural Economics and former Head of Department of Dr G. B. Ayoola, the applicant herein.
2. That I know Dr. G. B. Ayoola and I have his authority and consent to depose to this affidavit.
3. That I know as a fact that as the former HOD of Dr G. B. Ayoola, he takes all his assignments, teaching and research responsibilities seriously and has never shirked from it.
4. That I know as a fact that all through the time I was Head of department and even after he has never failed

to teach his students as I am in the same department with him and I do see him teaching regularly.
5. That I know as a fact that it is a practice worldwide and notorious in the university communities that a lecturer does not need to be sitting in his office from 8 a.m.–4 p.m. as civil servants or administrative officers do.
6. That I know as a fact that as an Agricultural Economist, like Dr G. B. Ayoola, after teaching you go out for data collections for research in market places, offices, government agencies, international agencies and so on and you do not need any permission to do so since this is the core of research duty.
7. That I know as a fact that when a lecturer does not teach the students will report formally to the HOD and in the case of Dr G. B. Ayoola, since he has been teaching as and when due, there is no basis for any student to report.
8. That I know as a fact that Dr G. B. Ayoola respects constituted authorities.
9. That I know as a fact that the duty of an academic staff such as Dr G. B. Ayoola is not only to teach but also to undertake research, extension and community services relevant to his profession and specialisation.
10. That I know as a fact that a university don in Nigeria such as Dr G. B. Ayoola belongs to the world community of scholars and should participate in local and international intellectual activities, which makes the scope of his duty very large.
11. That I know as a fact that a researcher such as Dr Ayoola has no stipulated range of time of day to be found in office like administrative staff, because he has alternative duty posts for him to be found at any point in time including laboratory and experimental field.
12. That I know as a fact that an agricultural economist and policy expert by specialisation such as Dr Ayoola undertakes data collection for research purpose in many places including markets, village communities, government agencies, private organisations as well as international agencies, among others.
13. That I know as a fact that what matters for an active academic staff and researcher in the area of agricultural

economics and policy analysis such as Dr Ayoola is his attendance at statutory meetings if proper notification of him at his office or laboratory or market among other places where he can be found on duty is made.
14. That I know as a fact that what is of essence in the performance of academic duty is the knowledge of his Head of Department about where the staff can be found at any point in time, rather than special permission for the staff to be somewhere other than his office at that point in time to perform his duty.
15. That I, N. I. Achamber, make this solemn declaration conscientiously, believing the contents to be true by virtue of the Oaths Act, 1990.

After advancing our arguments, the matter was adjourned to 8 March 2001 for reply by the respondents' counsel. The respondents' counsel countered all our arguments from all angles. One of such argument was that leave in any establishment was a privilege and not a right, and that leave was not denied me but rather that I was recalled from the leave I was enjoying, which did not deviate in any respect from the practice in Nigeria in the event of any emergency or issue of utmost importance, and that it would not be in the interest of students to allow me proceed on accumulated leave when students were there to be attended to.

Another argument in the case was in regards to my midstream motion that my counsel had moved for a mandatory order of court for my promotion to the rank of professor to be released by Gyang without further delay. The VC had withheld it for many years, even as it became open knowledge that the three assessment reports had since been turned in, all positive. My motion was supported by a many-paragraph affidavit in support, which both Gyang and Umeh vehemently opposed by deposing to separate counter-affidavits to destroy my own. However, my counsel observed that their counter-affidavits had raised new issues of facts and law, thereby necessitating me to depose to further affidavits. The most offensive, nay dangerous, part of their affidavit was the many paragraphs devoted to the legitimacy of my claims to promotion to the rank of professor, which formed the basis for me to expose Gyang and Umeh as co-travellers in academic crime regarding the promotion of academic staff. Excerpts follow.

24. That I know as a fact that:

   i. That I have merited promotion to the rank of Associate Professor since 1995/96 and to the rank of professor since 1997/98. Both were commenced and prima facie cases established. However, the VC (Gyang) has deliberately stalled the process since as part of his victimisation war against me.
   ii. Contrary to the claim in paragraph 35 (of Gyang's and Umeh's) affidavit, the VC uses promotion as an administrative instrument to manipulate individuals and the system rather than as a reward for intellectual labour.
   iii. The case of Dr Umeh is a typical example of how promotion was used by Gyang in this way.
   iv. I was HOD of Dr Umeh at the time that we were both senior lecturers in the department and I am conversant about the facts of his promotion to associate professor.
   v. The VC identified Umeh as instrument to witch-hunt me after the Abuja meeting so the promotion was used to entice and enlist him so as to enhance him over me in the department (preparatory to making him the HOD and using him to witch-hunt me of course)
   vi. At that time Dr Umeh's publications had been assessed against 1993/94 under the previous administration (but failed the external assessment);
   vii. It was one of those simply awaiting the announcement of the results of external assessment by the current VC (Gyang).
   viii. To the surprise of all against any conceivable tenable official explanations Prof E. O. Gyang (current VC) undertook fresh assessment for Dr Umeh (surreptitiously).
   ix. This action was clearly both an academic and administrative fraud, and was completely without the concurrence of the department and the college where recommendation for promotion and nomination of anonymous assessors should normally emerge from.

x. When one of the (external) assessors raised some serious preliminary issues that border on suitability of Dr Umeh, Dr Umeh was the one who himself carried the VC's letter to that assessor for the set of publications to be collected by him (Dr Umeh) and taken to another more amenable assessor.

xi. It was after this desperate shopping around that the VC made a tacit statement at Deans and Director's meeting that Dr Umeh had been promoted, without showing anybody the assessment report.

xii. Promotions under Professor Gyang were awarded not merited, awarded to his cronies and those serving as his instruments to hack other people down.

Nonetheless, as to the substantive matter, the contentions of both sides of the arguments were reviewed by the court, and in delivering its ruling, my application was dismissed.

Ruling

Dr G. B. Ayoola a senior lecturer with university of Agriculture Makurdi has filed this action in which he is seeking an order of certiorari, prohibition and Mandamus.

The originating motion is taken pursuant to S 6 A & B, s 341, s 42 S 46(1) of the 1999 Constitution and order 43 R 5(1) of the High Court Civil procedure Rules. There is a 63 paragraphs affidavit in support of the application and further affidavit of 43 paragraphs.

The counter affidavit of 2nd Respondent has 43 paragraphs while that of 4th Respondent has 41 paragraphs. There is a further counter affidavit of the legal officer to 1st Respondent that has 10 paragraphs.

Coming from the university community, most of the affidavits have the semblance of a thesis. The Case of the parties will be brought out in the course of this ruling as questioning the various affidavit will make the ruling unnecessarily bulky.

It is the submission of Okutepa J. S. applicant that the evidence tendered by way of exhibits consists of photocopies and as such the court should not make use of such evidence. He referred to s 97 (2) of the Evidence Act and s 111 of the same. It is the submission of the applicants counsel also that there is no evidence before the court that exhibit 1–4 were given to applicant on 2-1-2001.

Exhibit 7 that suspended the applicant is dated 3/1/2001. That the fact that the relationship between applicant and 2nd and 4th Respondents was not cordial is also not in doubt. It is argued on behalf of applicant that his suspension is based on the data the VC collected from another person. It is not based on the VC's opinion. That where ever the data on which the decision of the person vested with the discretion is known, it is no longer a matter of discretion. It becomes a matter of objectivity. That the VC is not expected to act whimsically but to obey the rules of natural justice. He referred to Adeniyi v. Yaba College of Technology (1993) 7 SCNJ (pt 11) P 304 at 322–333. At p 323 of the report Karibi Whyte JSC stated that there is no doubt that no determination involving the civil right and obligations can be properly made until the person whose civil rights and obligations may be directly affected has been notified of the matter and given the opportunity of answering the Case against him.

Mr Okutepa submitted further that by the senior staff Regulations of the university discipline can only be meted out where there has been a query and up to three warnings given to the staff concerned. That the regulations were not followed in the case of the applicant as his head of department had not given him even any warning. He referred to university Teaching Hospital Management Board v Hope Nwole (1994) 10 SCNJ 71 at 98 and contended that the regulation is mandatory and not regulatory. On the contention that the applicant refused to answer the query it is the submission of his counsel that time does not run out until you have received notice of what you are required to do.

As I stated earlier the affidavit evidence is in volumes and exhibits are many and diverse touching on various issues raised in the supporting and counter affidavit. The main complaint of the applicant however as it has become obvious from the supporting affidavit is that he was issued three queries and a reminder by his Head of Department and the said queries were kept away from him. That he was served with the three queries and reminder together on 2/1/2001. That he prepared his response and submitted but without hearing him the Head of Department reported him to the Vice Chancellor that went ahead and suspended the applicant in exhibit 7. J. C. Umeh, the applicant's head of department has confirmed in his counter affidavit at paragraph 3 that the applicant received all the three queries on 2-1-2001 because applicant deserted his duty post between 11th and 12th December 1999.

That the applicant reappeared on 14/12/2000 but submitted another application to travel and left without authorisation. Paragraph 7 states that when it became impossible for applicant to receive the queries personally, they were posted in dispatch book on 15/12/2000.

In paragraph 11 Dr Umeh deposed that the reply of applicant to the queries which he received in his office on 4/1/2001 was belated because twenty days had expired after the dead line given to applicant to respond. Chief Adejo Ogiri took a critical look at applicant's supporting affidavit and pointed out where it is either a conclusion, insult or speculative. He pointed out to several paragraphs. I agree with Chief Ogiri that applicant's supporting affidavit has many conclusions and contains insults therein. The language used is not polished and renders most of the affidavit to appear uncouth. It is amazing how the applicant blames every misfortune or hard luck on either the vice Chancellor or 4th Respondent. Quite a number of the issues raised could not be satisfactorily proved. The court will expect counsels to properly instruct their clients as to what constitutes a fact that can be deposed in an affidavit. Councils should avoid relying on the sentiments of their clients in order not becloud the court for the real issues for consideration.

10 exhibits before the court Chief Ogiri pointed out that the ones tendered by applicant are also secondary evidence. And certified, that at any rate the trial is strictly that based on affidavit evidence and that the standard of proof should not be as strict as in normal civil trials.

Chief Ogiri further submitted that there has been no proof of senior staff regulations before the court. That where there are contradictions between Regulations and the Act, the provisions of the substantive law will prevail.

It is also his submission that the applicant was suspended, and that a panel was immediately set up to investigate the allegations. That the work of the panel is administrative and should not be stopped. That as the VC has powers to suspend the applicant under S.15 of the university Act, the order of certiorari cannot issue to quash exhibit 7 as the VC acted within his powers.

That the court can issue an order of prohibition only where it is certain that if we stopped the proceedings what may follow will not conform to natural justice. He cited Head of state v Nwachukwu & ors (1976) NWLR 151. On mandamus it is the submission of respondents counsel that applicants leave has been approved. It is the exigencies of the office that will not allow him to enjoy his leave. He referred to Segun Ayewa University of Jos 7 NLR supra and urged the court to dismiss the application. It is the submission of Chief Ogiri also that the case of bias and hatred of applicant by 2nd and 4th respondents has not been made out.

On the submission of Okutepa for applicant that exhibits tendered by respondents do not conform to strict requirement of Evidence Law, I agree with Chief Ogiri that some of the exhibits of applicant are also not primary evidence and they have not been certified. If the court has to uphold his submission then his exhibits will also be thrown out. I however share the view of respondent's counsel that in a case tried strictly on affidavit evidence the strict application of the law of Evidence is relaxed to speedily dispose of the matter before the court. Also looking at the nature of the case and the injustice that will be occasioned throwing out the case on this technical point, I will ignore the lapse pointed out in the interest of justice.

On the queries issued to the applicant I need to emphasize that they were effective against the applicant on the date served on him. To merely post the queries in the department book of the university will not bring the fact of those queries to the attention of the person queried. To refuse to consider the response of the applicant on the ground that he did not respond when the query was not yet brought to his attention is mischievous and oppressive. There will be a special provision for a senior staff absenting himself from work. He is not to be punished by churning out queries to him in his absence and closing the door against him to reply.

Where the act of the 4th Respondent were the final stage in the disciplinary procedure to be taken up against the applicant, before a decision is reached on his guilt or innocence, the Court would have swiftly acted in favour of the applicant. The court has however considered the fact that the process has not been completed and has not yet reached a stage the court can cry foul play against the respondents. The Regulations allow the 2nd respondent to suspend a member of staff for the purpose of investigating the matter further with a view to determining the guilt of the person investigated. I do not think that the provisions of the university Act have been breached against the applicant at the moment as was found in Teaching Hospital v Nnoli supra.

Courts are not expected to constitute an impediment against the running of the country's institutions when no law or one's rights as guaranteed by the constitution have not been breached. The 4th respondent is certainly hasty in the manner he queried the applicant and proceeded to refer the matter to the Vice Chancellor. 4th respondent however maintained in his affidavit that he is only motivated by source to the institution and the country. The motive of the respondents is of no much value provided by what is correct and fair in respect of the applicant.

I do not believe applicant that the 2nd respondent hates him and 4th respondent has pathological hatred of him as he has claimed in his affidavit. The counter affidavit of the 2nd and 4th respondents pointed out particular times when their people acted humanely towards applicant or a member of his family. I think the applicant has driven himself to the state of thinking so many people hate him in the institution that any misfortune that comes his way is planned by one of his supposed enemies. I do not find the case of hatred has been established in the affidavit evidence.

On the leave of applicant that has accumulated over the years I do not consider it necessary to interfere in the day-to-day running of 1st respondent, as that is not the function of the Court. Leave of an applicant is a privilege created in his working place and dictated by the exigencies of the office.

While the court is left to wonder how a person will accumulate his leave for up to 13 years I do not consider it part of the function of the court to compel respondents to release applicant to proceed on leave.

On the terms contained in exhibit 7 they are in conformity with the senior staff Regulations and as such I do not consider them a violation of Applicants Fundamental Rights. What is required of the respondents is transparent fairness in handling the matter.

I decline from ordering the respondents to release the applicant to go on his leave. It is my view that in as much as the constitution allows one to go to court under 836 where he has genuine fears of threat to his fundamental rights, it is my view that the order of certiorari cannot be issued on what has so far transpired in applicant's case as it is not yet complete and has not yet amounted to a breach of applicant's' right. The court sees no harm to prohibit the process set in motion and I have also seen no basis for mandamus regarding the leave of applicant. The application is dismissed for lack of merit.

SGD.
Hon. Justice I. Hwande

12.4.2001

Plaintiff in court

1st 2nd and 3rd defendants represented by Mary Agogo

Mr S.J. Okutepa for the applicant with him is S. Nomji

S. P. Ejale for the respondents

Mr Okutepa: I have a motion for hearing. I was served with a counter affidavit this morning while in court. Because I am entitled to study it, I need 24 hours to go through it and react if necessary. I ask for another date.

Court: The application is adjourned to 8.6.2001 for hearing.

SGD.

Hon. Justice I. Hwande 11.5/2001

8.6.2001

Applicant in court.

Mr J. S. Okutepa for the applicant with him is S.O. Okpale

Mr S. P. Ejale for the respondents.

Mr Okutepa: We have a motion for information pending appeal.

We are ready.

Mr Ejale: We are not ready today. The applicant has filed a further affidavit containing a new ground and notice of appeal. This was served on me in the court premises yesterday. When I left the court premises I attended a seminar with Chief Ogiri where the Chambers was to deliver a paper. I did not have time to peruse the further affidavit and its attachment. I have not been able to file any counter affidavit if necessary. We ask for another date.

Mr Okutepa: I am not objecting because I had been told. The Respondents should be warned to "maintain the status quo while the motion is pending.

Mr Ejale: There is an affidavit to the effect that we are not doing anything in the interim.

Court: The matter is adjourned to 6.7.2001 for hearing.

SGD.

Hon. Justice I. Hwande

8.6.2001

3.10.2001

Plaintiff/Applicant in court.

1st–3rd defendant/Respondent represented by Mary Agogo Esq.

Mr J. S. Okutepa for the Plaintiff/Applicant with him is M. Adenyi.

Mr S. P. Ejale for the defendant/respondent.

Mr Okutepa: We have a motion for information. We are ready to take the motion. While we appreciate what has transpired in the matter, we are of the view that this matter be taken to avert the consequences of disciplining the applicant while this motion is pending.

Mr Ejale: My instructions are the same as earlier stated to seek settlement out of Court through the committee set up by the University Governing Council. We are desirous of settling matters out of court. I crave the indulgence of the court for a further adjournment. I will urge the counsel to plaintiff to focus on the leadership of the university rather than on what two individuals have said. A new Vice Chancellor has been appointed for the university. Whatever letters have been written it is my application that we suspend action in the case pending settlement efforts. These instructions were passed to me this morning by the Legal Officer.

Court: The matter is also adjourned to 22.11.2001 for parties to settle out of Court.

SGD.

Hon. Justice I. Hwande

3.10.2001

22.11.2001

Plaintiff not in court.

Mary Agogo represents 1st–3rd Defendants, 4th Defendant absent

Mr M. Adenyi for the Plaintiff

Mr Adenyi: We are yet to settle. I do not object to the application of defense counsel asking for another date.

Court: The suit is adjourned to 23.1.2002 for settlement.

SGD.

Hon. Justice I. Hwande

22.11.2001

23.1.2002

Parties absent

Mr J. S. Okutepa for the plaintiff

Mr S. P. Ejale for the defendants

Mr Okutepa: The matter is for us to settle. We were expecting a letter from the University. I understand that the letter has been written but it is yet to reach us. I ask for another date.

Mr Ejale: No objection.

Court: This suit is further adjourned to 15.3.2002 for parties to complete their settlement out of court.

SGD.

Hon. Justice I. Hwande

23.1.2002

Plaintiff in court.

1st–3rd defendants represented by Mary Agogo.

Mr J. S. Okutepa with him is Mrs Nwadieke for the plaintiff.

Mr S. P. Ejale for the defendants.

Mr Okutepa: We have fixed a sister case on 1.7.2002 for parties to renew a settlement out of court. I suggest same date.

Mr Ejale: I intend to see the VC with Mr Okutepa.

Court: The suit is adjourned to 1.7.2002 for parties to settle out of court.

SGD.

Hon. Justice I. Hwande 6.5.2002

1.7.2002

Plaintiff absent.

1st–3rd defendants represented by Mary Agogo Esq.

Mr J. S. Okutepa for the Plaintiff, with him is Mrs Nwadieke, Nomji, and Pepe.

Mr Okutepa: The matter is for report on settlement. I have instructions to withdraw the matter upon the directives given to my client by 3rd defendant. My client has communicated to me to do so. I have filed the paper and I hereby apply to withdraw the suit.

Court: On the application of J. S. Okutepa learned counsel to the plaintiff seeking to withdraw the suit so as to find an amicable settlement between the parties, this suit is hereby withdrawn and struck out.

SGD.

Hon. Justice I. Hwande

1.7.2002

Case 9

Direct Criminal Prosecution of Professor M. C. Njike for Defamation in the Matter of My Student Victor Ehigiator

In the Chief Magistrate Court of Benue State of Nigeria
In the Makurdi Magisterial District
Holden in Makurdi

Case NO/DCR/12C1/2000

Before His Lordships:
M. Odinya, Esq. (Magistrate/Judge II); A. K. Baaki, Esq. (Chief Magistrate I); E. A. Arii, Esq (Chief Magistrate I)

Between:
Dr G. B. Ayoola ....Complainant

And
Prof. M. C. Njike ....Accused

Case sequel to "Ninth Onslaught: The cause of action arose as a result of my discovery of a paper titled "Paper for Senate", dated 23/2/2000, produced and published by the accused person and relating to a thesis written by Victor Ehigiator, a student under my supervision, which held me out as personally interested and acting on material gain to pass the student. I felt that the said publication damaged my personal and professional character.

The charge sheet for this case was four-pronged, bordering on my prayer before the court to try Njike for:

1. Criminal defamation punishable under section 393 (11)
2. Injurious falsehood under section 393(4)
3. Framing incorrect document with intent to cause injury contrary to section 124
4. Giving false evidence contrary to Section 158 (2) of the Penal Code law

The case wobbled from the outset, when it opened on 22 March 2000, but it was not mentioned because the accused was absent. He was also absent on the next adjourned date, 20 April 2000, and my lawyer urged that he be served on a fresh hearing notice. The court ruled,

> There is therefore doubt in my mind as to whether the accused is aware of today's date. The doubt, which I realise in favour of the accused person... I have been directed by the Director of Area Courts and Inspectorate that I transfer the case to Chief Magistrate Court I Makurdi." In view of this, I order the transfer of the case to the Chief Magistrate Court I Makurdi. The accused should be served with fresh summons to be before that court on 5th May 2000 for the mention of the case.

Next, on 7 July 2000 was notice of preliminary objection by S. P. Ejale, Esq., but for which we were not served. The court ruled that my counsel should be served in court, who then asked for the case to be stood down till 12.30 p.m. to enable him to get legal authorities to reply to the notice right away. Playing a delay tactic, the counsel retorted to the accused person, "A stand down till 12.30 p.m. is not convenient to me."

Then my lawyer, Okutepa, declared, "I am ready to go on."

The hide-and-seek game continued until 3 September 2001, when my lawyer was pushed to the wall and was practically enraged. "The matter is for definite hearing. The accused is absent. There is no explanation. His surety is also absent. I ask for bench warrant and summons to issue."

Then the court ruled accordingly: "Bench warrant shall issue for the arrest of the accused". And, "The surety shall be summoned to show cause".

Eventually, hearing of the motion of the accused took place on 28 February 2002, in which the counsel to the accused, Ejale, S. P., Esq., prayed the court for an order striking out the case. The motion, which was supported by a nineteen-paragraph affidavit and was agued spiritedly, was vehemently opposed by my lawyer.

> Ruling:
>
> The Complainant filed this complaint before the Upper Area Court, Makurdi on the 10th day of October 2000. The matter was transferred to this court on the 28th day of April, 2000 on the order of the Director of Area Courts and Inspectorate.
>
> On the 7/7/2000 the case was mentioned before my predecessor, but plea of accused was not taken because Mr S. P. Ejale of counsel for the accused intimated the court that he has filed a preliminary objection which was never heard until it was withdrawn on the 8/2/2001 by the defense counsel. Plea was then taken but hearing did not start until the change of Coram of the court. The matter was mentioned before me on the 17th day of May 2001. Plea was taken on that day. The defense counsel asked for a hearing date, but that they "intend to file certain documents in the interim".
>
> This motion on notice was filed on the 17th day of July 2001 praying for an order striking out the case on three main grounds. First that the complaint need the sanction of the Hon. A. G. before the court can take cognizance of

it; secondly that it is an abuse of court process and; thirdly that it did not disclose any criminal offence.

In court, learned defense counsel started his submission on the second ground. He submitted that the complainant has multiplied the case in various courts. This fact was averred in paragraph 5 of their affidavit in support of this motion. It was there averred that exhibits 1 and 2 were annexed. The said exhibits are legal documents filed in the high court of justice Makurdi. The copies annexed are photostat copies of the said documents; and this fact is also averred in the said paragraph 5. Photostat copies of any document must be the secondary evidence of it. In this regard, learned counsel for the complainant argued that the exhibits are inadmissible evidence because they are public documents.

The learned defense counsel had no answer to the attack and I think he rightly chose not to reply to that because Section 113(1) of the Evidence Act 1990 clearly states that "any judgment, order or other judicial proceedings outside Nigeria, or any legal document filed or deposited in any court" is a public document. The proof of it shall be "by a copy which purports to be certified in any manner"

Exhibits 1 and 2 are not certified in "any manner". The documents are therefore not admissible.

In further submission on this ground, exhibits 4, 5, and 6 were also annexed to the affidavit in support. These exhibits are clearly not relevant to the issues raised in the complaint before me. And not only that only Exhibit 6 is certified, Exhibits 4 and 5 are also public documents, but are not certified in any manner. Exhibits 4 and 5 are therefore not admissible evidence.

With these exhibits remains of the averments in the affidavit in support is not enough to bring any facts to bear that the complainant has filed several cases based on same facts as contained in the complaint before me in other courts. The second ground therefore fails. There is no admissible evidence before me to warrant my holding that this complaint is an abuse of court process.

The first ground is that the complainant needs the consent of the Hon. A. G. as provided for under Sections 141and 142 of the Criminal Procedure Code before a trial under Section 393 of the penal code can be maintained.

With due respect, I do not agree with the learned defense counsel's submission on this ground. Section 141 Criminal Procedure Code clearly states that offences under Section 393 can only be maintained by a complaint emanating from the "person aggrieved by such offence"

This complaint was brought by the complainant - "the person aggrieved". He needs no sanction of the Hon. A. G. to bring the complaint.

It would be sound to so argue if the matter was brought by the police on a First Information Report without due sanction of the Hon. A. G. But that is not the position here. The first ground also fails.

We now come to the last ground. It is the contention of the defense that the complaint has either not disclosed any criminal offence or that if there is, it is so minimal for a tribunal to take note of.

The complaint is that the accused falsely and maliciously published of and concerning the complainant" a document which has caused actual damage to his reputation as a lecturer and Supervisor of M.Sc. and Ph.D. students.

On the face of the complaint, I think that the facts disclosed contain a criminal offence of the magnitude that this court should take cognizance of; and I so hold.

In totality, I hold that the preliminary objection lacks merit and it is accordingly dismissed. The case shall proceed to hearing.

(Sgd)

E. A. Arii, Esq., Chief Magistrate I.

19/3/2002

Coram: E. A. Arii, Chief Magistrate I

Accused present

S. P. Ejale, Esq., for accused Complainant present

J. S. Okutepa, Esq., with Mrs I. Nwadioke, Esq., for complainant Oklutepa: The matter is for hearing. I have three witnesses to call. They are in court. We wish to start with the complainant.

Evidence of Complainant:

Complainant: Adult, Male, Christian, sworn on the Holy Bible and states in English as follows—

My names are Gbolagade Babalola Ayoola. I live at No. 30 Senior staff quarters, University of Agriculture Makurdi. I am a Senior Lecturer with the University, engaged in teaching and research as well as community services. I teach Undergraduate level student in Agricultural Economics courses and postgraduate level students in Agricultural Economics Courses comprising postgraduate diplomas, masters and PHD courses. For supervision, I supervise research work of students at all the levels earlier mentioned. I know the accused person as Professor M.C. Njike with the Department of Animal production researching on Poultry in the same University. I knew him since 1988 when I joined the University. My area of specialisation is Agricultural Economics with specialisation in policy analysis and production economics.

The accused is not an agricultural economist. I was appointed the Director of Centre for Food and Agricultural Strategy in June 1995. I was appointed the Head of Department of Agricultural Economics Department in November 1996.

I occupied the two positions concurrently till December 1998. I know Victor Ehigaitor as a student in our Department; first as an undergraduate who finished his first degree with us and later as a master's degree student. He registered for M.Sc. Agricultural Economics in our

Department till 1991–92 session. He was first assigned to be supervised by Dr J. C. Umeh. Following difficulties between him and Dr Umeh, he was reassigned to me in 1997 as his supervisor. Before he was reassigned to me, he had successfully concluded his course work. When I came in as Head of Department in 1996, I intervened between Dr Umeh and Mr Ehigaitor to resolve their differences but I was not successful after about 5 months. At last I sought and obtained the permission of the University Senate to transfer Mr Ehigaitor to myself for supervision because I was the only one left in the department for the job.

Eventually, Mr Ehigiator sat for his oral examination in 1998 after a long delay caused by the accused and Dr Umeh. Dr Umeh petitioned the Senate about the change (but he was overruled, at which time there was no problem between me and the VC). Mr Ehigaitor passed his oral examination. A panel of 5 is usually set for M.Sc. oral examinations. For Mr Ehigiator the panel (members) had Prof. S. A. N. D. Chidebelu from the University of Nigeria, as external examiner. He was the chairman. I was one of them. The -third person was again myself as his supervisor. The 4th person was Dr J. C. Umeh (as Internal Examiner). And the 5th person was the Representative of the Post-Graduate School in person of Dr Gabriel Ehiobu.

The student appeared for the examination on time. The result of the oral examination was recorded in the standard form of the Post-graduate school. The standard form has four options from which the panel must choose one unanimously. The one chosen by the panel was that the Thesis was accepted and the degree was recommended to be awarded subject to minor corrections. All the members of the panel signed.

The accused was at the material time and still is the Dean of Postgraduate School ably represented at the panel by Dr Ehiobu.

The panel went further to describe in detail, the minor corrections the Candidate was to carry out. This is the photocopy of form 16—the Examiner's Report.

Okutepa: We seek to tender form 16 in evidence.

Ejale: I object to the tendering of the photocopy of the form 16. The law is that in a Criminal proceeding, Photostat copies of documents are inadmissible in evidence. This document sought to be tendered is the photocopy. And in trying to comply with the court order, the accused submitted what is in his possession. I have further instructions from the accused. And on that basis, I withdraw my objection.

Court: The document—Form 16—Examiners Report is hereby admitted in evidence and marked as Exhibit 'A'

Complainant continued: He carried out all the corrections as suggested by the panel and forwarded the corrected thesis to the Post-Graduate School. I have a copy of the statement of corrections carried out by the student, based upon which I attested my signature as the supervisor. This is the photocopy of the statement of corrections by the student.

Okutepa: I seek to tender the document dated 23/10/98 in evidence

Ejale: No objection.

Court: The document titled: "Corrections Made in the Thesis" is admitted in Evidence. And marked as Exhibit 'B'.

Complainant continued: I came across a document titled paper for Senate produced by the accused and published by him relating to this thesis in which the work pertaining to this thesis was rubbished; in which my professional character was damaged; and in which my personal character was destroyed.

I crosschecked the corrections made by the student and I was satisfied that the student has carried out the suggested corrections diligently.

There was only one area of unresolved matter which pertains to "instruction no 4". Instruction No. 4 directed that the remaining list of respondents should be submitted to the HOD and Internal Examiner for verification.

The Internal Examiner Dr Umeh had alleged at the Panel that he is aware of a list of respondents of only 194 famers while he was the student's supervisor. He tendered the list to the Panel as what the student gave to him at that time (i.e. when he was the Supervisor of the candidate). He said he was surprised that he saw a list of 258 respondents in the draft thesis sent to him. He urged the panel to find out what happened between the time he supervised the student and 1998 to explain the difference in the number of respondents. The panel took the student on and gave him the list Dr Umeh submitted to respond. His response was that the list submitted by Dr Umeh was incomplete. He counter alleged that he submitted more names to Dr Umeh than the list Dr Umeh produced to the Panel. He further alleged witch hunting by Dr Umeh to destroy his work to the panel. He requested for 10 minutes to get his list of 258 respondents, which he earlier submitted to Dr Umeh. The Panel did not grant his request. Rather the panel directed as in instruction NO. 4 in Exhibit 'A'.

Immediately after the oral examination, the student presented the longer list to me as the Head of Department in compliance with the Panel's directive. The student showed the list same day. That fact is "Obtained in Exhibit 'B'. I invited Dr Umeh to a meeting with the student when the student submitted that list with a memo. Dr Umeh refused to attend the verification meeting. Therefore when I was forwarding the bound thesis and my attestation as supervisor, I accompanied it with memorandum to explain what happened in relation to "instruction No. 4" of the panel.

With these the thesis passed through my own stage to the Post-Graduate School for onward transmission to Senate.

This is the photocopy of the "paper for Senate" published by the accused which I read.

Court: The document titled "paper for Senate" dated 23/2/2000 is admitted in evidence and marked Exhibit 'C'.

Complainant continued: The number of members of our university senate is about 50 to 60. Several members and some members of the University community have confronted me regarding the Content of Exhibit 'C'. Exhibit 'C' is complete falsehood against me. To substantiate this I refer to paragraph 2 of Exhibit 'C'.

The Panel never said that all the 7 areas corrections must be attested to by the Dr J. C. Umeh internal examiner and Dr Ayoola the major supervisor.

The Panel did not assign any job to any member of the panel.

It is therefore assumed that it is the supervisor that supervises the corrections. The motive behind paragraph 2 is to establish a false role for Dr Umeh.

Ejale: Motive is a matter of opinion.

Okutepa: Motive of the accused in his malice against the complainant is very important to this prosecution.

Court: I agree that the motive behind the malicious publication of falsehood against the "complainant is paramount to this prosecution. Evidence of motives therefore relevant. The witness can go ahead to adduce his evidence in this regard.

Complainant continued: Paragraph 2 has deceived the Senate of the University to believing that Dr Umeh has a role when indeed no such role was assigned to Dr Umeh by the Panel. It is the role of the supervisor to oversee all corrections by the students up to the point of award of the degree and therefore attest to it as I have done.

Paragraph 3 of exhibit 'C' stated that my attestation was a blanket certificate. I do not agree. Before I did my attestation, the student who carried out the corrections himself had documented the corrections in three pages to me. And these corrections relate to the issues raised at the panel - no less and no more. The student convinced me before I attested. The phrase in same paragraph stating, that "which did not indicate how the student handled every error highlighted "calls to question the meaning of "attestation". Attestation by dictionary definition is to certify that something has been done satisfactorily.

The accused wrote in Exhibit 'C' that spurious data were presented in the draft theses. That is total falsehood because there were no spurious data in the thesis I attested. A draft thesis is the thesis that a student produces for the purpose of oral examination. I was not the only one that read the draft thesis. It was read by all the members of the panel for about one month before the examination took place. None of the members of panel (Dr Umeh inclusive), raised issue of spurious data at the examination.

The statement on page 1 of Exhibit 'C' that estimates for variables X7–X9 were fabricated in the draft thesis is not true. I say so because I personally examined the estimates on the computer printouts of the student and they were present therein. The copy of the computer printout submitted by the student and given to the Post-Graduate School, which the University authority produced by the order of this court, has not got page 204. And that is where variables X7–X9 were printed out.

Okutepa: I seek to tender the "'computer printout with Page 204 removed by the University in evidence.

Ejale: We have no objection to its admissibility. It is my further instruction that the computer printout is what the student submitted to the University.

Court: The Computer printout is admitted in evidence and marked as exhibit 'D'.

Complainant continued: - When I saw a copy of exhibit 'C', I confronted the student. He denied any fabrication of variables. I then demanded evidence from him to show that indeed the variables were not fabricated in the draft thesis; and also to show that they were genuinely processed through computer like the other six variables—X1–X6. He produced a photocopy of page 204 for me. This is the Photostat copy of the computer printout of page 204 in evidence. The court ordered for the full set to be produced but Exhibit 'D' was produced without page 204.

Ejale: It is my instruction that the document sought to be tendered was not submitted to him by the student. And since it came from their custody, the original ought to be tendered. That is the basis of our objection.

Okutepa: I urge the court to dismiss the objection. It is the defense of accused that the page was not there. In criminal proceedings Section 91 read together with Section 97 apply only in civil proceedings.

(At this stage the accused, Njike, broke down in health. His head suddenly dropped with a loud groaning sound out of his mouth in apparent deep pain, thereby disrupting the court session; so he was helped out by a number of people before he would collapse in the open court)

Case further adjourned to 9/8/2002 for ruling and continuation of hearing.

(Sgd)

E. A Arii, Esq.

Chief Magistrate I

13/5/2002

9/8/2002

Coram: E. A. Arii, Chief Magistrate I

Accused present

S. P. Ejale, Esq., for accused

Complainant absent

Counsel absent

Ejale: This case was instituted by direct Criminal Procedure. The complainant is absent and his lawyer is also absent (by which time I had taken decision to take the case out of court at the instance of the university Governing Council, and my lawyer had filed a notice in court to that effect already). And speaking from the Bar, his counsel told me that he has filed paper for withdrawal of this case. Whether he has done this or not, the fact remains that complainant is absent. I therefore apply that the complaint be struck out.

Court: The complaint is hereby struck out. Accused is hereby discharged under Section 165 Criminal Procedure Code.

Case 10

Originating Summons in the Matter of General Maladministration of the Federal University under Professor E. O. Gyang

In the Federal High Court
Holden at Abuja

Suit No. FHC/ABJ/CS/222/2000

In the Matter of an Application for the Proper Interpretation of Decree No 48 of 1992 and Decree No 11 of 1993

And

In the Matter of an Application Pursuant to Order 1 Rule 2(2), Order 6 and Order 39 of the Federal High Court (Civil Procedure Rules), 1999.

Before His Lordship: Justice B. F. M. Nyako

Between:

1. Arc. Victor S. Daudu
2. Dr Oluwabiyi I.A. Shoremi
3. Dr Gbolagade B. Ayoola
4. Dr Olusola O. Agbede
5. Mr Peter O. Ododo

6. Mr Sylvester Agha
7. Mr Michael Idachaba
8. Mrs Nancy N. Allagheny
9. Mrs M. N. Yaor
10. Mr R. O. Ozioko
11. Mr T. K. Yesufu
12. Dr E. O. Omoregie
13. Dr Sule Ochai
14. Mr A. I. Omoike

And

1. The University of Agriculture Makurdi
2. The Vice Chancellor University of Agriculture Makurdi
3. The Senate, University of Agriculture Makurdi
4. The Governing Council University of Agriculture Makurdi
5. The Hon. Minister of Agriculture and Rural Development

Defendants

This case was not sequel to any particular onslaughts. The originating summons was anchored on the absence of provisions in the enabling law of UNI-AGRIC Makurdi (then known as Decree 48 of 1992, as amended by Decree No 11 of 1993), to backup the several actions of Professor E. O. Gyang as the vice chancellor of UNI-AGRIC Makurdi since the inception of his tenure in 1996. It rendered such actions nugatory, illegal, and bordering on maladministration of the university by Gyang and under him.

Accordingly, we prayed the court to hold as follows.

(i) There is no provision in the said Decree that allows the 1st–3rd defendants herein, their servants or agents to perform, do all or any of the functions/duties of the 4th defendant specified in sections 3 (2), 6, 10, 15 and 16 or any other section of Decree No 48 of 1992, when the said 4th defendant was not duly constituted.

(ii) There is no provision in the said Decrees which permits or allows the 5th defendant herein, to assume the roles, duties and functions of the 4th defendant specified in sections 3 (2), 6, 10, 15, and 16 or any other section of the said Decree No 48 of 1992, when the said 4th defendant is not constituted and in place.

(iii) Every decisions reached and or ·taken by the 1st–3rd defendants and the 5th defendant in the areas of:

    (a) Approval of budget/expenditures/capital projects.
    (b) Creation of new offices, and or re-designation of offices/posts.
    (c) Appointment of senior staff lasting more than one year.
    (d) Promotions of senior staff.
    (e) Discipline of senior staff such as termination of the appointments of the 4th–14th plaintiffs herein; suspension of the 2nd–3rd plaintiffs from supervision of their postgraduate students and warning letters issued to the 1st and 3rd plaintiffs without the approval and or sanction of the 4th defendant were ultra vires, null and void, illegal and a breach of Decree No 48 of 1992.
    (f) Members of the 4th defendant newly constituted and or appointed cannot ratify any decisions taken by the 1st, 2nd, 3rd and 5th defendants before the appointment of the said members of the 4th defendant in July, 2000 or there about having regard to the provisions of Decree No 48 of 1992.

Plaintiffs' Claims:

1. The 1st–3rd plaintiffs herein are currently senior staff of the University of Agriculture Makurdi, (hereinafter called "the University") and are residing in Makurdi, Benue State within the jurisdiction of this Hon. Court. The 4th–14th plaintiffs herein were also senior staff of the university until, by the publication in the "University of Agriculture weekly News

Bulletin" dated 23–27/11/98, they were purported terminated and dismissed from their employment in the University.

2. Plaintiffs aver that the termination and the dismissal of the 4th–14th plaintiffs was due to "the recommendation of UNIAGRIC Administrative committee on Disciplinary cases that sat 3rd–5th September, 1998 and the subsequent approval of the Hon. Minister of Agriculture and Natural Resources Abuja, on behalf of council".

3. Plaintiffs aver that the 1st–5th defendants herein are creation of law, which clothes them with juristic personalities to sue and be sued.

4. Plaintiffs aver that by Decree No 48 of 1992 as amended by Decree No 11 of 1993:

   (a) Disciplinary proceedings and discipline of all categories of staff of the 1st defendant such as suspension from duties, issuance of warning, termination of appointments, and or dismissal from office are the exclusive preserve and duties of the 4th defendant.

   (b) Creation of new offices and or posts, re-designation of existing offices, posts, establishment of new schools, units, colleges, department and so on are the exclusive duties and preserve of the 4th defendant.

   (c) Appointment of professors and senior staff lasting beyond one year and promotion of such staff are also the exclusive duties/preserve of the 4th defendant.

5. Plaintiffs aver that between 31st day of December 1995–11th day of July 2000 A.D., the 4th defendant herein was not constituted to enable it carry out its statutory duties and functions as provided for by Decree No 48 of 1992 as amended.

6. Plaintiffs aver that even though the 4th defendant was not constituted between 31/12/95–11/7/2000, the 1st, 2nd, 3rd and 5th defendants herein were purportedly performing or doing the functions of the 4th defendant between January 1997 till 11th July 2000 A.D.

7. Plaintiffs aver that in consequence of the illegal actions/decisions of the 1st, 2nd, 3rd, and 5th defendants, plaintiffs herein suffered the following detriments.

> (i) The 1st and 3rd plaintiffs were warned 'vide letters dated 1/12/98, and 1/11/99.
> (ii) The 1st plaintiff was stripped of his duties and had his office split into two, viz, department of Budget and planning and department of physical facilities instead of physical planning department, which was the creation of the council.
> (iii) The 2nd and 3rd plaintiffs were suspended from the supervision of postgraduate students vide letters dated 23/11/98 and 7/7/2000, even though supervision of postgraduate students is inherent in teaching.
> (iv) The 4th, 5th and 6th plaintiffs had their appointments terminated on the purported approval of the 5th defendant.
> (v) The 7th–14th plaintiffs were dismissed from service on the purported approval of the 2nd defendant when the 4th defendant was not duly constituted and in place.

Questions for Determination

> (vi) Whether there is any provision in Decree No 48 of 1992, as amended by Decree No 11 of 1993, that allows or permits the 1st, 2nd and 3rd defendants, their servants or agents to perform all and or do all or any of the functions, and or duties of the 4th defendant herein as specified in SS. 3 (2), 6, 10, 15 and 16 or any other section of Decree No 48 of 1992 in the absence of the 4th defendant being duly constituted and or without the sanction and approval of the 4th defendant.
> (vii) Whether there is any provision in Decree No 48 of 1992, as amended by Decree No 11 of 1993 that

permits or allows the Hon. Minister of Agriculture and Natural Resources as it was then known, now the 2nd defendant, to assume the functions, role and duties of the 4th defendant specified in Decree. No 48 of 1992 when the said 4th defendant is not constituted and in place.

(viii) If questions (i) and (ii) above are answered in the negative, whether all actions done and all decisions taken by the 1st, 2nd, 3rd and 5th defendants without the approval of the 4th defendant, in such areas as:

(a) Approval of budget expenditures (b) creation of new offices, posts, schools, colleges, departments, re-designation of offices (c) appointment of senior staff lasting more than one year (d) promotions of senior staff (e) discipline of senior staff such as warning letters issued to the 1st and 3rd plaintiffs, suspension of the 2nd–3rd plaintiffs from supervision of postgraduate students, termination of the appointments of the 4th, 5" and 6" plaintiffs and the dismissal of the 7th–14th plaintiffs, were null and void, ultra vires; illegal and a breach of the provisions of Decree No 48 of 1992.

(b) If questions (i), (ii), and (iii) above are answered in the negative, whether members of the 4th defendant recently constituted can ratify all the actions and or all the decisions taken by the 1st, 2nd, 3rd and 5th defendants in the areas enumerated in question (iii) hereof, before the appointment of the said members of the 4th defendant having regard to the provisions of S. 9(2) of Decree No 48 of 1992 read together with the 2nd schedule thereto.

Reliefs Sought

(i) A declaration that there is no provision in Decree No 48 of 1992 as amended by Decree No 11 of 1993, that permits or allows the 1st, 2nd, and 3rd defendants, their servants or agents to perform or do all or any of the functions/duties of the 4th defendant specified in S. 3 (2), 6, 10, 11, 15 and 16 or any other section of Decree No 48 of 1992, in the absence of the 4th defendant being duly constituted and or without the approval/delegation of the 4th defendants; and consequently every action or decision taken by the 1st, 2nd and 3rd defendants which ought to have been taken by the 4th defendant and which were taken by the 1st, 2nd, and 3rd defendants in the absence of the 4th defendant or without the approval or sanction of the 4th defendant between January 1997–11th July 2000 A.D; were ultra vires, null and void and of no effect whatsoever.

(ii) A declaration that there is no provision in Decree No 48 of 1992, as amended by Decree No 11 of 1993, that permits or allows the 5th defendant herein to step into the shoes and assume the role, functions and duties of the 4th defendant as specified in SS. 3 (2), 6, 10, 11, 15 and 16 or any other section of Decree No 48 of 1992 when the said 4th defendant is not constituted and in place and consequently every approval purportedly given to the 1st, 2nd and 3rd defendants by the 5th defendant from January1997–11th July, 2000 A.D; on behalf of and or in place of the 4th defendant is ultra vires, null, and void" and a breach of Decree No 48 of 1992 as amended.

(iii) An order quashing the warning letters issued to the 1st and 3rd plaintiffs, letters of suspension of the 2nd and 3rd plaintiffs from supervision of the postgraduate students, letters of termination of the appointments of the 4th, 5th and 6th plaintiffs and the dismissal letters of the 7th–14th plaintiffs on the grounds that the said warnings, suspension, termination and dismissal were done contrary to and in breach of the provisions of Decree No 48 of 1992.

(iv) A declaration that the 4th–14th plaintiffs are still in employment of the 1st defendant and are entitled to their salaries, wages, allowances and other benefits accruing thereto from the dates of their purported termination and dismissal until they leave office or removed from office in accordance with the provisions of Decree No 48 of 1992 as amended.

(v) A declaration that the 1st, 2nd and 3rd defendants herein cannot create in the 1st defendants, new offices, schools, colleges, departments, units, posts, divisions and re-designating the office of the 1st plaintiff and split same into two, without the approval and sanction of the 4th defendant and consequently every such schools, colleges, departments unit, offices, post divisions and re-designation of the office of the 1st plaintiff by the 1st, 2nd and 3rd defendants between January 1997–11th July, 2000 A.D. is null and void and of no effect whatsoever.

(vi) An order restraining every members of the 4th defendant from ratifying or approving every action done or decision taken by the 1st, 2nd, 3rd, and 5th defendants on behalf of or in place of the 4th defendant between January 1997–11th July, 2000 A.D.

(vii) Any other legal or equitable remedies that this Hon. Court may deem fit to grant in the circumstances of this case.

In a fiercely argued response, the defendants came by way of statute bar, citing the Public Officers Protection Act. The court ruled on this on 12 February 2001.

Ruling

This was a motion on notice challenging the jurisdiction of this Court and seeking certain reliefs on 4 grounds—

(1) An Order striking out the names of the 7–14th plaintiff on the grounds that they did not authorize this action on their behalf.
(2) An Order striking out the plaintiff's claims for being statute barred by virtue of Section 2(a) of Public Officer Protection Act. (POPA).

(3) An order striking out the claims of the 4th, 7th, 9th, 11th, 13th and 14th plaintiffs as this court lacks jurisdiction to entertain the matter by virtue of Section 3(3) of Public Officer Protection Act.

(4) The relief sought by the Plaintiffs are entirely academic.

The motion was supported by a 15-paragraph affidavit and another 7 paragraph further affidavit. They relied on all the paragraphs.

On the 1st ground, learned Counsel to the applicant - Mr Kondoun argued that by the letter marked as Exhibit 'CA' signed by Michael A. Idachaba PhD being the authority to Mr Okutepa to institute this action on behalf of the 7th–14th Plaintiffs cannot be admitted as such because the Originating Summons was taken 'out on the 17/7/2000·while the said authority i.e. Exhibit "CA" was dated the 7/12/2000. As such the names of the 7–14 plaintiff should be struck out because at the time the action was initiated, they had not given their consent to be joined as parties. -

I am not going to dwell too much on this ground because as by the authority of Busari vs. Husaini (1992) 4 NWLR (pt.237) 557 at 584, only the person whose name has been made a party can complain that he did not authorise his name to be used and by the authority of Tukur vs. Gongola State (1988) 1 NWLR (pt.68) 39 at 52, the appearance of Counsel on behalf of parties imputes that he was briefed. And as such only the 7–14 plaintiffs can challenge his authority to represent them. I therefore, dismiss this ground.

I shall take the next 2 grounds together as they are both dealing with the jurisdiction of this court by virtue of the provision of Section 2(a) of the Public Officers Protection Act (POPA) and that the determination of the appointment of the Plaintiffs having been done by the Head of State by virtue of Decree 17 of 1984 the plaintiffs are barred from challenging the action. It is very important to note that it is not in dispute that the termination of the appointments of the plaintiffs was conveyed to them vide their various letters of termination dated sometime in September 1998 and also by the letter signed by the Secretary to the Government of the Federation (SGF) Dr Gidado Idris dated 25/3/99 conveying their termination by the Head of State by virtue of Decree 17 of 1984, with effect from 30th April, 1999. What the plaintiffs are challenging is that their alleged termination by the Minister in the absence of Council to the University in 1998 was illegal, null and of no effect as the Minister has no legal backing to stand in for Council in its absence. Also, that the purported termination by the Head of State can only be done in accordance with Section 1(1) (a, b & c) of the Decree. The applicant is however saying that if the plaintiffs were in receipt of these termination letters since September of 1998 and they decided to go to sleep they cannot now wake up in the year 2000 to challenge the action of the applicants and that the subsequent termination by the Head of State caps the case. First of all I shall take the issue that by virtue of Decree 17 of 1984 the act of the Head of State cannot be challenged and adopt the views of these judges before now whom have held that that Decree will not avail anyone by virtue of Decree 107 and associate myself with the decision in the unreported case of Geofrey Saaondo Ingye vs. Military Administrator Benue State & 1 or Suit No. MHC/108/97 by Honourable Justice Kpojime. However, on the 2nd leg of the argument if the termination of either September 1998 or 30th April 1999 are to be given their natural implication in relation to Public Officer Protection Act (POPA), they are clearly outside the 3 months limitation period within which to institute an action against a public officer as the Originating Summons was carried out in 17/7/2000.

To determine if this law will avail the applicant, we must decide if the Minister is a public officer in this context and if so if he was acting within the color of his office as found in the Ibrahim vs. J.SC. Case (1998) 12 SCNJ 255. By virtue of the interpretation section of the Constitution and the authority cited above, the minister is a public officer and by virtue of Section 19(9) of the decree 48 the visitor i.e. the Head of State has the final say on staff and students discipline. Also, by virtue of section 3 of the Decree puts the University under the supervision of the Ministry of Agriculture.

By virtue of all the above, I find that the plaintiffs have been caught by Section 2 of the Public Officer Protection Act (POPA) and as such the case is statute barred. Be this as it may, there is no need for me to look into the other issues raised as the plaintiffs have no legal right to be before the court. I hereby dismiss this action.

Justice B. F. M. Nyako, (Judge)

12/2/2001

With this unfavourable ruling to us, probably we had caught a tiger by the tail. The need to take cover became obvious. As usual, Okutepa immediately filed a notice of appeal and hurriedly entered the federal court of appeal afterwards. Even though I concurred with him in doing that, I was not less convinced that the case at hand was significantly an academic exercise, having not been practically provoked. Much later I was compelled to withdraw from the case, in partial fulfillment of the terms of the out-of-court settlement agreed with the succeeding university administration.

Part Four
Afterword

♪
*"Then sings my soul, My Saviour God, to Thee,
How great Thou art, How great Thou art
Then sings my soul, My Saviour God, to Thee,
How great Thou art, How great Thou art."
—Stuart K. Hine (1939)*

"There is a certain enthusiasm in liberty, that makes human nature rise above itself, in acts of bravery and heroism."
—*Alexander Hamilton*

In August 2001, Professor Erastus Gyang-Gyang—he who became hostage to a messianic agitation of his ethnic clan, engendered by a group violently seeking control of a federal university located in his state in order to assert an ethnic superiority—left office as vice chancellor of the institution. The poster child for a highly defective system of patronage that sacrificed merit-based appointments of staff and admission of students because of ethnic and nepotistic considerations came to such an ignominious end that not one student was prepared for convocation in his five years of farcical leadership. Unlike when he assumed office amidst fanfare and great jubilation, Gyang left quietly, his reputation in tatters. He was a pariah rejected by the same people who'd agitated for his appointment to take place the way it did, through the back door. It was a fitting end for a misfit, as the unavoidable outcome of a warped system that permitted such misfits to be hoisted on public institutions in Nigeria.

It has been some three decades since Professor Francis Idachaba, then a member of Babangida's Presidential Advisory Committee, first proposed the idea of establishing a specialised university of agriculture in Nigeria. I, as a research assistant, helped in proofreading the policy proposal before submission to the president. Unfortunately, Idachaba died in August 2014 in active service as the chairman of the governing board of the Nigeria National Merit Award (NNMA), a quasi-academic agency of federal government for maintaining an ethical focus on the sector, with a view to promoting meritocracy and rewarding excellence and innovation in the knowledge society. The primary responsibility of the NNMA is to confer the Nigerian National Merit (NNOM) Award on deserving Nigerians who have contributed outstandingly to national development in the areas of science, medicine, engineering and technology, and the humanities, including arts and culture and other fields of human endeavor.

Fortuitously, within six months of his deserved appointment to that post in January of 2014, I became the Secretary and chief executive officer of NNMA in May of the same year, barely three months before Idachaba passed away; that being at his instance for which I feel so much gratification. Perhaps his parting gift to the agency and Nigerians at large was his last-minute choice of the theme for the annual forum of NNOM laureates of that year: The National Value System. What a glorious exit for Francis Idachaba, a scholar of world renown and a stickler for merit and excellence in academia and public service!

The proposal to establish an agricultural university was targeted towards scientifically transforming the agricultural sector and making the country sufficient in food production, as well as joining the select group of leading exporters of agricultural produce in the world. In the span of time between that moment and the five years that followed the highly eventful Idachaba administration, Gyang defined a different era: the running of UNIAGRIC Makurdi into the ground, the massive brain drain of the university, and the progressive institutional decay that we witnessed. These were fallouts of Gyang's administrative misadventure, but they also engendered a toxic sense of entitlement amongst his people, who came to see the vice-chancellorship of an academic institution or the chief executive position of any other federal institution located in Benue State as their exclusive preserve, a birthright to be passed from one Tiv person to another. Indeed, very soon after his exit from the university, Gyang rather shamelessly did a self-appraisal of his tenure as VC at a public occasion, saying if he had not recorded success in any other aspects, he had succeeded to reclaim UNAGRIC from ukes (strangers) for the Tiv nation to pocket in all conceivable areas: student's admission, staff appointments and promotions, contract awards, etc.

This trend can only portend one danger to the university system in Nigeria: eventual diminishment of the concept of a university, from universality as a member of global intellectual community to mere ethnic enclaves. This trend is up to the federal government, the owner of the much-troubled Makurdi varsity, and similar institutions located anywhere in the country, to reverse it as a matter of urgency.

This book wouldn't have been necessary if Professor Ikenna Onyido, a first-class brain in chemistry and a proven university administrator under Idachaba as deputy VC, had assumed the helm of affairs at UNIAGRIC Makurdi. A manipulation bordering on outrageous fraud perpetuated by senior ministry officials under the watch of Alhaji Jimeta Gambo (then minister of agriculture) effectively ensured that any hope of having Onyido as VC never materialised. Perhaps General Sani Abacha, for all his desperation to perpetuate himself in office in self-succession as president of the country, had initially gauged the mood in the university and realised the precariousness of announcing an unsuccessful candidate for such a vital post. This probably informed his decision to delay making the announcement for close to one year. The fact that Abacha still went ahead to make the dubious announcement (or a faceless cabal in his office did) robbed the country of a golden opportunity to reap the benefits of years of hard work put in place under the Idachaba administration. The administration had placed so much emphasis on practical agriculture and cutting-edge research in different areas of specialisation, which had begun to yield results. UNIAGRIC had begun to produce value-added products and had become a choice destination for Benue consumers seeking bargain deals for crop products (tubers, grains, oilseeds, etc.) and livestock products (dairy products, eggs, beefs, pork, and others), all gotten from the university's research and commercial farms and student farms. Some of these value-added products were already at stages of market testing and venture investment. There was also the aspect of dissemination of knowledge to farmers through the university's outreach programme.

The fateful decision to appoint Gyang not only stymied these processes, but it also set in motion the wheels of dismantling key structures that gave UNIAGRIC its identity as a specialised university and it differentiated it from the generalised ones. Three important policy centres—the Centre for Food and Agricultural Strategy (CEFAS), the Cooperative Extension Centre (CEC), and the Centre for Agrochemical Technology (CAT; this at the instance of Onyido)—were made to rot away because of Gyang's excessiveness in office, coupled with the inordinate ambition of members of his ethnicised cabinet, their criminal tendencies, wanton frivolities, and near-absolute incompetence demonstrated during Gyang's time as vice chancellor. Idachaba had envisioned an agricultural extension system in which the largely unenlightened rural farmers would learn practical skills on how to improve their productivity and keep abreast of best farming practices. He envisioned an agricultural university in such an intimately close relationship with the agriculture ministry at the federal and state level to be able to directly feed the public policy authorities with global best practices in taking policy decisions for the benefit of the agricultural economy. He also envisioned an agricultural university that would offer a platform for raising a generation of students who, in addition to studying the traditional courses taught in a conventional university, would acquire practical skills that would prepare them for the working world.

The thrust of Idachaba's policy was derived from the Morrill Land-Grant Act, which had proved to be such an effective policy tool for transforming the agricultural sector of the United States over the years. The Morrill Land-Grant Act was based on a tripartite mission of teaching, research, and extension integrated both in terms of simultaneity of the activities involved and also in terms of their mutual coexistence under the same administrative umbrella.

This triple helix model formed the basis for the establishment of the agricultural universities in Nigeria, and Idachaba had established from the outset two special-purpose vehicles for implementing the model in UNIAGRIC Makurdi—the Cooperative Extension Centre (CEC) and the Centre for Food and Agricultural Strategy (CEFAS)—as vehicles for building UNIAGRIC as an institution that, in addition to the classical model of teaching and research as obtains in faculties of agriculture in general universities, would also deliver the benefits of practical agriculture to the nation. Onyido was instrumental to the establishment of the third centre, the Centre for Agrochemical Technology, with the funding of the Canadian government—a feat that Gyang, as an ignoramus, had reported to law enforcement agencies as a breach of national security during the draconian administration of General Abacha.

Gyang not only began his administration by targeting non-Benue indigenes for victimisation; he also seemed bent on destroying all the good works of the Idachaba administration. My first suspicion of Gyang's asymmetrical vision for the university came when, while offering me the HOD position in his official residence, he told me that he didn't care about CEFAS—an organ of the university he likened to a mere public relations outfit. But for my quick intervention to educate him about the value of CEFAS as a vital policy analysis organ of the university, Gyang had decided to appoint an administrative officer to take over from me as director of the centre so that it could die off naturally. At that point, it became clear that the real motive of Gyang to offer me two administrative posts at the same time wasn't because he believed in what we were trying to achieve at the centre; it was more a ploy to kill the centre and eventually co-opt me into his network of do-gooders—a network populated by lackeys and hangers-on whose relevance mainly derived from the putrid system Gyang created.

My service as director of CEFAS had heightened my professional visibility in large measure, occurring within the last six months of Idachaba's tenure as VC. He was very happy with my performance in office. I had put up a proposal for repositioning the centre and establishing its coordinate on the global intellectual map, which he expressly approved: an upgraded library, a systematic hunt for quality staff, and the institution of an annual Makurdi lecture delivered within three months of my appointment, which not only popularised the centre specifically but also accrued limelight for the university as a whole. In particular, Idachaba was most fascinated by the success of the first annual Makurdi lecture delivered by Allison Ayida, a highly respected personality in the public service system and the very first head of federal civil service after independence, under the chairmanship of the agriculture minister, Professor Ademola Adesina. In bringing Ayida to Makurdi to deliver the lecture, I had capitalised on his previous role as the permanent secretary in the ministry of economic development when the Malaysians came to take oil palm seedlings from Nigeria, which Ayida had happily approved. Idachaba was so elated by my imitative that he devoted substantial space to pour encomiums on me in his valedictory lecture when his term ended in December 1995.

Ayida's lecture was so well thought out, with an excellent job at intellectual memory recall. Indeed, the lecture filled a gap in our knowledge of how it happened when the Malaysians came. He recalled that a letter was written to him by the government of Malaysia asking to buy oil palm seedlings from Nigeria Institute for Oilpalm Research, located at Benin and at that time a member of pre-existing, pan-territorial, institutional legacies of the British colonial government prior to independence in 1960. The aspect that we never knew as students of agricultural policy history, and which Ayida mentioned, was that at about the same time, Ghana also sent its request to buy oil palm seedlings from Nigeria. It was Ayida's discretion to give both countries our seedlings free of charge. Ayida noted with astonishment that whereas Ghana literaly jumped at the free gift, the Malaysians replied to thank him for the gesture but insisted on paying for it. Years later, as recounted by the lecturer, Malaysia became a world exporter of tannin and palm oil and other palm oil products, even into Nigeria, but Ghana never recorded such a feat in its palm oil economy.

I had planned for the second annual Makurdi lecture to be held in December 1996. Former head of state Yakubu Gowon had agreed to be the guest lecturer, based on the reason that he was the apex policy authority in the country when the very first Federal Ministry of Agriculture was created immediately after the coup d'état in 1966. However, when I returned from my scholarly visit to the United States later in 1996, General Gowon was no longer available. At this time, Gyang had become VC, and I dug in my heels to organise the second lecture in the series, delivered by Mr Oladosu Akinyemi, a retired director in the federal ministry of agriculture. This was equally successful, to the admiration of Gyang himself. However, Gyang was to subsequently frustrate my efforts to hold the third lecture in 1997 and the fourth one in 1998, in the wake of the intense hostility against me. The series of public policy lectures petered out into nothingness at the instance of Gyang. My successor, Odoemenem, was not cut out for performing scholarly works.

It wasn't surprising that Gyang displayed so much impunity in office. It was, after all, the Abacha era—the most brutal in the country's history, when there was so much lawlessness in the land. But the Obasanjo administration had ushered in hope to many law-abiding Nigerians. For many of us who had been wrongly victimised by the Gyang administration, our spirits had been particularly buoyed by Obasanjo's pronouncement about giving protection to whistle blowers and those who were ready to help his administration end corruption in public service. This included academic corruption in the universities, where according to the new president (as if he had heard what was happening to us at Makurdi), "certain staff members with strong views had been earmarked by VCs to be crushed at all costs".

Alas, it was mere platitude. There was nobody to bail us out when we entered into trouble with one such VC at Makurdi. Even when we wrote to the appropriate quarters apprising them of Gyang's excessiveness and targeting of university staff for victimisation, the government turned a deaf ear, and we helplessly wallowed in the trouble for many years. But for the opportunity of court to seek refuge (at what a heavy financial and other cost, though?), someone like me would have been forgotten as an academic, or grass would have been growing on my grave a long time ago at the behest of Gyang. When one looks at the insensitivity of the two ministries, agriculture and education, at the federal level—which were reached for help, but none came—it became clear that government was obviously its own enemy.

The erosion of key structures and values that gave UNIAGRIC its identity as an agricultural university didn't end with the Gyang administration; successive administrations also contributed to this bastardisation of the institution. In subsequent years, the Centre for Agrochemical Technology (CAT), the Cooperative Extension

Centre (CEC), and the Centre for Food and Agricultural Strategy (CEFAS) were scrapped, no thanks to Ayatse and Uza, who built on the destructive foundation Gyang had laid for them. Instead, several irrelevant courses were introduced. Policymakers also played their part, especially with the unwarranted transfer of the agricultural universities from the Ministry of Agriculture to the Ministry of Education by administrative fiat, even when the enabling statute still subsisted. Clearly this was an act of illegality or failure of the government to obey its own laws, or policy irresponsibility to say the least. This action signified a further departure of the agricultural universities from their initial targeted focus to a generalised type, which has now atrophied the specialised agricultural universities to the miniature status of agricultural faculties in general-purpose universities. The agricultural universities had been an integral part of the Ministry of Agriculture according to their enabling law; they were intended to play strategic roles in the ministry's day-to-day problem analysis and solution processes through the Agricultural Universities Coordinating Agency (AUCA). AUCA, a coordinating unit for all the agricultural universities, was established as an agency under the Ministry of Agriculture, and so the transfer of the agricultural universities to the education ministry has robbed the agricultural ministry—and by extension, the entire nation—of the capacity of the agricultural universities to provide the technical backup support for policy decision making by the agriculture ministry through AUCA, which as originally planned would have provided the central coordination services for agricultural universities to identify and analyse problems facing the ministry of agriculture and deployed their researchers, extensionists, and other developers to act on them.

We are in an era when the over one hundred land-grant universities in the United States are more active, liaising with farmers and proffering solutions to peculiar farming problems. The same is true in India, Brazil, and other countries that have agricultural universities. Nigerian politicians and policymakers are manipulating the few in this country to suit their aims, making the agricultural universities more and more inaccessible to farmers as the central focus of these institutions. Central to the success of the agricultural universities is their accessibility to farmers. The bastardisation of the universities by Gyang and his successors in office makes them agricultural universities only in name, and their programmes are no different from those offered in the agriculture faculties of conventional universities. These programmes are hardly affordable and offer little by way of preparing students for the working world or providing solutions to farmers' problems.

It is important to note that the concept of agricultural university is part of the country's policy experimentation process. This process was successful when the necessary structures and leadership were in place, but it became confused or vindictive when the structures and leadership disappeared. It was vindictive as in the case of Professor Onyido's Centre for Agrochemical Technology and the Centre for Food and Agricultural Strategy, which from outset I was instrumental in putting up the concept paper for it and later managing its affairs for three and a half years. Little wonder that the change of priorities has led to a worsening situation in the country's food supply. Unfortunately, when Gyang chose to frustrate Onyido's effort at the Centre for Agrochemical Technology (CAT), he also succeeded in frustrating the efforts of the university itself towards researching and developing fertilisers and pesticides that would benefit the country's agriculture. And when Gyang stifled CEC and CEFAS out of action—ignorantly labelling them as mere public relation units of the university, where they were to be further strangulated and then cremated by the combination of Ayatse and Uza in quick succession—they had also denied the farm population and public authorities the benefits of workable farmer support policies and programmes.

A major fault line with policy implementation in Nigerian universities is the rearing of ethnic interests above merit factors, as played out in the case of Makurdi Agricultural University. Many times when a candidate is foisted on a university as vice chancellor, it is not necessarily because he is the best qualified but because he serves a local group interest. In UNIAGRIC, since Gyang's emergence, the vice chancellorship position has continued to be occupied by the Tiv ethnic group. It's not that I have anything against the Tiv people in becoming VCs, but reducing such an important appointment to a mere exercise in ethnic assertion is counterproductive. It deprives the country of its most brilliant minds and their valuable intellectual contributions to nation building.

Lessons Abound

Perhaps the first lesson for me to learn was that disappointments could transform themselves into blessings. As things turned out, the Farm and Infrastructure Foundation (FIF), an organisation for promoting policy best practices in agriculture and rural development, originated from the hullabaloos. I managed to found the organization in the face of the hullabaloos, which has now grown out of the infancy it was in when I founded it at Makurdi to be an icon of popular reference across the country and abroad. Ironically, the vision of FIF developed innately from my intellectual devotion to CEFAS during my time as the director. As the latter's vision was destined to be scuffled with the arrival of Gyang, it soon crossed my mind to found a more resilient outfit to better do the job of focused analysis and resolution of food and agricultural policy problems through an independent body outside the sphere of government institutions.

Fortuitously, as if I had a premonition of the looming hullabaloos back home, the vision of FIF came to me in the latter part of the three-month intellectual stocktaking I did while at Iowa State University in 1996, as well as in the trepidation that followed the news of Gyang's appointment as VC of my home university. Thus through thick and thin, I succeeded in managing FIF for ten years at Makurdi before moving its headquarters to Abuja in 2006, which I had as a ready-made organisation in the civil society, suitable for carrying on with academic works after my premature exit from UNIAGRIC Makurdi in 2009. I am most gratified to see how, purely due to my effort at intellectual entrepreneurship, combined with the efforts of staff and associates, FIF has grown from stage to stage as a force to be reckoned with and a foremost non-state actor in delivering its mandate of a specialised nature yet to be equaled in the country, rendering services in public-spirited policy advocacy, knowledge-driven policy brokerage, and evidence-based policy research.

Lessons in Human Nature

One thing that astounded me was the deep-seated animosity Umeh and Odoemenem exhibited towards me. Much as I tried not to be bothered by the individual and joint actions of this duo in crime by constantly ignoring them and carrying on with my work life, I wasn't free from trouble with them. I ascribe this to the human nature of my three stalkers.

I'm of the opinion that the success of any government policy is delicately anchored to human nature in those to implement the policy, particularly to the stochastic outcomes of human behaviour by its very nature. Stochastic outcomes of a human nature are those outcomes wherein the parameters of their probability distribution are not known but can only be estimated; the estimates have margins of error no matter how narrow that can be. Succinctly put, you can never predict with certainty the outcome of a person's action in advance of that action. People are full of several unknown variables governing their behaviour in specific circumstances. Of course, some variables are known to have deterministic outcomes, whereby the parameters of their probability distribution are known exactly and predictable in definite terms. This is why, econometrically speaking, if you can reach the entire population of a parameter value, or you can reach all the samples of a parameter value possible, you can find the central tendency of a parameter of that population without the usual statistical inexactitude accompanying it. However, in a policy experiment like appointing a vice chancellor for a university, you can only reach some samples of the population, not all, and this makes the parameters of the probability distribution of the human nature involved practically stochastic and not deterministic in this case.

This analogy provides an econometric context to explain the behavioral dispositions of my three stalkers towards me, including their stooges like Mrs Lawal as well. With these people, I couldn't have predicted their stochastic behaviours with certainty. On the one hand, Umeh and I had known each other from our days at the University of Ibadan, and we were meant to be true friends, but it turned out that we were not. How on earth could I have predicted that except by analysing the stochastic properties of his human nature? For Umeh to have developed such a bitter hatred for me and stalked me all the way at Makurdi, let alone for him to be the architect of the downfall of two postgraduate students of mine for whom I had a duty of care as the major supervisor of their research work - Magit and Ehigiator, even when I was practically instrumental to his (Umeh's) coming to Makurdi in the first instance; this though I did in good faith was literally akin to pulling down the tree branches on myself with the ants to bite me all over. Then the evidence of analysis suggests that something behaviourally stochastic must be wrong. On the other hand, it was less a surprise to me that Njike or Odoemenem acquired similar capacity to Umeh as my stalkers, given that I didn't know either of them from Adam, and yet they developed such a bitter hatred for me at Makurdi where we only met by chance. The human nature in them, as also in their principal Gyang, was very manifest alright, but which was not necessarily attributable to an aberrant stochastic behavior.

Side by side with all of that, was also the human nature in Achamber (of blessed memory), in whom I found one Tiv person in my department and college (and even the whole university) who volunteered a witness statement in support of my case in court at a time I needed a colleague to debunk Umeh's allegation of frivolous travels against me in his report to Gyang. In his witness statement for me, Achamber, a Tiv man like Gyang himself, willingly deposed to a fifteen-paragraph affidavit to portray me in good light. His lone affidavit proved so useful that the judge believed him at that point, not Umeh, thereby ruling in my favour on that score. Even though Achamber regrettably passed away so untimely, and so soon after my exit from the university, his good deed to act on my side at that material time, lives on in my spirit forever.

From Achamber's human nature, I was inclined to prove myself utterly wrong in believing that the problem I faced at Makurdi was necessarily because I was not a Tiv man. After all, there were the likes of Mrs Lawal, who belonged to the same tribe like me (*Yoruba*), yet she acquiesced halfheartedly in the plot to nail me down for Gyang as an accessory after the fact of the various crimes committed by my stalkers against me. Rather, it was more the human nature of a few Tiv elites with a tint of inherited xenophobic traits, who had sworn a secret oath that after Idachaba, never again would a non-Tiv person be allowed to become chief executive of a federal establishment, university, or other institution– located on the soil of Benue State. It is in such an inherited trait that is coded the genotype of the stochastic properties of human nature, which now constitute a prominent part in the lessons of life's experience I gathered as a university don at Makurdi during some two decades or so of dwelling in Benue State.

Lesson in the Grace of God

My story line is one like that of a proverbial dog walking on its hind legs. It does it poorly, but one wonders how it is possible to do it at all. In my own case, it was possible for me to have survived the sporadic onslaughts of Gyang and his hatchet men by nothing other than the favour of God, not the least my deliverance from a strange sickness, the desperate gunmen in search of me and my wife, and other such instances and circumstances beyond my own control. Looking back years after my travails and successfully navigating through the hullabaloos at Makurdi varsity, I am hard put not to see how I would have been consumed if not for the grace of Almighty God.

Notarization

J. S. Okutepa, SAN & Co.
(GRACE OF GOD CHAMBERS)
Legal Practitioners, Consultants and Notary Public

26th February, 2018

Mr Henrick Abella,
Publishing Consultant
Xlibris, LLC
Victory Way, Admiral Park
Crossways, Dartford,
DA2 6QD, United Kingdom.

Dear Mr Abella

RE: MANUSCRIPT OF PROF. G.B. AYOOLA

Please refer to your e-mail to Prof; G. B. Ayoola in December, 2017 on the above subject, copy of which was made available to me.

2. Pursuant to the said mail and the request therein, I have notarized the manuscript and put my seal thereon on each page of the manuscript.

3. I also wish to confirm that the court processes given to you by Prof G.B. Ayoola, have been duly certified as required by law and they are public documents within the meaning of Sections 102 and 104 of the Nigerian Evidence Act; 2011. These processes can be published having been duly certified as required by law.

Accept the assurances of my professional respect always.

Yours Faithfully

J.S. Okutepa SAN
(Notary Public of Nigeria)
J.S. Okutepa SAN & Co.

J. S. Okutepa, SAN
LL.B (Hons), Notary Public
(Principal Partner/Managing Solicitor)

ABUJA OFFICE: Eleojo Court, Plot 2202 Apo Resettlement, Adjacent St. Paul's Anglican Church, Apo Abuja.
MAKURDI OFFICE: House 3BR/3B No. 11 Hudco Quarters High Level Makurdi, Benue State.
TEL: +234 8147336388, 8035896910, 7036818104 **E-mail:** info@jsokutepa.com **Website:** www.jsokutepa.com

Appreciation

I am to appreciate the doggedness of the other endangered species like me at UNIAGRIC Makurdi during the same period, namely Professor Ikenna Onyido, Professor Olusola Agbede, and Arch. Victor Daudu, to whose families mine was tightly bonded in friendship that held so dear and in faith that lasted so long - most endearing the weekly joint family fellowship sessions we had together, rotating from one house to the next in many cycles of Fridays at which we prosecuted the war only on our knees.

In writing this book, I received professional contributions and varied assistance from several sources, without which this book may never have been written, herein acknowledged. These include the indefatigable Okutepa the father (Jibrin Okutepa SAN), who notarized the huge record of court proceedings in the many cases that he himself had earlier prosecuted for me; then Okutepa the son (Ocholi Okutepa Esq), who though he was a little boy when his father locked horns with UNIAGRIC Makurdi for years on my behalf, but now a legal luminary and a budding intellect in his own right, he helped in the compilation and synthesis of the records and put up a philosophical teaser for the manuscript that I found useful in the organization of the book in the present form it eventually appears.

I am also grateful to S. O. Okpale Esq, who commenced the legal fireworks for me at the instance of the late Eche Ada and subsequently subjected himself to the seniority of Okutepa in handling some of the litigations for me; as well to Babatunde Babajide Esq for his painstaking job of penultimate legal vetting of the book prior to press time.

Next is Christopher Okonkwo, a *ghostwriter* of immense worth, who marked me up so closely and stayed on with me as a partner in constantly discussing the subject matter and message of the book till the end of a zero draft manuscript; then is Dr. Steven Ogundipe who helped in reading an initial draft to make his valuable professional input into the manuscript, and who, alongside my bosom friend Professor Ademola Ladele, they tarried to give me the encouragement I needed at successive stages of writing the book in the face of competing demands for my scarce time and the many distractions emerging from stage to stage.

Furthermore my gratitude to Moremi Soyinka-Onijala (Esq) and Uye Ogedegbe (Esq), who were so favourably disposed to sharing their thoughts in the early stages with me on the potential contributions of the book to knowledge generally and to the legal profession particularly; and many others, who as members of my staff or as professional and personal associates of mine at UAM, IFDC, FIF and NNMA at different points in time, have provided considerable technical or other forms of assistance in different capacities, namely: the late David Adamu, Busola Coker, Ahmed Agbo, John Ogbodo, Jerry Hyacinth-Osai, Temitola Arasi (Esq), Adeola Adegoke, Abiola Bayode, Ayodeji Taiwo, Joel Olorunshola, Bosayo Kanjuni, Chidinma Anyawu, Tope Davies, Iyanu Ajayi, Omotola Aweda and Daniel Adamu, among others.

Finally, I am to thank the brethren at Makurdi including those ones in the multiple fellowship groups I belonged; especially the chaplain of Living Bread Chapel at the material time, Sam Baba Onoja, who superintended over the many prayer sessions for me and others in travail, and subsequently he also acted true to type at the instance of my wife Bose who, having failed to persuade me against writing the book at all, she wished the pastor prevailed on me in order to ensure that the manuscript was totally purged free of acrimonious expressions, hateful statements or any language of vengeance, which advice I heeded as much as humanly possible in the circumstance. For my children – Taiwo, Kehinde, Iyinoluwa and Similoluwa, my awful experience at Makurdi was testimony of the atmosphere of protracted hostility and trepidation in which they grew up at tender ages, ever being most regrettable.